# ENGLAND'S
# SEA-OFFICERS

SAMUEL PEPYS, THE FOUNDER OF NAVAL ADMINISTRATION

# ENGLAND'S
# SEA-OFFICERS

## The Story of the Naval
## Profession

BY

## MICHAEL LEWIS

M.A., F.R.HIST.S.

*Professor of History*
*Royal Naval College*
*Greenwich*

LONDON

GEORGE ALLEN & UNWIN LTD

FIRST PUBLISHED 1939
SECOND IMPRESSION 1948

PRINTED IN GREAT BRITAIN
in 11-Point Baskerville Type
BY HENDERSON AND SPALDING
LONDON W.1

# INTRODUCTION TO NEW IMPRESSION

THIS book was written just before the Second World War. It reappears when the effects of that encounter are still very fresh in our memories. It would be presumptuous to the verge of folly to pretend that so vast an affair did not in any way affect our professional Sea-Officers, their status, their tenure and their way of life. Of course it did.

But the difficulties of printing and publishing are such that, at this juncture, many additions and revisions are technically impossible, so that, for the most part, this version must be content to remain—as in fact it describes itself— a reprint, not a new edition. This is much less serious than it might be; than it *would* be were the officer-personnel of the Royal Navy a sudden "brainwave", invented in a hurry to meet a sudden emergency, instead of—as it is— a slow-moving evolutionary phenomenon. What in fact has happened is that the Royal Navy officer, considered generically, has continued to evolve, on the whole slowly, though in some directions at rather more than his normal tempo, since War is an occasion when things—even English evolutions—tend to be speeded up. But he has not, in any notable respect, suffered a radical change. Whether he will do so in the immediate or foreseeable future is another matter, which it would not be in order to discuss here. I concluded the 1939 version by declaring that I was trying to purvey not Prophecy but History, and I should like to repeat that now.

So the reader need not fear that the whole is irretrievably "dated". I think it is not: I would even claim that no

considerable portion stands in need of rewriting—now, in
the fall of 1947. But I am fain to admit that one section
of a few pages may—very likely will—stand in need of very
important *additions* in the fairly near future. The section
to which I refer is the concluding part of Chapter VII,
where the past sources of officer-supply are analysed and
compared with the modern sources. The *past* sources, of
course, if they were historically correct when they were
set down, remain so still: they do not, and will not, require
revision. But the modern sources may—nay, I think *must*—
need *adding* to: and perhaps, as a result, a change of
emphasis in relative importances may be necessary: also—
perhaps—the whole comparison between the past and the
present-that-is-to-be may have to be re-written. But that,
as yet, is a prophet's work, not mine.

There is one other point. In the light of this latest war,
I might, on a casual view, be accused of a very grave
omission. No one who studies the naval side of the 1939-
1945 war, can fail to be struck by the tremendous part
played by those great Reserves, the R.N.R. and the
R.N.V.R. Why, then, it might be asked, is there nothing
about the officers of these bodies in a book like this?

Such a criticism, I hold, would not "lie" (as the lawyers
say). I yield to no one in my appreciation of their importance
to the Navy and to the country; in evidence whereof I
would cite my own book recently out in which a major
attempt is made to correlate them with the Royal Navy,
and to estimate their immense service to the State. They
are indeed an integral part of the Navy of Britain. But
they are not, by definition, part of the *Royal* Navy: they
are not men who have taken up the naval profession as a
whole-time occupation. Now *England's Sea-Officers* is, as
its sub-title proclaims, "the Story of the Naval Profession"—
i.e., of the Royal Navy Officer—and of that alone. It
should be regarded, therefore, as a part—a large and
important part, but still only a part—of a larger and more
important theme, the *whole* Navy of Britain. It is in the

new book (which bears that name), and not here, that an appraisement of our great Reserves will be found.

The differences between this text, then, and that of 1939 are very small, involving verbal modifications only: some resulting from sheer misprints, some from factual changes, easily described or added, which have happened in the years between; and others in rectification of minor discrepancies and errors, which friendly readers have been so kind as to point out to me.

Of my equally friendly critics, I would reply to only one. He (who came from somewhere north of the Tweed) took me to task over my title. "Why", he asked, " 'England's Sea-Officers'? Why leave *us* out of it?". Well, I can only say that it was intentional: not at all to hurt the feelings of these our most trusted friends and partners in a quarrelsome world, but because the vast bulk of my story is, both in time and in its own peculiar nature, essentially *English*; not British, because, in the main, not Scottish at all. By that fortunate year 1707, almost all the foundations of the profession were well and truly laid; at least, so definitely as to ensure that the edifice, when erected, would match them in its style of architecture. Built on such characteristically English foundations, it was inevitable that the profession should be characteristically English too: and so it was. But let me add, by way of amends if I can make them, I believe that the Scots, had *they* designed it from the start, would have been careful to begin with a much clearer blueprint of the whole, and there would not have been so much appearance of "muddle-through" about it. Yet I must not be asked to admit that their Naval Officers would have been, by and large, a *superior* breed: as good—perhaps: better—no! And I believe my critic would agree. Surely this latest war has shown, *nemine contradicente*, that they could hardly have been that?

# FOREWORD

THE attitude of the ordinary Englishman towards the Navy seems, at first sight, remarkable. He does not ignore its importance: he realizes—perhaps a trifle vaguely—the part it has played in the moulding of his particular civilization, and the creation of his particular Empire: and he is, in his own undemonstrative way, proud of it. The Navy, he feels, is a "good thing", and he probably pays out that proportion of his income-tax which is to go towards its upkeep with comparative equanimity.

But at this point his interest in the Navy begins to fade. It is not altogether his fault. He does not receive much encouragement to pursue the subject further. The Navy is the Silent Service: it does not advertise; it does not invite diurnal inspection from without; yet it is the soul of efficiency in that it is always there, or thereabouts, when the ordinary Englishman suddenly becomes aware of the fact that he wants it. So, in characteristic English fashion, he just takes it for granted.

Why is this? It is all very simple really. It is just a case of "out of sight, out of mind". The naval profession is very much alive, though we seldom see it in the act of living. And the Naval Officer certainly does not help us. He shuns the publicity of uniform when not afloat. When he has a shore job, he will always go to his work in plain clothes, if allowed, so that, even when we do see him, his disguise is too effective to penetrate. This leads to a vicious circle. On those few occasions when he does appear in uniform, he complains that his grateful countrymen mistake him for a railway official; which has the effect of keeping him out of uniform; which only makes the public more prone to the unfortunate mistake.

When he is afloat, or safely inside some naval establishment, he wears his uniform, of course. But that is not enough to dispel the mystery which surrounds him. We other professional men, when we go into our offices, our consulting or lecture rooms, or behind our counters, are reasonably accessible to all and sundry. But our naval colleague goes into *his* office behind a foot or so of impenetrable steel. To visit him, or even to see him at work, we have to take a special boat—not an excursion steamer, or one which runs to public schedule—or else we have to penetrate the gap in a high dockyard wall, where a big policeman glares out at us and wants to know our business. In fact—save on such special occasions as "Navy Weeks"— we never see our colleague in his office: and even then he is not really at work, because he politely knocks off in order to show us round.

No wonder we take him for granted, and overlook the fact that he is a member of one of the most highly-organized and efficient professions in the world, with a long and vitally interesting history behind him: a profession which has grown up gradually and instinctively, yet very surely, to meet all the calls that may be made upon it: a profession which is as typically English as any institution in the land.

So much, indeed has it been overlooked that nobody, I believe, has ever devoted a book exclusively to it: and that in an age when books are pouring from our presses on almost every conceivable subject. Naval Strategy and Operations have received some slight attention: the Navy's administration and its present condition have not been entirely neglected, nor the careers of individual officers. But the Naval Officer in general, in his professional aspect, and as heir to many generations of previous naval officers, has never yet found a biographer.

This task I have attempted here. It has seemed to me to be of the utmost importance that we of the "laity" should penetrate for once the steel plates of today and the wooden walls of yesterday, to learn how the men upon whom we have so often and so trustfully relied came to be what they are.

And twenty-six years of close association with the Naval Officer have taught me one thing more. He will not contradict me, I am sure, if I affirm that the ordinary member of his profession knows little of his own origins. This is by no means through lack of interest: he is too alert and intelligent not to know full well that the story of his own evolution has much to teach him: that *how* he came to be what he is has a big influence on *what* he is. All he lacks is the opportunity of finding out, for he cannot often have the facilities, even when he possesses the inclination, for historical research. That opportunity, too, I hope this book will give him. He will find in it the story of the beginnings, the growth, the adolescence and the maturity of that great profession to which he belongs, together with brief biographies of each principal rank and branch in it. What he reads will not, I am very confident, detract from his already great loyalty to the Service, but rather enhance it, by revealing something of the age-old tradition upon which that loyalty is so largely—if unconsciously—based.

The story, which is one of the organic growth of living tissues, is sometimes involved, often circuitous, and always slow. The intricacies have been, where possible, smoothed out; but not unduly so, since the essential interest of the story lies in that organic evolution, and this must on no account be lost. Technicalities, however, have been avoided where possible, and so have notes, though the authorities for most of the conclusions are incorporated in the text.

I have relied, in the main, on three kinds of contemporary sources—The Regulations and Instructions, from 1731 onwards: Admiralty Orders in Council: and the various Navy Lists themselves, from the time of Charles II to the present day; in these latter, apart from their obvious importance in the story, there appear many ephemeral orders not included in the other authorities.

Other sources are many and varied. I feel that I owe a good deal to a great many of these—too many for separate enumeration—but no overwhelming debt to any one of them, since no considerable proportion of the subject-matter which I have sought has anywhere been collected together in one place. But it would be graceless not to mention two very large and important *groups* of such sources, to which, collectively, I am tremendously indebted. The pages of the *Mariners Mirror*, the journal of the Society for Nautical Research, have been raided again and again, especially for the earlier portions of the story. They are mines of erudition on all branches of naval and nautical matters, and no one interested in any such subjects can afford to ignore them. And the same acknowledgment must be made, in only a slightly lesser degree, to the Navy Records Society's publications, where a mass of material, otherwise all but inaccessible, is brought within easy reach of all.

For valued assistance in the completion of various chapters, I should like to thank the Chaplain of the Fleet, Archdeacon T. Crick, R.N.; Engineer Captain E. C. Smith, R.N.; Instructor Captain A. E. Hall, R.N.; Paymaster Captain A. F. Cooper, R.N., and Commander (E.) A. D. Bonny, R.N.; and, for their kind help with the illustrations, all the Staff of the National Maritime Museum. To its Director, Professor Sir Geoffrey Callender, I am particularly indebted. He has not only read the whole book in typescript, but has given me the most practical and valuable advice at all stages in its creation.

Lastly, I would tender my grateful acknowledgments to the Trustees of the National Portrait Gallery, and the Visitors of the Ashmolean, for permission to reproduce the portraits of Samuel Pepys and Lord Clinton respectively; while to the Trustees of the National Maritime Museum I owe a still greater debt for allowing me to reproduce no less than seven illustrations—those mentioned in the list on page 13 as being in that Museum.

# CONTENTS

## BOOK FOUR

# THE NEW OFFICERS

# ILLUSTRATIONS

## BOOK ONE

## The Antecedents of the Naval Officer

### CHAPTER I

# HIS ANCESTORS

WHEN we think of a Naval Officer nowadays, we visualize a paid servant of the State, belonging to a profession in which he rises from the lowly position of Cadet to (perhaps) the lofty station of Admiral by a series of steps, or "ranks". He is a man who studies his profession carefully from a very early age and continues in it, as a rule, as long as he is allowed. He is, in fact, a "whole-timer" —every bit as much as other professional men.

But in one respect he differs from them. He belongs really to *two* professions. The Doctor is a body-healer, the Lawyer is an exponent of the law, and so on. Also, the Soldier is a fighter, and the Sailor is a manager of a ship. But the Naval Officer is *both* the last two; and they are, in their real nature, two quite different things, which call for quite a different set of abilities and quite a different sort of training. This distinction is perhaps a little blurred in our own time. Nowadays, the Naval Officer tends to specialize, like everybody else, and the man who makes the ship go, for instance, has nothing to do with the firing of the guns: indeed, does not know very much about them: and vice-versa. But this is only a recent development. If we go back a mere hundred years, we shall find that all naval officers—at least, *commissioned* officers, were essentially both fighters and seamen. We are all aware, for instance, that a man like Nelson knew pretty well all there was to know about both the sailing and the fighting of his ship.

B

But there existed a period in our history when this dual being had not been evolved; when not only was there in England no naval career possible, but actually no naval ranks, no naval officers, no naval personnel—not even a navy, as we understand the word: a period, in fact, before fighting and seamanship had coalesced into one. It is in that dark age that we must first look for the ancestors of our Naval Officer.

The Fighter, needless to say, was always there, and even the professional fighter has existed for longer years than History herself can remember; and so has the seaman—for ages, probably, before Odysseus sailed the Mediterranean or the Phoenicians came to Cornwall for tin. But they did not coalesce to form the Fighting-Seaman until comparatively recently. Nor, when they did coalesce, did they do so at once: the finished article did not sprout up, as it were, overnight, like a mushroom. He grew slowly, with that almost exasperating deliberation which is so characteristic of any English institution.

The first—and most obvious—reason why he failed to appear for so long was the absence of the Navy—the Navy, that is, in its modern sense, a "Permanent National Maritime Fighting Force". Notice the epithets: they each refer to something which is there now, but was once absent. "Permanent" and "Maritime" are self-explanatory: by "National" we mean to suggest a body which belongs to the whole of the people, as opposed to a section or an individual, even when that individual was a person so important as the King; and by "Fighting" we mean to suggest a force that exists, if not necessarily to fight, at least to be *able* to fight when necessary: a force whose principal function is fighting.

Now in England throughout the Middle Ages there *was* no such specialized force—neither the ships nor the men. But there were its component parts, which, if coalesced, would *almost* have made it up. These component parts were—normally—three in number, and—sometimes—four.

The normal three were, first, the ordinary ships of the ordinary merchants and fishermen from the ordinary commercial ports of England; second, the ordinary plain seafaring men who normally sailed them: and third—a class very far removed from the last-named, and relatively very "'superior"—there was the professional fighting man: and, in the Middle Ages, it is scarcely necessary to emphasize, it was he who counted for more than anyone else. *The* profession *par excellence* of the nobility, the profession of anyone who professed to be anybody, was fighting.

The fourth component part which sometimes existed—yet, very often, did not—was a collection of ships called "The King's Ships", or, to give it its much rarer, and—to us—more misleading name—the "Royal Navy": which is just what it was—in the most literal sense but not in ours. Not by any means all English Kings before the time of Henry VII possessed such luxuries as ships of their own—and when they did, they had but few. But when they did possess them, they were very much their own—their own property throughout, built with their own money, to their own specification, and used exclusively for their own purposes: and naturally they tended to be rather super-ships, for after all the King was usually the most wealthy and important man in the realm: and in the matter of ships he was competing, not with the big barons, who were not normally at all interested in the sea, but only with the comparatively humble merchants who were. And the story of the evolution of the King's ships is very largely the story of the evolution of the modern Royal Navy's ships—a story which we shall not attempt to follow here. The point to grasp now is that, in the Middle Ages, the King's ships, which appeared so sporadically, did in no sense constitute a Permanent National Maritime Fighting Force.

Then was there never such a thing? Not exactly; but

there was a rough substitute for it when an emergency arose —a real emergency, that is: not just a passing whim on the King's part to cross the Channel and conquer a piece of France. That substitute was a rally of all the component parts mentioned just now, tumbled together for that emergency and dispersed when it was over. By age-old custom and tradition, on emergency the King could call upon the whole *maritime* community to assemble in their own ships: and he could call upon the whole *fighting* community to go on board these ships and fight the enemy. Each profession does its job, and there is no overlapping: the seaman, as ever, works the ship, and the fighter, as ever, does the fighting. If the King had ships of his own, so much the better: they would form a very useful nucleus to the otherwise haphazard collection. But that was all. We shall go badly astray if we think of the King's ships as being in any way "ships of war" and therefore different from the others, or "merchantmen". There was no such distinction in England: there was, normally, no such thing in England as a specialized ship of war. We shall be much nearer the truth if we regard all the ships—King's and Merchants' alike—as common-or-garden merchantmen. The "Old Navy" of England was simply the whole mercantile marine of England, or such of it as the King thought fit to summon. There was nothing else that he *could* summon, because, even if he had any, his own ships were merchantmen too.

Now it must be admitted that we are generalizing here: and our excuse must lie in the fact that this chapter is essentially only the introduction to the story of the Naval Officer: it is not the story itself. Yet generalization is notoriously dangerous: in the interests of accuracy there must always be qualifications. Thus we must not wholly omit certain exceptions to the general rules laid down above. Two such, ephemeral or partial in their nature though they were, call for some notice.

First, there existed once, very early in our history, a

body of men who appear to have been, in their essence, "soldier and sailor too". They were called "Buscarles", or "Butsecarles", and they were enrolled into an organized corps under the later Saxon kings. They were apparently a counterpart of the "Huscarles", or Royal Bodyguard on land. But their functions were purely naval. Their headquarters were at the mouth of the Thames, and they had their own officers, the principal of whom was the "Batsuen"; or, as we should now say—for the name is still with us— the "Boatswain". But these men disappeared at the Conquest, or were merged in the next experiment which we must mention, and became as though they had not been: so that it is safe to say that they have little or no direct influence on the story we are tracing.

The other exception is the Navy of the Cinque Ports—a bigger and more durable affair. The "Five Towns"—the original ones were Sandwich, Dover, Hythe, Romney and Hastings; though others were added later, so that the term became generic—were, of course, the Channel Ports of their day, and were in some small degree the furnishers of "specialized" ships, in that they long enjoyed a special contract with the King to provide him with ships for his own particular purposes. Their main obligation under the bargain was to produce fifty-seven ships, all found, for fifteen days per annum: if the Crown wanted them for a longer period, or wanted more of them, it paid extra, at fixed rates. But their "specialization" did not extend to differentiation of build or construction. They too were ordinary merchant ships, and for far the larger part of any or every year they acted as such. Their principal duties, when employed, consisted of guarding the Narrow Seas and furnishing transport for such of our monarchs—not a few— who had military "business" in France. On such occasions they might, and sometimes did, engage in naval actions. These functions, while important in themselves, were not important enough to justify the Crown in calling up the

full "Old Navy". The King was, in fact, doing by contract
with a quasi-public body what he might have done, had he
thought it worth while, by building private ships of his
own. Indeed, a monarch like Henry V, who went further
than his predecessors in this latter experiment, did in some
measure substitute his fleet for that of the Cinque Ports,
which were already falling into decay and tending to silt
up. After his time, his successors reverted to the "contract"
system: only now they made, for the most part, more
strictly private contracts with individual merchants or ports,
instead of with the larger organization.

A certain number of the leading Cinque Ports' seamen,
by dint of frequent, though sporadic, employ in ships thus
hired to the King, received, no doubt, a rough sort of
"fighting-experience", and were in their day the nearest
approach to the modern Naval Officer. Some of them even
attained to high-sounding titles, and positions of real
national authority, as we shall see when we come to discuss
in greater detail some of the "Old Officers". But they were
exceptional, and it would be over-emphasizing their importance to see in them the ancestors of the modern officer,
whose real descent is somewhat different. The Buscarles
(certainly) and the Cinque Ports' leaders (probably) are
better regarded as two early exceptions to the general rules
which we have formulated.

"But," it may be asked, by the reader who remembers his
classical history, "what about the naval warfare of the
Greeks and Romans? What of Salamis, and Aegospotami
and Actium? And what, even, about the great battle of
Lepanto, fought as late as 1571, when—or so *we* always
understood—the highly-trained *battle*-fleets of the Mediterranean performed tactical manœuvres which were miracles
of intricacy, precision and practised skill? Surely those
fleets were composed of specialized ships of war?"

It is true. They were. But they were confined to the
Mediterranean, or at most to a little way up the outward

seaboard of Spain: and they were composed of galleys—
long, agile, but relatively frail craft, propelled in battle by
oars. We, however, are discussing England—England who
always does nautical things differently from everybody else,
and almost always does them a great deal better, even when
she does not quite grasp what she is doing, or why. We do
not affirm that no galley ever appeared in England. That
would be quite wrong. What we do say is that this particular type of ship never acclimatized itself in the rougher
waters and the tougher weather of the Channel and the
Northern Ocean, and that its influence on our story is
practically *nil*.

The kind of ship which concerns us—the medieval
English "cog"—was diametrically the opposite of the galley.
The former was long and thin, the latter short and fat—
the ordinary cog having a length of only twice its breadth:
the one was light and of very shallow draught, the other
was an affair of massy timbers, with a huge pot-belly; and
it wallowed deep in the seas: for the one was propelled by
oars, and was designed to move fast over short distances in
comparatively calm waters, while the other, propelled only
by sails, was built to carry bulky cargoes over long distances
and in heavy swells, with the maximum possible safety,
albeit with the minimum conceivable speed. After all, there
was no great hurry in the world in the days before Columbus
discovered America. In short, the galley—the *Navis longa*—
was built for war, and was useless for trading since it had
no cargo-space: while the cog—the "Tall Ship", or (as a
French writer has called it) the "Round Ship"; was built
for trade, and was the clumsiest imaginable weapon of war.
The Southerners, of course, had both sorts, but they
specialized throughout, using the galley exclusively for war,
and the round-ship exclusively for trade. Where we differed
from them was simply in this, that we used the cog for both
purposes: found out at last, in our muddled way, what a
shocking weapon of war it was, so cut down its height,

pulled it out lengthwise and continued to tinker with it
until we had turned it into that most graceful thing that
ever sailed the seas—the Ship-of-the-Line: and when one
day—in 1587 at Cadiz to be exact—we pitted this new
thing against the galley, the whole world, including ourselves, was amazed when it blew the marine heir of all the
ages sky-high inside an hour.

This is perhaps a digression; but the point had to be
raised, for—to come back to our Naval Officers—it goes a
long way to explain why it was the English—the new-
comers in Naval Warfare—and not the old hands, the
Southerners, who invented the Fighting Seaman. In the
galley, the gulf between the High and Mighty class who
fought, and the utterly degraded pariah-dog who was the
motive-power—the galley-slave—was never bridged: was
indeed unbridgeable. The English Seaman, on the other
hand, whose duty it was to wait upon the wind—*our* motive-
power—was, it is true, a humble soul, but at least he *had*
a soul—he was a free man. Add to this the undoubted fact
that the English nobleman was never anything like so High
and Mighty as the Don of Spain, and we find that the river
to be bridged was formidable indeed, but still bridgeable.
How that river was at length crossed, we must now try to
explain.

Let us see what happened, in medieval times, when, shall
we say, the *Christopher of Dartmouth* was called out at
the King's summons, either on "general emergency" or on
the King's private hiring. She sailed from her own port,
carrying her own "officers"—the men, that is, appointed
by her owners. It is worth taking a look at the principal
trio, because they all bear names which are still very familiar
to us. They were the Master, the Boatswain, and the Carpenter. The Master was "the skipper"—the responsible
man—responsible to his owners for the safety of the ship:
for the navigation and the steering of her. He remains to
this day, absolutely unchanged: and if the modern *Chris-*

*topher of Dartmouth* is not a proud big ship, but just a modest sort of tramp, we shall find that the responsible man in her is still the Master. Only if she is a liner, or something of that kind, will he have acquired the more pretentious, but not grander—because in the sea-sense *younger*—title of Captain. The Boatswain was the man of the ship who "made her go": his "opposite number" in these dingy days would be, no doubt, the Chief Engineer. He had fallen already from his high estate of Buscarle days, when he was the Commanding Officer. But he was still a most important personage, since he had under his charge all connected with masts, yards and sails, and was second only to the Master. The Carpenter was in charge of repairs—to the hull, the masts, all the canvas, all the hemp—everything in fact. These were the Big Three—until they came to the place appointed, which was usually, though not always, London.

Here certain curious rites had to be performed. They brought the *Christopher* up the Thames and dropped anchor off the Tower. The Carpenter, instructed and aided by the King's carpenters, then set to work, and built up those curiously fragile upper-works in bow and stern which people called the "forecastle" and the "after" or "Somer-castle". What was their purpose? Exactly the same as that of a castle on land. They conferred the boon of *height*. While furnishing cover to the fighter behind their crenellated breastworks, they also gave him the advantage of that essential principle in all pre-cannon missile-warfare— gravity. The whole system was based upon the incontrovertible fact, grasped for long ages before Newton, and by monkeys as well as by men, that missiles, like cocoanuts, rocks, hot pitch, flaming darts and boiling water are launched far more readily downwards than upwards. Till about 1400, these "castles" were, as a rule, taken down again when the campaign was over. After that date they usually stayed where they were, and ultimately always

did—one may suppose because the owners found a similar
use for them when the ship was following her normal peace-
time avocations. The only other war-preparation was a
temporary change of name. Our ship was now *The Christopher of the Tower* and remained so until the crenellations
were taken off her.

Then when all was ready, came the fighters—a troop of
men-at-arms complete, of course, with *their* officers: two in
number, the Captain and his Lieutenant: the "Caput",
the Headman, and his "Locum Tenens", to take his place
if anything untoward happened to the Great One himself.
Soldiers both, let us notice. The Captain of course took
charge at once. He was the King's Man; the Master was
not. He was the Gentleman: the Master was not. He had
the orders in his pocket. He told the Master where to go,
and when. But, unless he was a fool, he never told him *how*
to go. That was the Seaman's job, the Master's, and even
the great man himself had orders from above not to interfere here. It was only common prudence. Nor did the
Captain, at any rate directly, have any dealings with the
sailors; that too was the Master's job. But he governed the
soldiers entirely, and, when it came to fighting, he and
his soldiers did it all.

And now the *Christopher of the Tower* was a warship
—as near, that is, to being one as she could ever become.
And what is more, she had on board, in embryo, all the
really essential executive officers of the present day; and the
two classes into which they were then divided—absolutely
clear-cut as they were—have come down to us, equally
clear-cut in status on shipboard. The soldier-officers were
then the men who had the King's authority to command—
that is, in terms which are both medieval and modern, the
"King's Commission". Their descendants are the Commissioned Officers of today. The Seamen officers, as we have
said, were very much smaller fry. In fact they were so little
regarded by their new employer, sad to relate, as to be

counted as merely part and parcel of the ship—as *things*, hired along with it. So it came about that, when in Henry VIII's time a Board was appointed to look after the "things" of the King's Navy—the "matériel" as we say now, as opposed to the "personnel"—the seamen officers still found themselves classed as "things", and so came under the charge of that Board. It was called the Navy Board, and could not deal in commissions—only the King could do that. It could only issue "warrants" for things. So it issued them to these seaman officers, who thus became at once—what they are today—"Warrant Officers".

A curious illustration of how entirely these men were regarded as chattels is to be seen in their other, and, in earlier days, commoner name. Those parts of a ship's rigging which are most permanent, which are not hauled upon in making or reducing sail, are called the "standing" rigging. They are regarded as an integral part of the ship, and are only shifted when they break down or wear out. Well, the Warrant Officers, who were also regarded as an integral part of the ship, and were only shifted when *they* broke down or wore out, were called the "Standing" Officers. And, indeed, right up to a century ago, a "standing" officer remained planted in his ship throughout his career, unless one of the great ones took a fancy to him and got him specially moved. A pleasant example of this occurs in a State Paper of 1632, where mention is made of an old "ship-keeper" (that is, one of a ship's old-time "officers", left on board as caretaker when she was put out of commission) who was a hundred years old. Provided that ship had lived long enough, there is no reason whatever why the old gentleman should not have been in the same ship, man and boy, for ninety years!

Now this medieval system of "dual-control" which we have just described undoubtedly worked: at any rate until some particularly foolhardy captain came along and tried to sail the ship as well as fight her. But dual control, it must be admitted, is not usually the *best* method of getting things done; nor the safest when, as in this case, the dice are so heavily loaded in favour of one controller. A very elementary knowledge of medieval social distinctions will suffice to make us realize which party would win if it ever came to a clash of authorities; and that might—nay, certainly would—endanger the ship and all her company. No, one person must lead, must make the ultimate decision, must take the ultimate responsibility. And men soon began to realize this. They would probably have done so in any case, but, as it happened, the realization was suddenly hurried on by circumstances. Early in the sixteenth century there began to arise a new type of marine warfare which was in itself specialized: which was, in fact, *naval* fighting as opposed to just "fighting". This new mode came into being almost exclusively as a result of the introduction of one quite revolutionary weapon—the "Great Gun".

# CHAPTER II

# THE WEDDING OF SEAMANSHIP AND FIGHTING

Up to the moment of the great gun's appearance on shipboard Seamanship and Fighting were professions which existed side by side in England, but they were quite distinct. They were even accustomed to associate closely with each other on the constricted deck-space of the medieval ship; yet they had quite failed to unite. We must now see how union was ultimately achieved: how Seamanship was finally wed to Fighting, and what was the result of the match.

Up till the early 1500's our military captain and his men could walk on board the *Christopher* one afternoon, and next morning, with cheerful hearts could fight a battle; for they fought on shipboard exactly as they would have fought on land with the firm earth under their feet and the stone rampart at their breasts. There was, in fact, no other way in which they could fight: the ships were mere fighting platforms, laid side by side, whereon to perform one's deeds of prowess. Indeed, the principal difference between a medieval land fight and a medieval sea fight lay in the fact that the latter was the more desperate affair, for the simple reason that one could not run away with any reasonable hope of safety.

But with the Great Gun there came at last a "ship-killing" weapon—the very first of its kind in sailing-ship warfare. There was artillery before. Tradition says that the first gun ever on ship-board was carried into the very ship

which we have been discussing—the *Christopher of the Tower*
—in the year 1410. But these guns were small—effective
man-killers, indeed, but quite unable to do any vital
damage to a ship. From now onwards, however, the naval
battle was destined to develop into something quite different
from the land battle. "Off-fighting" began. The object
came more and more to be the *sinking* rather than the
*taking* of ships.

This touches our story very nearly. "Off-fighting"—even
when the distance between ships was only a matter of
yards—meant that the ordinary soldier—the "man-at-arms"
—immediately lost importance. In other words, requirements changed: one no longer needed an "infantry-man":
what one wanted now was a "gunner". . . .

This "gunner" was the immediate result of the Great
Gun's arrival; and, if we consider for a moment, we shall
see what an enormously important bearing he has on the
breaking down of the "dual system". For the naval gunner
was, by his very nature, the first person to appear on
board who not only *should* be "fighter-and-seaman-too",
but practically must be. His was a difficult job—far harder
than his army brother's, whose piece never pitched and
rolled at the moment of firing. But the naval gunner's did,
and unless he knew something about the way in which his
ship would behave in any particular condition of wind and
sea, he could not hope to make anything of his task. Listen
to Sir William Monson, the most eminent naval authority
of his day, a commander in the later stages of the Spanish
War, and a veteran of the Armada Campaign:—"A principal thing in a gunner at sea is to be a good helmsman,
and to call to him at helm to loof or bear up, to have his
better level, and to observe the heaving and setting of the
sea, to take his aim at the enemy." Here then is the first
"fighter-cum-seaman", the first true combination of the
two functions, and perhaps the first living proof that the
complete fighting seaman was a practical possibility.

And the Soldier-Captain, too, is becoming something of an anachronism. He can no longer fight in a medieval sense (that is, hand-to-hand); and it would be undignified and distasteful to a gentleman to stand idly by while his expert Master navigates the ship, and his expert Gunner fights the battle. No, the time has clearly come when something must be done. The question is—what?

The happy solution obviously lay in some form of combination, like that already achieved among the inferior sort of officers in the person of the gunner. There were only two alternative possibilities: first, that the fighting leader should learn the seaman's art; and, second, that the seaman should turn fighter. Both look feasible enough at first view, yet both had their special difficulties inherent in the social life of the times.

As to the first possibility; in the days of Henry VIII— for it was then that the problem began to come up for solution—it was very difficult for the fighting leader to take to the sea really wholeheartedly. That Sea is, even now, a hard master: it is a commonplace to say that a seaman cannot be made in a day. And it was a far harder master in Tudor times—and in Tudor ships—than it is now. Its apprenticeship was long, and the life was rough—too rough perhaps for the high-born youth of that age. Not that he minded roughing it in what he considered a good cause— that is, if he thought that advantage would thereby accrue to his personal honour: the early Tudor gentleman undoubtedly set great store by that. But here was the crux— *would* a sea life, connected in the minds of himself and his contemporaries with the inglorious drudgery of inferiors, help his honour? The answer was clearly "No!" We must remember, moreover, that he had not in any great degree that other inducement which was so soon to replace the merely selfish sense of personal honour with the more generous sentiment of England's honour—the inducement of "Patriotism". England's national consciousness is largely a product of Elizabeth's reign, and was in great measure fostered, as it so often is in peoples, by the appearance of a hateful and fearful danger from without—in our case by the terrifying menace of Spain.

So the long and short of it is that the fighting gentleman of Henry VIII's time seldom took to the sea, though here as elsewhere in our story there are partial exceptions. Such a one was William FitzWilliam, an early example of the "Gentleman Seaman". He commanded the fleet in 1520, and was made Lord High Admiral in 1536, and Earl of Southampton a year later. But even he was only a "part-timer" compared with modern officers. Henry VIII was certainly fully alive to the welfare of his Navy—for who should know better than he that it stood between him and the vengeance of the continental potentates whom he flouted? He seems, indeed, to have been anxious to have as captains in his great ships men who had been brought up to the sea, but it is certain that he did not often get them: and when he could not, he chose, as the convention of his day dictated, a gentleman who was *not* a seaman. A much more typical commander of the period was Sir Thomas Knyvett, captain of the *Great Harry*, who was Master of the Horse, and a soldier by profession. The day of the "Gentle-man-Seaman-Captain" had not yet dawned; and the problem of acquiring suitable naval officers was not solved by tempting "blue blood" to a sea career.

There remained the alternative of the seaman turning fighter. This may seem the obvious solution, since Nature and the ordinary conditions of contemporary life made him half one already. And indeed, the seaman *did* become the fighter. Thus simply may we explain the origin of the "rank and file"—the *men*: the "ratings", as we say today. The process of turning the common seamen into fighters may be measured by contemporary figures. If we compare the proportion of "soldiers" in the complements of repre-sentative ships with that of "mariners", we shall soon obtain a broad idea as to how things are going. This can be done, and we find, as we should expect, that the change-over from a "soldier" to a "sailor" majority on board coincides very exactly in time with the introduction and rise in importance of the Great Gun. The century following the appearance of that weapon, in fact, ends with the total disappearance of the soldier as a permanent member of the ship's company, as the following figures will show: though in some respects this was going too far, and it was not very long before the Marines appeared to redress the balance.

| Year | Ship | Soldiers | Mariners | Gunners | Number of Soldiers per 100 Sailors |
|------|------|----------|----------|---------|------------------------------------|
| 1512 | *Mary Rose* | 251 | 120 | 20 | 209 |
| 1520 | *Great Harry* | 349 | 301 | 50 | 116 |
| 1558 | *Victory* | 100 | 268 | 32 | 37 |
| 1603 | *Triumph* | 120 | 340 | 40 | 35 |
| 1624 | *Speedwell* | 0 | 100 | 64 | 0 |

The apparently low figures of "gunners", and their big increase in the last-named ship, call for some explanation. In the first four cases the classification is the age-old dual one of "soldier" and "sailor". The gunners mentioned are what we should now class as "warrant" and "petty" officers —the comparative experts. Their figures here are not intended to indicate the total number of men who actually plied the guns. These—the "rank and file"—would be drawn in the first two ships from the soldiers, and in the third and fourth from the mariners. But in the last-named ship's company, another, and more modern, method of classification is attempted—a triple one. The hundred men termed "mariners" in the table above have been sub-divided into two classes of fifty men each—fifty actually to man the sails and to attend to the propulsion of the ship, and fifty, called "small-arms-men", to act on deck for boarding and repelling boarders. We are justified in classing these two sub-groups together as "mariners" for the purposes of our statistics, because they all were, in fact, seamen, and not soldiers, even though half of them were assigned duties which the soldiers used to do, and which the Marines were destined to do in the future. The other group here—the sixty-four "gunners"—include *all* the men, "ratings" as well as "warrant officers", who were given the task of plying the guns.

It is clear from these figures that the first, and far the greatest, move from soldiers to seamen took place in the reign of Henry VIII, the monarch responsible for the great gun's appearance. The second stage may be regarded, to some extent, as a result of experience gained in the Anglo-Spanish War. But by then the process had really gone some way further than the figures in the table indicate; for many of the soldiers serving on board ship, especially in such critical years as 1588, were sent thither simply to make good the shortage of seamen, which always occurred when there was suddenly a big demand; and they seem to have been employed afloat for strictly nautical duties. They were not, like the Spaniards of the same period, segregated on board in their normal military formations, but were mixed indiscriminately among the ordinary seamen.

Thus, then, the "mariners" became fighting seamen, though the interrupted nature of their fighting employment obviously rendered them much less expert than their modern counterparts. The warrant-officers, too, who were their natural commanders, and always had been, could hardly help participating in such a revolution, and becoming fighting seamen too: and perhaps even more efficient ones, since the nature of their employment was far more constant than the men's.

But the story of the "Commission" officer is not quite so simple, for he did not normally exist in the old ship-

hierarchy, and there was still that one serious obstacle to
overcome—the *class* problem. The universal consensus of
medieval opinion still supported the belief that "gentle"
blood was essential in the battle leader. This was no mere
snobbery—nor, we hope, will the emphasis here placed on
the class-question be attributed to snobbery. Medieval
opinion was *right*: the custom of centuries sanctioned it,
and the social facts of the time justified it; for it is certain
that the habit of initiative and even of independent thought
was then far more nearly the monopoly of the upper classes
than it is today. It is a fact, very regrettable but none the
less true, that in Henry VIII's day there existed in England
practically no member of the regular seaman class who
could command a ship, let alone a fleet, in War.

But the man we are looking for was already there, and
was, even in Henry VIII's life-time sometimes sailing the
seas. He belonged to a class that was still comparatively
new in England, that had been encouraged and coaxed
by Henry VIII's shrewd old father into setting foot on the
deck of his own ship. We mean the Merchant. There were,
even in Henry VII's time, business men (mostly in the
West of England) of sufficient enterprise to be interested in
the new-fangled ideas of their monarch about the New
Found Lands: they had even—greatly daring—sent their
ships as far as Iceland before the first Tudor arrived; though
it is not so clear whether they had ventured there themselves. And they were eager enough in their questioning
of the dark-haired Italian, John Cabot, when he came to
Bristol *en route* for the West on the King's business. No one,
perhaps, could possibly suspect it then, but here in fact
was the answer to the puzzle—that enterprising eldest child
of the Renaissance on its commercial side—the Merchant
who wanted to see the new wonders for himself: or, perhaps,
who thought his interests would be better served on shipboard if he were there to look after them himself; in a word,
the "Merchant who took his own ship to sea."

Just such a one was old William Hawkins of Plymouth:
not the first Hawkins to be a merchant of Plymouth, but
perhaps the first to go to sea in his own ships, and certainly
the first to take them so far afield. We know that he made
several voyages to Brazil, and very likely went to other
remote parts as well. He must have been a man of initiative and a lover of adventure, for he had little help or
recognition from his government, such as he would have
had in Henry VII's time. Henry VIII was much too busy
pulling down the Pope, scandalizing his neighbour kings
and escaping their vengeance by building a colossal fleet.
This makes a curious and rather interesting contrast. Here
was the King, furnishing himself with a private navy un-
equalled heretofore in England, and officering it, for lack
of anything better, with all the distinguished *soldiers* he could
find: and there at the other end of England, was old William
Hawkins, bent mainly on his own financial advantage,
unconsciously engaged in solving the "officer" problem
that baffled the all-powerful monarch all his days.

For William Hawkins *was* solving the problem. By the
end of his life, he was a prime seaman who was not of the
seaman class. He was not, of course, quite a "gentleman";
nowadays, no doubt, we should think him a pretty tough
old customer. But he was a distinct cut above the seaman,
and—which was very important—he died *rich*: for then, as
now, "money talked". In a word, his family was "on the
rise". So it came about that his sons, young William and
John, were a distinct cut above their father, socially speaking.
They were brought up, for instance, to dress well—even a
trifle ostentatiously perhaps—and to have nice things about
them. Yet theirs was a canny stock, and they all knew
well enough which was the goose that laid the golden eggs;
so it happened that young William and John were "brought
up to the sea," and not only made the voyages themselves
but were even seamen by profession.

The brothers prospered exceedingly. Young William,

indeed, only became a very rich man who on several occasions filled the office of Mayor of Plymouth to his own, and everybody else's, satisfaction. But John went much further, for John was a great man. He died Sir John Hawkins, Treasurer of the Navy, Rear Admiral of the Fleet which defeated the Armada, and, to a very considerable extent, the man who created it. Still, "not quite one of us" in the eyes of the real old English families, but quite gentleman enough for most purposes.

Yet even John Hawkins was primarily a merchant, secondarily a Naval Administrator; and only as it were thirdly, a fighting seaman and a Naval Officer in embryo. His pose was always that of a respectable business man, with a reputation to keep up of steadiness and trustworthiness. That may sound a little odd to anybody who only knows of him as the founder of the English Slave Trade from Africa to the Spanish dominions, but it is none the less true. He was so respectable that, when set upon at San Juan de Ulua in a most treacherous and murderous manner, and deprived violently of most of his merchandise and many of his men, he gave up the trade altogether. And he was so trustworthy that the cautious Elizabeth entrusted to his sole and uncontrolled care the maintenance of her entire fleet, and did not trust in vain. No, Hawkins was a great man, but his greatness lay in the arts of peace and in the administrative (as opposed to the executive) side of war. He was one of the makers of modern business, and one of the makers of the English ship-of-the-line, but not—primarily—a fighting seaman. The distinction of being the first of this latter category—or at any rate the first really typical specimen of it—must go to an even better known figure—Sir Francis Drake. He and his fellow-fighters, brought up and blooded in our first great national war, may, more than any others, be called the eldest sons of Seamanship's union with Fighting.

# CHAPTER III

# THE BIRTH OF THE NAVAL OFFICER

IN plucking one exceptionally bright gem like Drake out of the brilliant setting of his contemporaries, we are now running the risk of particularizing—a risk no less grave than the peril of generalization to which we have already called attention. And our excuse must be the same. This is not a treatise on Elizabethan seamen; and more can be achieved in fewer words by dealing with one type-figure, one outstanding example of the special gifts and tendencies which we wish to illustrate, than by spreading our net to catch the many. Not that any of the great Sea Captains of Elizabeth had the same characteristics. While all were, in greater or lesser degree, essentially the sons of Seamanship and Fighting, they each had their own particular fortes and foibles: they were essentially *un*alike, essentially divergent personalities. Hawkins, we have seen, was Merchant, Seaman, Administrator and Fighter—perhaps in that order. Frobisher was Explorer, Seaman and Fighter, yet, though a fine seaman and a very fine fighter, perhaps more just "Fighter" than "Seaman Fighter". Grenville was Colonizer, Imperialist and Fighter, with yet a streak of the berserk about the latter which makes him not quite the "seaman-fighter" of the new tradition. Gilbert was Geographer, Explorer, Colonizer and Seaman: Raleigh was—very nearly everything *except* Seaman-Fighter; and so on. A process very much akin to elimination leaves us at last with Francis Drake as, not in any sense the *only* son, but the outstanding one in our particular aspect of the Elizabethan story.

This astonishing man was a kinsman of Hawkins (though exactly what the relationship was no one has ever been able to discover). We will attempt no consecutive account of his life: that is too well known. All we shall do is to try and show where he stands in the biography of the Naval Officer. After he came to fame, there was a brave attempt at the Herald's Office to equip him with a watertight set of ancestors, but that should not blind us to the fact that his family was probably very similar in origin to that of Hawkins: only the Drakes were not nearly so prosperous, and Francis himself was certainly not born in what has been called the "Purple of Commerce". To be exact, his boyhood was spent in an old ship laid up in the Medway, where his father, a rather fanatical Protestant, who had made his native Devon too hot for him, acted as a kind of lay preacher. Francis, too, as a young man, was present at San Juan de Ulua, and again a little later he had a second experience of Spanish double-dealing. His reaction took a very different form from Hawkins's. He made it his life's work from then on to wipe out the affronts. He became the deadly enemy of Spain and everything Spanish.

Such a man, with such an aim, and at such a moment in our history, had the ball at his feet. His resolve to down the Spaniard coincided almost exactly with the beginning of the Spanish menace to England. That menace, and the situation it occasioned is well known. It is enough here to say that, from being a man with a private grudge against Spain, Drake very quickly worked up, *via* the rôle of guerrilla leader under the Queen's uncertain patronage, into the position of leader of England's fleet, and—for one short but rich moment—not only the director of England's naval strategy, but even the director of England's conduct of the War.

England and the Navy both owe Sir Francis Drake a great

deal. It was he who first formulated that strategic doctrine which has since become the main plank in the platform of British Naval Strategy—a doctrine later to be summed up in the words—"The frontiers of England are the ports of the Enemy." It was he, too, more than anyone else, who was the originator of all sailing-ship tactics. Henry VIII had introduced the great guns, but it was Drake and his immediate school who taught the world how to use them, and who laid for ever the ghost of the galley's superiority. But there was something else that he may almost be said to have invented—a side of his life's work less advertised than his singeing of King Philip's beard or his harrying of the Armada. It was, in fact, Sir Francis Drake who, more than any other one man in our history, really created the Naval Officer. The other debts we owe him must not be forgotten, but here we must concentrate on this one.

He did it in many ways, of which we shall only indicate two: first, by the very fact of his own career: by forcing himself, on sheer merit, into a position unheard of before for the son of a poor preacher. In 1588 he was Vice-Admiral of England's Navy—England's *Old* Navy, that is: the whole might of Maritime England, headed by the Queen's ships, but supported by five times as many of her subjects' ships, summoned on emergency, as described earlier, to defend her shores. Many have wondered why it was that he was not higher still: why he was not its Admiral. The reason is very apposite to our subject. In fact, he and his colleagues did all the planning and most of the leading: in name only he was not Admiral, for such a thing was an impossibility. Drake had done wonders, but he could not work miracles. No one of his standing had ever before risen so high: far from being annoyed that Lord Howard of Effingham was "put over his head", he was intensely proud of his Vice-Admiralty. Besides, Howard was not *put* over his head. Howard was, already—and automatically—over every seafarer's head, for he was the "Lord High Admiral", as per-

manent a feature of the Ship of State as the figure-head
was of the Ship-of-the-Line, and, for sheer technical knowledge in handling ships and squadrons, just about as much
use. We shall explain later the significance of the Lord
High Admiral—and he was a most important person. We
may dismiss him here by saying that he is best regarded,
not as an Admiral in our modern sense at all, but as the
representative of that part of the Queen's Sovereignty which
related to the sea. Ashore, he was the whole Board of
Admiralty rolled into one, but with none of the sea-
experience conferred on that body nowadays by the
presence of the Sea Lords. Afloat, his position would be
analogous to that of the First Lord of the Admiralty, if the
latter found himself sent off in the *Nelson* to command the
Grand Fleet. Professionally—and in practice—Howard was
no rival to Drake, but did just what, we may be sure, the
First Lord would do under such circumstances today—he
put himself entirely into the hands of his naval advisers.
In fact, it was Drake and his fellows who fought and beat the
Armada.

And this Drake was a seaman *and* a fighter—or a fighter
*and* a seaman: it is hard to decide which to put first. Not
"blue-blooded", of course, yet a born leader of men, with
certainly enough "initiative and habit of command" to
carry him through any ordeal. And everybody had the
opportunity to know him for what he was—the prime
Seaman, the expert Fighter, the far-seeing Strategist: the
great Invention whom necessity bore for the great occasion:
neither poor and humble seaman, nor rich and powerful
Lord, but, socially speaking, the Perfect Compromise: the
typical product of that backbone of the nation, even then
just coming into its own—the Middle Classes.

Here then, are surely all the essentials of the modern
Naval Officer, we may say. And the answer certainly is,
Yes. The *main* thing is there—the Fighting Seaman Leader.
But there are several minor features still lacking. Let us

recall our original definition of the modern Naval Officer, and we shall see. He is to be (*a*) a "whole timer" and (*b*) one who rises step by step—rank by rank—through his profession.

Now Drake fulfilled neither of these conditions. He was certainly no whole-time Naval Officer. If we were to add up the whole sum of the periods when he was *strictly* in the service of Queen and Country we should perhaps be amazed at the smallness of it. For Drake was many other things as well—Queen's Counsellor, Member of Parliament, and of several Select Committees, Country Gentleman, Public Benefactor of Plymouth, Soldier, Merchant-Adventurer, Explorer and Privateer. The modern Naval Officer could hardly find time to adorn a quarter of these professions; and therefore, until we can find a man who is a "whole-timer" we can hardly be said to have reached our goal.

Next, what was Drake's naval *rank*? There too the answer may surprise some people. It is—He had none: and that for the very good reason that there was not such a thing to have. Of course he had a *post*—many of them in his time: many *jobs*, that is: or, to use the very accurate term which they used then, many "offices". So he was an "officer" in the Tudor sense—that is, a man who held an office: but not in the modern service sense of a man who holds a *rank*. This distinction is by no means pettifogging. It is most important to grasp it if we are to understand the later stages of our story, and we shall have cause to mention it again. When Drake was officially made Second-in-Command of the Anti-Armada Fleet, he was appointed, not "Vice-Admiral", but "Vice-Admiral of" that particular fleet, assembled for that particular purpose. The qualifying "of" is really all-important, for, both then and for long afterwards, the title itself simply did not exist without the "of": and this is true of all naval titles from Admiral down to Lieutenant. When the Anti-Armada fleet was dispersed, therefore, Drake did not remain Vice-Admiral, nor even revert, say, to Captain. He was still, of course, *Sir* Francis, because "Sir" was, even then, a rank—a social rank to be retained, normally, till death or promotion to something higher. But he had no naval rank. Again, on those occasions when he commanded an expedition, the Lord High Admiral being absent, we find that Drake's official title is "General": that is, he held the *office* of general, or Leader; not the rank. In these cases nobody is likely to make the mistake of calling him "General Drake". Yet it is really just as bad to call him Admiral Drake—or just as good. For if we do but qualify the title with that significant "of", and add the name of the expedition or fleet, we are quite entitled to call him by either name.

One contemporary example—again from Monson—of the Tudor use of the word "officer" is worth recording. That authority gives a list of the "officers" belonging to the King's ships at sea. They are:—"the Captain, Lieutenant, Master, Pilot and Coaster, Boatswain, Gunner, Carpenter, Purser, Trumpeter, Surgeon, Corporal, Cockswain, Quartermaster, Cooper, Swabber and Liar, Steward and Cook." It is clearly a very comprehensive term which includes the all-powerful Captain and the necessary but humble Cook. But it is in that picturesque "officer" the Liar that the contemporary meaning of the word is fully revealed. For Monson, having explained exactly the "office" (i.e. the duties) of each person, goes on thus quaintly:—"The Swabber is to keep the cabins and all the rooms of the ships clean within board, and the Liar to do the like without board. The Liar holds his place but for a week, and he that is first taken with a lie upon a Monday morning is proclaimed at the mainmast with a general cry, 'A Liar, a liar, a liar!': and for that week he is under the Swabber, and meddles not with making clean the ship within board, but without." The Liar's duties, obviously, were to be strictly corrective and deterrent. How deterrent they were we shall understand when we realize that what polite house-agents now call "usual offices" were not installed at that date in His Majesty's ships, the outboard of the bows being used as a substitute. We of today might call the poor Liar an office-*holder*, for he had a very necessary office to perform: but hardly an "officer".

There was not, then, such a thing in the Elizabethan ships as the modern officer. Yet Drake was always busy doing his utmost to create him. He laboured all his life, with that half-conscious groping so characteristic of the founders of England's best institutions, to improve the status of the seaman leader class: the class which he represented in its struggle against its natural enemy, the "gentleman-amateur-seaman". He was always waging this war in small ways, so one example must suffice. In 1577 he sailed on his famous voyage round the world, and took with him, as was then the custom, a number of "voluntary gentlemen", as they called themselves, who joined for the love of adventure or the chance of profit. Among these was his own dearest friend, one Thomas Doughty. Now, although Drake did not know it, this Doughty was something of a viper in the bosom, for he was bent on wrecking the expedition. His reasons for attempting such a thing are disputed, but his methods are not; and the important point for us to notice in this extraordinary story is how he went about it. He tried, in effect, to set the young "gentlemen-officers" against the mere "tarpaulin" or "shell-back" officers whom Drake had, very naturally and very properly, put in command of the ships. He could not attack Drake in person, but he could —and did—appeal to the age-old and hitherto accepted instinct of "blood" superiority. It was a cunning approach, and it speaks volumes for the personality of Drake himself that it was not instantly successful. It was not: on the whole, the Volunteers had come sufficiently under the spell of the great man to resist. And Drake did the rest. Having learnt what was happening, he gave the offender solemn warning once—twice: then, realizing that half-measures were useless, struck with dramatic suddenness: arrested

Doughty: constituted a court to try him: charged him with treachery in attempting to ruin an expedition undertaken on the Queen's service: secured a conviction—for the crime was obvious enough once one allowed the competence of the Court—and then summarily executed him. Thereupon he delivered to the rest a harangue of which some words deserve to be remembered yet: words which are, in a sense, the very charter of Naval Discipline. "I must have," he said, "the gentleman to haul and draw with the mariner, and the mariner with the gentleman"; that is, in the Gospel according to Sir Francis, "If you come on board my ships, you shall obey my officers, whoever *you* are, and whoever *they* are!" It was a salutary lesson, and it enshrines for all time the real essence of service discipline—*nothing* must stand between the responsible officer and his authority.

In Elizabeth's later years, the exploits of such men as Drake, and perhaps still more the wave of patriotism which was born of the war, at last brought the old gentry and even the nobility into the new profession in ever increasing numbers. They had discovered that there *was* honour in it, not to mention money, if they were lucky. So we find that, by the end of the century, quite a few really high-born people had taken to the sea, and acquired a very real proficiency; though not, of course, a proficiency comparable with that of the real "old hands" like Drake, Hawkins and his son Richard, Frobisher, Fenner, Cross and many more. Still, people like Sir Richard Grenville, Lord Thomas Howard, the Earl of Cumberland, the young Earl of Essex and Sir Richard Leveson·were by no means contemptible as seamen. Incidentally they contrived to win the Queen's ear, and to have a hand in driving out Drake himself: which only goes to emphasize how strong class-feeling still was, and how remarkable was Drake's feat in rising so high and in keeping it at bay for so long.

There follows a very gloomy period in the maritime history of England. James I and Charles I, for reasons

which cannot be discussed here, seriously let down both the
Navy and the Merchant Service. James stopped the war
and—what was perhaps as bad from the gentleman-sea-
man's point of view—he also stopped privateering. The
first cut out possibilities of honour, the second possibilities
of profit. With neither of their two primary inducements
left, almost all the better classes ceased to "follow the sea".
They were hardly to blame: James forced them out of the
profession. The few "gentry" to remain seamen—men like
Sir Francis Verney, Sir Antony Shirley and Sir Henry
Mainwaring—only remained at the price of becoming what
would now be called out-and-out pirates. There was nothing
else for them to be.

Yet, oddly enough, it was in this very dark period that
there began to appear the first symptoms of a naval personnel organized on a more permanent basis, and divided
into more appreciable and durable grades. Our closer study
of the Service as a profession will begin, when the time
comes, in this period. The first developments were rudi-
mentary and tentative, but they were there: and—what is
even more important—we now begin to find, for the first
time, indications that men are waking up to the desirability
of procuring some body of professional "sea-officers". It
was the unfortunate Charles I who was largely responsible
for these things. Like all the Stuarts, he had a great love for
ships, though he never had enough money to indulge that
love to the full. And this was decisive, since the "Royal
Navy" still consisted of "the King's Ships", and it was he,
and no one else, who was still supposed to maintain them.

Herein lay Charles I's great contribution to naval history.
He saw the shocking results of having no fleet capable of
guarding even Home Waters: he saw pirates flourishing
in the very channel, raiding our ports and capturing ships
in them, landing on our shores and carrying off the country-
folk for galley-slaves: and he said, "This is a job for the
nation to tackle. There should be a National Maritime

Fighting Force always at hand to protect our shores: and all Englishmen should be responsible for the upkeep of the force which guards the honour and the property of all Englishmen." This was unquestionably his idea when he levied the famous Ship Money, and no one today would think of disagreeing with it. But, unfortunately, most of his subjects did disagree—not with the providing of the fleet, nor even with the paying for it, but with the question of who should control it. The King's theory was, "The Nation pays, but the King controls." That was his view of his duties and rights, not only as regards the Navy, but in all departments of State affairs: indeed, as ill luck would have it, he was even then in the midst of his long attempt to break Parliament for good, as Richelieu had lately done in France. No wonder his people mistrusted him. Yet he was right in his main contentions that a fleet adequate for the defence of the nation should exist at all times, and that the nation, as principal beneficiaries, should pay for it. His antagonists opposed him then, but that did not prevent them from making the reform themselves as soon as they could alter the formula to "Nation pays, *Parliament* controls": and at the Restoration both King and Parliament acquiesced in the principle of a Standing Navy, paid for by the nation.

In Charles I's time it was around the ships that controversy raged most hotly: but the crews to man them—and especially the officers—were unavoidably part of the same problem. Anyone who requires a permanent fleet can hardly avoid trying to acquire a permanent body of reasonably expert men to officer it. And so it was that Charles, who wanted the former, began to take steps towards obtaining the latter. They did not amount to much, because, on the whole, he failed in both respects. He wrung sufficient money from his unwilling subjects to build a few good ships, but it ran out before he could pay, clothe or feed his personnel: with the tragic result—for him—that, when the clash came, they almost all, officers and men alike, deserted to the other side.

Yet that other side, as we have seen, quickly borrowed both his projects, and, having the money this time, went ahead with them. Thus it was that, after the arrival of that amazingly efficient body of men whom we know as the Commonwealth Government, things began to advance very rapidly, first in the matter of ships, but soon in the sphere of personnel too. Everyone knows that, in their "New Model", they created the English Army. What is perhaps less well known is that they really created the New Model Navy as well—the *new* English Navy, that is, as opposed to the old "Emergency" hotch-potch of King's Ships and Merchantmen: they created the Permanent National Maritime Fighting Force of today: and it was only a question of time before someone would create an adequate corps of Permanent National Maritime Fighting Officers to run it.

Briefly, it all happened like this. During the Great Civil War the Parliament had no cause for anxiety on the naval side since they had secured at the outset practically all the King's Ships. But after the main war was over—just before the King's execution in fact—about half the ships revolted, and went over to Prince Charles in Holland. Faced at last with a maritime problem of the first magnitude, they tackled it with their usual common sense and clearness of vision. They reorganized the whole service from the bottom, built ships (for which, at last, the public and not the King were made to pay), equipped them as they had never been equipped before, and made the Navy attractive once more by raising the pay handsomely all round—with the people's money—improving the victualling, and introducing prize-money in lieu of the lost privateering benefits. Thus they had no difficulty in procuring men: nor even the more junior officers. But for fleet-leaders it was not so easy. Once more they found themselves lacking in "class", since a vast majority of the "high-borns" hated them like poison. Indeed, very few people in the whole of England, outside the ranks of the Army itself, were on their side. This, in one way, however, actually made their job more obvious, for there was only one type of man with the habit of command from whom they could choose. And he was, without doubt, a magnificent fellow for their purpose—the Army Colonel, thoroughly trustworthy, and thoroughly skilled in "war": not in *naval* war, indeed, but they had to chance that. They proceeded to select three Colonels who had more experience of the sea than the rest, and put them in command of the New Model Fleet with the title of "Generals-at-Sea". They "picked a winner" first time. Two of the three were comparatively ordinary folk who soon faded out, one by a natural death, the other by having the ill-luck to be hit by a chain-shot which cut him in half. But the third was Robert Blake.

Now once more we shall have to particularize, and, regarding the Alpha Star as the type of the whole Con-stellation, focus our telescope upon it to the exclusion of the rest. But in doing so let us not forget the existence of those other stout heroes of the First Dutch War—Popham, Deane, Monck, Penn, Lawson, Bourne, Ayscue, Badiley and a host of others. Nor must we forget, in assessing Blake's contri-bution, that some of these men, like Penn and Lawson, were far more "professional" seamen than he was, while Monck at least was a far more "professional" fighter, being, in fact, England's leading soldier. These things must be borne in mind in what follows.

Blake, then, must rank as a very important figure in our story, for he was—or at least became in the end—a "modern naval officer" in every essential sense. Those who have been accustomed to regard him merely as an eminent soldier, who turned sailor at the advanced age of fifty, may be disposed to deny this. But in fact he was *not* a soldier —at least, in no sense a professional one. It is true that, in

D

middle age, he enlisted, as we used to say some years ago,
"for the duration", and made himself in a very short time
into a remarkably competent officer. But he was no more
a soldier really than tens of thousands of business and
professional men still living who had their four years of
soldiering from 1914 to 1918. He was, like Drake and
Hawkins, of merchant or business stock, and at first tried
to become a don at Oxford, staying up ten years for that
purpose. Then something called him back home—probably
the fact that the family business was suffering, like everybody else's, in the vast slump caused by Charles I's neglect
of the sea. For many years he disappears from our view,
but probably what he was doing was voyaging in his own
ships—a practice which had become very common for
merchants by that time. Only when the Short Parliament
met do we find this versatile man emerging as a Member of
Parliament. Then came his soldiering, and at fifty exactly
he became General-at-Sea. Why, then, was he chosen?
Well, partly because he *was* a good soldier, no doubt; but
more because he already knew a good deal about the sea:
and most of all, perhaps, because he was an educated and
a cultured man who could *think*: who could plan wisely
and well—and far beyond the mere limits of a ship. We
cannot go into details of his service here: it is enough to
say that there never has been a more consistently successful
sea-officer.

He became one late in life and so did not, like a modern
officer, work up from the bottom; but *once* he became so,
he remained a "whole-timer": not, like Drake, called upon
for a single cruise, and then shelved: once started, he served
continuously. So, then, he fulfilled one of the two conditions which Drake lacked. And he fulfilled the other
condition too. He had "rank", or something as near to it
as was then possible. It was in the middle of the First Dutch
War that the Generals-at-Sea had conferred upon them
for the very first time one portion of the powers of Admiralty.

The punishment of all offences at sea was a part of that power, and had been vested for centuries in the High Court of Admiralty. Now the right of holding Courts-Martial at sea was granted to the commanders afloat; and with that right came, too, the title and—within the limits to be described later—the *rank* of Admiral. In fact, the only essential respect in which Blake's naval position differed from, say, Nelson's, was in the comparatively minor circumstance that the former went to sea at fifty while the latter went at twelve.

As for the lower officers, the Commonwealth made some advance in their appointment and tenure, though not much. That will be discussed later. It remained for the Restoration Government to set the seal on the Commonwealth's labours. The latter had given England her ships; now she was to have her own Sea-Officers, and the whole was to be called "the Royal Navy".

The Royal Navy! How paradoxical is the story to the last. There is something quite irresistibly English in the fact that, so long as the English Navy was the King's own navy, it was seldom if ever called the "Royal Navy". That title was blandly bestowed upon it by the first King who ceased to own it!

*     *     *     *     *

Now that we have brought our story, in broad outline, down to the Restoration Period, the first part of our task is done. We have shown how Seamanship, from being a profession altogether separate from Fighting, came first to be associated with it, and finally wedded to it: and how, from that union, sprang the Sea-Officer of the seventeenth century. By 1660 the Naval Profession had come into existence, and it had come to stay. But it was still quite amorphous, and in no sense yet an organism. How it became one we must next try to discover.

BOOK TWO

*The Profession in the Making*

# CHAPTER IV

# THE ESSENTIALS

THE main intention of this book is to tell the story of how the modern Naval Officer arrived at what he now is: how he first came into existence, how he acquired the various titles of command which have distinguished him for so long: how those titles gradually hardened into standardized ranks, together with a large number of other considerations which will arise in the telling.

So it seems rather important that we should get clearly into our minds exactly what we do mean by "Naval Officer": or rather, since we all *know* what we mean by that term, even if we cannot put it briefly and clearly into words, let us put the question in a slightly different form, and attempt to answer it briefly.

What, let us ask, are the main and essential conditions which must obtain before there can exist, in its modern form, a permanent, fluid and efficient, professional corps of naval officers?

*First*, there must be the provision of a continuous flow of entry of young officers, of the required material, and in the required numbers. It is clearly of no use to obtain the wrong sort, and it is equally clear, if we consider for a moment, that the modern system would not work if we procured, say, five hundred in one year, and none the next: for there would then be such blocks at some points that the whole machinery of promotion would break down: and there would be such hiatuses at others that there would be no officers in existence of certain seniorities, and required to do certain kinds of work. This aspect we will call "Entry".

*Second*, there must be the provision of an adequate system of training the young officers as they enter. This aspect needs no further elaboration here, so we will label it "Training" and leave it for the present.

*Third*, there must be the provision of *regular* employment for the officers thus trained, and of an adequate remuneration while so employed. Now this condition of employment, in an absolute sense, is an impossibility. Under no system of organization of a Service like the Navy could the Authorities guarantee that on every day of the active service life of every officer he should be employed. So we must modify our condition, or rather, split it into two sub-conditions.

(*a*) Employment must be as regular as possible, and
(*b*) When it is not forthcoming, the officer must still be maintained.

This aspect of the Service—the "place" or "job" which is to be found for the officer we will call "Post". The old name for it was "Office"; the modern is "Command". But both these terms give rise to difficulties, for, as ever, people have not been very careful in the use of words, and "Office" and "Command" have each come to bear, in English, several very different meanings. As words, in fact, they are seriously over-worked. And this verbal errancy is still more pronounced in the case of the original words' derivatives, "Officer" and "Commander". The former always used to mean "a man who holds an office, or place": but now, in the fighting Services, it almost always means "a man who holds a rank", which, as we shall shortly see, is a very different thing: while the latter has strayed even further from the original, and is now used to identify a *particular* rank-holder. So we shall, throughout, use the

word "Post" when we refer to the naval man's "Office",
"employment", "place", "job", or "command",

"Adequate remuneration" is, of course, much more easily
labelled. The straightforward three-letter word "Pay" has
always been good enough for the Navy. And "Half Pay" is
the obvious label for the maintenance of an unemployed
officer.

*Fourth*, there must be the provision of reasonable chances
to the individual officer of rising gradually in professional,
financial and social status, according as by his character,
his ability, his acquired experience and his enlarged professional knowledge, he becomes capable of bearing greater
responsibility, and thus giving more to the Service and the
State. This condition is summarized in the word "Rank":
and the corresponding condition in the remuneration plane
is "Scales of Pay". Both these will furnish that necessary
stimulus to patriotism and ambition which healthy competition invariably promotes. They put a premium on merit,
in the widest sense of that word, and a discount on
stagnation.

*Fifth*, there must be provision for a steady exodus at the
upper end of the Service. Here again—for obvious reasons—
absolute steadiness is impossible: for even if every Cadet
who entered were designed by nature for the ultimate rank
of Admiral of the Fleet, not one in fifty could reach it, and
promotion would degenerate, after a while, into an indecent
scramble to remain alive longer than one's contemporaries.
But also, in real life, where every cadet is *not* so designed,
such a horrid spectacle must be avoided at all costs, if only
to allow the really important posts to be held by men not
past their prime. This aspect of Service life used to be
called "Superannuation", or, later, "being put on the
Reserve".

The *Sixth* and last condition follows close on the fifth,
and is now, in most cases, axiomatic to it. It is pecuniary
provision for the retired officer—whether he retired as a

result of superannuation, sickness, or wounds, or through just being passed over—and for his dependents in the case of his death. But it was not always axiomatic, for it existed, in the form of half-pay, before there was any such thing as retirement in the modern sense. It must therefore be mentioned separately. Nowadays, the term Pension is reserved for grants for special circumstances, while the ordinary remuneration of a retired officer is "Retired Pay". We may combine the two under the one term "After-care".

Thus we have the Six Ages of the Naval Officer—Entry and Training; Post and Rank; Superannuation and After-care—all essential to the proper smooth running of a modern Service, and all, save sporadic appointment to posts, and rather more sporadic payment for the same, quite unknown throughout the period covered in the previous chapters. In a word, though Drake and his companions had much of the spirit of the modern Naval Officer—and that, as we tried to stress, is perhaps the main thing—they had nothing of the detail: the machinery of the profession was altogether wanting.

Nor did it come suddenly. Our English institutions have never done so, and the English Sea-Officer is a typically English institution. He was never deliberately created: he has "grown up", just as our Constitution has grown up, and our Common Law, our Judicial Procedure, our Local Government—even our Church. Indeed, it is sometimes tempting to say that he has "just happened"; but this would not be true, for it would fail to reveal the secret of his strength. He is rather the spontaneous and common-sense supply of an urgent, if inarticulate, demand.

> There's a divinity that shapes our ends,
> Rough-hew them how we will.

The British Naval Officer is, in very truth, one of those ends that we have rough-hewn: but assuredly it is our tutelary deity who has shaped him.

It is this process of shaping which we must now try to follow, for it is a vital step in our story. But here, the tale will be told without any consecutive attempt to trace out the history of the individual ranks: their fortunes we will follow in the last part of this book. Here we confine ourselves to the principal mile-stones on the long road from Monson's strangely assorted band of "Officers" to that other highly regulated and respected band which fills the pages of the current Navy List.

For our immediate purpose, we may further group our "Six Ages" under three headings:—"Entry and Training," or *"Supply"*: "Post and Rank", or *"Service"*: and "Super-annuation and After-care", or *"Retirement"*. But we shall not deal with them in this order, which is only the order in which they happen to the individual. It is not the order either of their true importance, or of their historical emergence. In any profession of a life-time, Service is, after all, the primary fact. The other two are important, but not vital. In the old Navy, many a man *did* serve, faithfully and well, without training—even without formal entry; with no option of retiring, and certainly without any after-care worthy of the name. But no man who merely entered, and was properly trained, or who went out and was properly cared for, would be of much account if he had not also served well between-whiles. It is but natural, too, that History brought Service first, and only added the other two as it were by afterthought.

So that shall be our order:—first, Service; second, Supply, and third, Retirement: the latter pair running, chrono-logically speaking, a very bad second to the first-named, and ultimately finishing in almost a dead heat.

# CHAPTER V

## "SERVICE"

### POST AND RANK

THE most important landmark in the creation of the officer personnel of the Navy is the long struggle between the principle which we have called "Post", and the much more familiar idea of "Rank".

In the old days, as we have seen, "Officer" meant simply "office-*holder*", and nothing more: and a man was only a "commission" officer at such times as (*a*) a ship was in commission and (*b*) he was a definite part of that commission. It is this way of looking at the matter—the conception that the *post* is everything, and nothing else anything—that we have called the Principle, or the Idea, of "Post". The other —and more modern—way of looking at the matter introduces the principle of "Rank"—a state personal to every individual (not to the ship at all) which permits him to be a "commission" officer of (or in) the Navy as a whole, and not only while of (or in) a ship: not, that is, a "commission" officer every now and then, but continuously one. The distinction is vital, because the two ideas are antagonistic: they pull in opposite directions, and a Service entirely ruled by the "Post" idea will be an utterly different thing from one in which "Rank" has triumphed. The former can hardly be a whole-time profession at all: the latter is almost bound to be one.

For "Post", which concentrates upon the Ship as the

basis of all command and appointment, implies a break, a series of breaks, in the continuity of service. It is like a row of high peaks with bottomless abysses between them. When a man has an appointment he is a "commission officer"— he is in and of the Service: but when he has not, he is not a commission officer at all: he is not even an "officer": he is nothing. But Rank is essentially relative and essentially enduring. The metaphor here is the etymologically correct one of a ladder. Once a man has his foot on it, he will go on, mounting continuously—fast or slow according to his luck and his abilities—until he reaches the top, or falls off for ever, whichever happens first. Now any modern, organized profession which is worth while is, and must be, in the nature of a ladder rather than of a succession of peaks with gulfs between: above all if the profession is a highly specialized one, as is the case with any of the fighting forces. For in these a man will never become really efficient, and therefore capable of the highest command unless he spends his whole working life on the job in hand. And so the old English Navy could never become the Modern British Navy until the idea of "Post" and all that underlies it had given place to the idea of Rank in all its implications. Not, as we shall see, that "Post" is dead, or ever will be. The issue at stake, in the struggle we are about to describe, was not which should slay the other, but, rather, which should be the predominant partner. Rank won, and, in winning, made the British Navy a modern profession.

The change from Post to Rank began inevitably with the most permanent office-holders—the "Standing" or "Warrant" officers—because in the matter of employment they had always been in the position of enjoying much greater continuity than their "commission" brethren. Let us recall that they were "whole-timers", or very nearly so, at quite an early date, for they had snug posts on board at all times, whether the ship was "in commission" or not. Now the normal service term, until quite recently, for the state of a ship *not* in commission was "in ordinary". And, as old terms so often are, this one is particularly significant. It was, in its own day, literally true. A ship was ordinarily laid up: it was in an *exceptional* state when "in commission".

The reason for this must be sought outside the immediate precincts of Naval History. It was inevitable so long as, by constitutional practice, the Crown was expected, as folk said then, to "live of its own", and not to depend upon its subjects to finance its normal undertakings. It could seldom do more than *just* manage this, even when comparatively well-off; and therefore it never could afford the luxury of putting fleets, or even single ships, into the obviously more expensive state of "commission", unless it was absolutely necessary; and even then it returned them to "ordinary" at the first possible moment—often too soon, as witness the famous and disastrous Medway Raid of 1667. In fact, this state of things really continued until the long struggle between Crown and Parliament had ended in favour of the latter, and at last the Parliament, presumed to represent the people, took over the finances of the country in general, and of the Navy in particular. The only seeming exception was in the Commonwealth times, and that is really no exception at all, since, for that short period the Government of the day did really control the country's finances, albeit by force. But even subsequent to the "Bloodless Revolution", and for a long time afterwards, the country itself was not rich enough to keep its fleets all ready for action for a moment longer than was necessary: and so the custom of keeping the bulk of the fleet "in ordinary", whenever such a course was possible, continued long after 1688.

During all this period, when strict economy was essential, it was inevitable that the idea of "Post" should predominate, and that the poor "commission officer" should spend long periods, especially in peace time, "out of a job"—at least out of a *naval* job. In practice, we know, the majority of

these men refused to starve in consequence, because they
expected such periods of naval unemployment, and were
not therefore taken by surprise. They knew perfectly well
that they were *not* whole-timers, but "piece-workers", so
they just entered other professions between-times and came
back, or not, more or less as they liked. That was all right
in itself, perhaps. But so long as such a practice was almost
universal we cannot possibly think of the naval officer's
profession as a *modern* one.

The three most usual professions to be thus "worked in"
with the Navy were, for the lesser sort, the Merchant
Service, and for the more "gentle" and highly placed,
Politics and the Army. The first-named substitute had quite
a little to recommend it: it was as good a *pis aller* as one
could expect, for at least the officer concerned kept up,
and even added to, his sea-experience. The second was
bad in principle, and "political officers" caused many a
regrettable incident before Authority, led by Lord Barham
in the year of Trafalgar, finally put an end to them. The
practice of soldiering between-whiles was, again, *not* a bad
thing in itself. It was, after all, only a survival from medieval
times when "fighting" was *the* profession, and "land-
fighting" and "sea-fighting" were nothing but rather ill-
defined specializations of it.

We meet with many cases in Tudor and early Stuart days
which, if we are not wise as to how men looked at things
then, will appear most anomalous. We tend to be surprised
to hear of Drake in the front line of a purely military assault
on the Castles of Cape St. Vincent. We ask ourselves how
on earth Frobisher came to lose his life leading infantry
to an escalade of earth-works in Brittany. And, on the other
hand, we marvel to see great Elizabethan *Generals* like Sir
Francis Vere and Sir Roger Williams commanding ordinary
ships at sea.

Later still, in the Commonwealth period, some historians
have made much of the selection of Colonels to command

the Fleet. But—even apart from the fact that the Government had no other suitable source available and that they undoubtedly tended to choose the colonels who had the most sea experience—such an action was not regarded as anything out of the ordinary by contemporaries who could remember the ill-fated expedition to Cadiz of 1625 sailing under a comparatively unknown soldier, and the ridiculous La Rochelle adventure commanded by one who was not even a soldier, still less a sailor.

The same phenomenon is still visible in the Restoration period, when George Monck and Prince Rupert are well known examples of "Fighters"—and very brilliant examples too—shining equally in both of the specialized branches. Even in the next generation the distinction has not crystallized. Arthur Herbert, Earl of Torrington, though best known as a sailor, saw a good deal of military service too; while at the great naval battle of Solebay, in 1672, we find, receiving his baptism of fire as a volunteer (or, as we should now say, as a Naval Cadet), one John Churchill. But Samuel Pepys was even then on the eve of his great creative work, and Churchill had quickly to take the decision which ultimately made him Duke of Marlborough and first soldier of Europe. Indeed, the last important occasion when one man, in his own person, combined the offices of C.-in-C. on land *and* at sea belongs actually to the eighteenth century. In the Spanish campaign of 1705–6, the brilliant but erratic Earl of Peterborough was vested with both powers, with almost disastrous results.

After that, the most innocent reader can no longer be mystified. Anson, Hawke, Rodney and Nelson patently belong to a profession in every way distinct from that of Amherst, Wolfe, Moore and Wellington. And why? Because the two have become separate whole-time "jobs".

How was this accomplished? We are not concerned here with the Army: but in the Navy it was done by creating an organized Naval Hierarchy, employed whenever possible, and "retained" for the rest of the time. This latter condition is most important: it is, in fact, the inauguration and growth of the principle of "Half Pay", which, more than any one thing, has created the whole-time service as we know it, and is mainly responsible for making the cardinal idea of "Post" subservient to that of Rank.

This latter assertion needs, perhaps, some explanation.

Let us first remember that, up to Charles II's time, every "commission" officer from highest to lowest was packed ashore as soon as the ship was paid off, and his pay ceased forthwith. But then comes a day when a government decides to change this, and to pay officers something during the time when they cannot employ them: they fix upon half-pay as the correct remuneration. But now comes the question, "How shall they assess it?" Officers will inevitably expect a graded half-pay, corresponding with the posts which they have been accustomed to occupy. Every man in command of a ship will demand—and in equity will be entitled to enjoy—half the pay he received when in command. And every lieutenant will make a parallel claim to receive his just dues. What can Authority do? There is only one thing, and they cannot escape it. They must make a list of all claimants, according to their demands. They must group all the "commanding officer" claims into one section, all "lieutenant" claims into another, and so on. In short, they must divide their officers up into *ranks*; and the principle of "Rank Seniority", already present vaguely and in a quasi-recognized state, will be officially recognized ostensibly for "half-pay" purposes, but actually also as a vital principle in the Service.

This is, we need hardly add, exactly what happened. But, by one of those not infrequent interventions of our kindly Providence, the actual course of events was such as to bring about very quickly yet another refinement, that of "Seniority within Ranks".

E

It happened thus. Charles II inaugurated the scheme, but in a very small way, as one would expect from any pre-Revolution monarch. His enthusiasm for the fleet made him anxious to have it commanded by the best possible officers: and his natural shrewdness taught him that he could only keep them by offering them a "retainer" of some kind. So in 1667 he extended to the Captains of First and Second Rates, who were, presumably, the pick of his officers, the privilege of being kept "on half-pay to the very day peace is proclaimed". That was something, if not very comprehensive. In 1672 the same lucky ones were accorded half-pay "while on shoar this winter season", and, two years later, when the Third Dutch War was at an end, "so long as they are unprovided for". Two years later still, the junior commission officers were "retained", in a less expensive way, by being allowed officially to serve in commissioned ships in the lowly station of "extra midshipmen", or—as the original wording went, "Midshipmen Extra-ordinary".[1] But even this was found too expensive for the exiguous resources of the Crown, and the numbers were soon rigorously limited. In an age, too, when even ordinary pay was by no means certain, there is reason to believe that half-pay was in the precarious position of an ordinary dividend in a concern whose directors were hesitating over payment of preference shares.

But in 1693, almost as soon, that is, as Parliament had obtained complete control of the government (and therefore could afford what would probably have been impossible at any earlier date) they decided to be very generous indeed: to increase pay all round—and therefore half-pay: to extend that half-pay down to First Lieutenants and Masters, and—most important of all—to pay it in periods both of peace and of war. But apparently they had gone too far, and soon discovered that they had "bitten off more than they could chew". The result was that in 1700 they

[1] See under "Midshipmen", p. 219.

recanted somewhat, and reduced the liberal privileges they had just conferred, by the rather unjust operation of restricting the numbers to receive half-pay to fifty Captains, a hundred Lieutenants and thirty Masters. The motives underlying this retrogressive and even slightly parsimonious action were not of the best, for the "high-ups" had been complaining, and the onus of the blow therefore fell on the lower officers. But that must not blind us to the immense and lasting importance of the step, of which, we may feel sure, the ruling authority had little or no conception. Who were to be the fortunate recipients? Obviously those in each grade who had served longest in it: who were, that is, the *senior* fifty or the senior hundred.

The immediate result was the first "Seniority" Navy List, printed in 1700, and arranged, for the first time, according to the date of each man's first employment in each type of post: or, as we may now truthfully say, for the first time, according to each man's *seniority* in his *rank*. The Admiralty used it solely in order to discover to whom half-pay was due, and so the earliest Seniority *Navy List* was never issued for sale to the public. But in making this discovery, they contrived—inadvertently, no doubt—to inaugurate a type of volume which has gone on with but few yearly breaks from that day to this, and has imprinted upon the Service with ever increasing firmness the idea of *Rank*.

The *Navy List* is, in fact, so important a clue in our story that it will be by no means digressive to add a few words about its history, both prior and subsequent to 1700. All the earliest lists known are, as anyone who has followed the argument so far would guess, *Ship*-lists—lists set down, usually in manuscript, for the use of the Authorities. They are such natural phenomena that we need not attempt to trace them back to their origins. And they are not our immediate concern either, though some, from quite early times, included the names of the officers commanding the squadrons and ships. Of such a sort is the still extant list of the "Anti-Armada" fleet, which gives the names of Captains and the few Lieutenants then serving afloat.

The earliest *printed* list known is one of 1641 which contains the same sort of information, and in the same form, as the Anti-Armada List. But it is in no sense a "Seniority" List, nor is there any great change in form until we come to the famous "List of Flag Officers", and "List of Sea-Commission Officers" made by Samuel Pepys. These typically painstaking works of the great little man are in manuscript, and are arranged, for the first time, under officers, and not under ships. They claim to include all Flag-Officers, Captains and Lieutenants who had held any post in His Majesty's Ships from 1660 to 1688. They are not arranged, however, in "seniority", but in alphabetical, order. Indeed, they furnish proofs at every turn that even Pepys, who had more to do with the creation of the Service than any other man, was still thinking exclusively in terms of "Post". The very names he uses show it. His first list is called "Flag-Officers"—men, that is, suitable to take command of Squadrons or Fleets: not Admirals in their own right as it were; even though, against the dates of their various commissions we are given their titles when in command—thus:—"Vice-Admiral of the Blue", "Admiral of the Fleet in the Straits", "Commander-in-Chief of the Squadron from Portsmouth, to wear Union Flag at Mizzen Top". The Union Flag in this last example was a high honour, reserved only for officers who were in supreme command of a fleet. But the point is that both Flag and Command were *temporary*: the officer must haul down the one when he gives up the other: in fact, in some case he may only wear the flag assigned to him in specific localities. Nay, he may—and quite often does—revert to plain "Captain" again, and that without derogation to his character. Let us look, for instance, at the record of Sir Robert Holmes, the officer whose holocaust of Dutch ships in the Vlie has earned the name of "Holmes' Bonfire". By

putting the two lists together we find that he was, first—
after 1660, of course, when the lists begin—the Captain of
various small ships: then C.-in-C. of a detached Squadron
to "Guinny", and allowed "to wear the Union Flag at the
mizzen top while out of the Channel": then Captain again:
then Rear-Admiral of the Red, a post which became *later*
a definitive rank: then C.-in-C. of another detached
Squadron: then Captain of two third-rate ships in turn,
and finally Captain of a First rate. Or again, Sir John
Harman, in one hectic year—1665—was, first, First Lieutenant of the *Royal Charles* (First rate): Captain of two
different Third rates, Captain of a Second rate, Rear-
Admiral of the White, and Rear-Admiral of the Blue.
Notice the last move: after what seems like a meteoric rise
in a single year from Lieutenant to Admiral, he falls a little
before the end of it, for the White Squadron was senior to
the Blue. Next year he rises a little, getting a small independent command; but in 1667 and 1668 he has dropped
sharply, to become the captain of a mere Third rate.

The "lower" list reveals the same peculiarities. Pepys
shows very clearly how he regards them in the name he
applies—"Sea-Commission Officers": that is, obviously,
officers appointed to Sea-Commissions.[1] Some of the records

[1] In describing this type of officer during any part of his career up
to the close of the eighteenth century, we have purposely used the
noun-adjective, rather than the past participle—"Commission-Officer"
rather than "Commissioned Officer". The latter is a late importation,
practically unknown before the nineteenth century. It is now the
recognized term: but even now, we are not being particularly logical
in using it. For if we call an officer a "commissioned officer" because
he is appointed by general commission, as he now is, we ought, in order
to be consistent, to call an officer appointed by warrant a "warranted
officer". Still, it must be conceded that "Commission*ed*" is more logical
now than it was in the days when it was really the ship which was
commissioned, and not the man; and so we have followed the modern
usage in writing of the modern officers. It is significant, and apposite
to our story, that the change of name begins to occur at just about the
time when the officer is changing his nature, i.e. between 1794 and 1860.
(See below pp. 75 and 76.)

look very odd to eyes which are accustomed to "rank"
only: as for instance one Thomas Berry, who achieved the
following, in this order: Lieutenant, Captain, Second
Lieutenant, First Lieutenant, Captain and Master (i.e.
"Commander"), First Lieutenant, Captain: or the poor
fellow who was successively *de*moted from Captain (1670),
to First Lieutenant (1672), and to Second Lieutenant
(1673)! But in terms of "post" there is nothing strange in
these moves. A modern officer might still suffer such seeming
vicissitudes in his appointments, and still be rising in rank
all the time. Thus, he might be, first, Lieutenant-in-command of a drifter; then "Number One" in a destroyer, and
lastly, the second-most-senior Lieutenant in a battleship.

No advance in Navy Lists is noticeable between Pepys's
effort and the revolutionary 1700 ones. After that, however,
the "Seniority" List has come to stay. By far the most
famous series, the "Sea -Officers" List, containing Captains,
Masters and Commanders (i.e. Commanders),[1] and Lieutenants begins in 1718 and continues yearly up to 1846. In
1732 a first "List of Surgeons" was published, also compiled
for half-pay purposes, with date of first warrant: in 1747 came
the first List of Flag Officers in order of seniority. The first
"List of Marines" dates from 1757, and the "Royal Calendar"
of 1767 added Chaplains. In 1780 a List of Masters (also
with the "half-pay" motif) was issued by the Navy Board
who were responsible for them. In 1810 Pursers, Gunners,
Boatswains and Carpenters had their own Seniority-List.

Another well-known list of this period is Steele's List of
the Royal Navy—begun in 1779, much improved and enlarged in 1783, and lasting till 1817. It contains, in addition
to Seniority, a great deal of other information. It was this
work, published for so long by the private enterprise of
Mr. David Steele, that served as a model for the first official
*Navy List*, published, for the first time "By Authority", in
1814. Indeed, the Admiralty seem to have treated Steele's

---

[1] See below, p. 199.

heirs—he was himself dead—rather shabbily by first modelling their own compilation very closely upon his, and then driving them incontinently out of business by withholding the necessary information.

But though the "Seniority List" thus came to stay in 1700, gradually and almost imperceptibly familiarizing Englishmen with the idea of naval "rank", we must not suppose for a moment that this new idea gained the day at once. There was not just one pitched battle, complete with victor and vanquished. That is not our way. We generally like to pretend that what has been, is, even when it has ceased to be for many a long year. And so, just as we still proclaim publicly that our laws are made by the Sovereign, with the *advice* of the Lords and Commons, so, in this matter, we went on assuming for over a century and a half that no officer could hold a "commission" unless appointed to a named ship in commission: that he could never be *promoted* unless so appointed and that every time he was appointed to a ship he must have a separate commission to it. Nobody seemed to notice that this proceeding sometimes caused considerable inconvenience to all concerned: was, in fact, sometimes unworkable. When that happened we got round the obstruction either by quietly ignoring some portion of the convention, by more or less shamelessly dodging it, or by flat contradiction of it.

One example of each process must suffice. When in 1747, as we shall see later, the first attempt to ease the promotion-block was made—an attempt which really started the principle of "retirement"—the Admiralty was faced with the problem of having to commission their unwanted Captains *to* some appointment where they would be out of the way. That is undoubtedly how they looked at it. "We can't do anything with the man," they argued, "unless we commission him *somewhere*: it is not done!" They therefore hit upon the brilliant expedient of appointing him to fly a flag in a squadron which did not exist. They did not

call it the "Yellow" Squadron themselves: their phrase
was "without specifying any squadron or division of colours
used in the fleet". But the Service and the Public called the
process "yellowing", perhaps because that was the colour
of the quarantine flag, under which people not very much
in demand for other reasons were safely stowed away.

This process was so patent as to be practically a relaxation
of the convention. It is the first time that any officer was
promoted "generally"; i.e. to no specific "post". The next
example is one of shameless dodging. The authorities were
often hard put to it to find opportunities to promote the
man who was obviously due for it, even in time of war,
when most of the ships were in commission. But in peace
time, when they were mostly laid up, and therefore very
few officers were in "commission" at all, things became
desperate. In the last few decades of the eighteenth century,
however, they hit upon the expedient of promoting an
officer as usual (i.e. by appointment to a ship in commission)
and then promptly removing him from the new ship back
to a smaller one such as he was commanding before the
performance began. In the contemporary appointments
we find many entries like this:

1773. 25th June. Richard Pearson to be Captain of the *Juno*—
                 (a frigate, and therefore a command which
                 entitled its commander to be posted as
                 "Captain").

1773. 26th June. *Captain* Richard Pearson to be *Commander* of
                 the *Speedwell*—(a sloop, and therefore only a
                 Commander's appointment).

In this way they had dodged the convention, for Pearson
was now—very deservedly—entitled to the *rank* of Captain;
and they had not upset any of their own command arrangements. Yet it would undeniably have been simpler could
they simply have announced: "June 25th. Commander
Richard Pearson to be Captain."

The third example reveals the Admiralty driven into a

corner by the force of their own untenable logic, and having, in self-defence, to bite back. It appears that, early in the nineteenth century, certain quite lowly lieutenants had "got away with it" owing to the accident of finding themselves, while in distant waters, promoted, through the death or other misadventure of their seniors on board, to the post of Captain in a ship, the command of which automatically implied Captain's rank. So, according to the convention, they *were* Captains, and nothing could unseat them. But the Admiralty felt—quite rightly—that such a passing whim of Fortune ought not to be allowed to put them above the heads of scores—perhaps hundreds—of other, and possibly better, officers. So they turned at last, and in an Admiralty Order in Council of 1808 they said in effect: "We can't deny that you *are* a Captain, so you must be allowed to be one while in command. But you shan't remain so afterwards. Still"—and here is the farcical side of the business—"since you undoubtedly *are* a Captain really, we will allow you *one* rise—in rank—to Commander. But, convention or no convention, you shall not hold the *rank* of Captain." This is indeed a very instructive example, because it shows Authority's almost ostrich-like refusal to acknowledge the defeat of "post". Such a situation could not arise now because "post", *per se*, has at last been recognized as quite a separate thing from "rank". There is no difficulty nowadays in a Lieutenant commanding a ship. They simply call him "Lieutenant-in-command", and pay him a little extra by way of "command-money"; and he remains a Lieutenant by rank.

Yet there exist to this day two pleasing conservatisms among the officers themselves. First, many newly-promoted officers will not don the distinctive badges of their new ranks while still occupying their old posts. Thus the Commander of a ship, promoted to Captain, will often refrain from adding the fourth stripe to his arm so long as he remains as Commander there. He feels, after all, that he is still

Commander-of-the-ship—and, incidentally, is paid as such. Though now a Captain by *Rank* (and figuring as one in the *Navy List*), he will only appear as one when he relinquishes his Commander's *Post*. This, it should be observed, is not an *order*. It is a custom, and it is not universally observed in the modern Navy.

Again, Lieutenant "X", commanding the drifter or the submarine "Y", will almost always find himself referred to, locally and colloquially, as "the Captain", or "Captain of the 'Y' ". And the title is, historically speaking, a very sound one. He is Captain *of* the "Y": that is his post, and the word "captain" is being used in the perfectly good historical sense of "Commander-of-a-ship". And yet—so real is the victory of "Rank"—that no one, not even the latest-joined boy, would dream of calling him "Captain 'X' ".

These customs are, as we have said, conservatisms: possibly—who knows?—continuous traditions from the days when they still represented the facts. A fairly topical instance from the late eighteenth century proves this very well. We have most of us, perhaps, been suitably thrilled not so long ago by a certain film which was all about that brutal fellow, Captain Bligh of the *Bounty* and his most attractive young Lieutenant, Fletcher Christian. That the portrait of the Captain there depicted was a mere travesty of a man who, being dead, could take no action for libel, and that Fletcher was hardly the bright boy he is made out to be, is neither here nor there. What *is* to the point is that "Captain Bligh" was not a Captain, and Lieutenant Christian was not a Lieutenant—by rank. Search the lists of the year—1789—and we shall see. But if we look among the Lieutenants we shall find the name of William Bligh there: and—if the list we consulted contained the names of Masters' Mates we should find Fletcher among them. Yet here at least the film-makers were not wrong: by the ordinary nomenclature of the time, and by the logic of history they were altogether right. Bligh was Captain *of* the *Bounty*, and Fletcher in a very literal sense was *his* lieutenant, because Bligh, acting quite within his rights, had made him so—Lieutenant *of* the *Bounty* for that voyage —nothing more. Had they returned home in the *Bounty* together, and paid off the ship, Bligh would have reverted to Lieutenant, and Christian to Masters' Mate, because the *Bounty* was not a Captain's Command—or Post Ship, as they used to say—and Bligh could not promote anybody to any "commission" rank whatever, because he was neither the Sovereign nor the Lord High Admiral.

On the whole, perhaps, it would be a safe generalization to say that "rank" had really won the battle by the end of the eighteenth century—won, without annihilating the enemy. Indeed, the first official admission of defeat took place in the 1790's, when a small alteration was at length made in the wording of officers' commissions. Up till then, every post on board, from Captain to "Gunner's Taylor" was meticulously defined, and jealously limited to exact numbers: not a soul "above complement" was admitted, and everyone who came aboard was promptly assigned his exact berth in the Ship's Pay Book. So it is not surprising to learn that a lieutenant had invariably been appointed to as exact a post on board as possible. His commission appointed him, for instance, "First Lieutenant of the *Bellerophon*", or "Fourth Lieutenant of the *Victory*". But now came the first loosening of the "post" bands, and he was appointed simply as "Lieutenant of" the ship. But even then, he still had to have a new commission to each ship he joined, and could still be promoted only on commission to a ship. His was still a "Ship-Commission", as the one reproduced between pp. 76 and 77 makes plain. It belongs to this period, and in it, we see, Mr. Michael Turner is appointed as "Lieutenant of His Majesty's Ship the *Royal Adelaide*": not as he would have been earlier, "*Fifth* Lieutenant of H.M.S. *Royal Adelaide*", nor yet, as he would be now, "Lieutenant in His Majesty's Fleet".

Men still living were born in the days when this was yet
the case, for it was not until 1860 that the final step was
taken. "At the Court at Buckingham Palace, the 9th day of
June, 1860, Present, the Queen's Most Excellent Majesty
in Council," it was proposed—and approved—that, owing
to the "inconvenience to Your Majesty's service, . . . the
present practice of issuing Commissions and Warrants to
Officers on their appointment to ships . . . be discontinued and abolished": instead, "that in the cases of Commissioned and Warrant Officers in Your Majesty's Navy, only
one Commission or Warrant as the case may be, shall be necessary for each *grade of rank* . . . and that after a Commission
or Warrant shall have been granted to an Officer . . . it
shall not be necessary, so long as any officer shall continue
of the same rank, to grant him any other commission or
warrant; but he shall do duty, *and be an officer*, according to the Commission or Warrant which he holds . . . ."

The "General" Commission has come at last, and the
long fight is over. Rank has won, for a man can now be an
officer by virtue of that alone, even when he is not an
officer by reason of the post he holds.

The story may be carried one stage further—to the
present day—and left there. On July 30th, 1938, it was
announced that "Half-Pay" was to be abolished from the
Service. Looking back over the story of the long struggle,
and seeing what an important—if not decisive—part
Half-Pay has played in it, are we not entitled to look upon
this event as the last shot fired? Up till now the principle
of "Post" retained at least this significance—never under-
estimated by the sufferer, even though outsiders did not
always realize it—that the ordinary rates of pay still depended
upon the possession of a "post": and the victory of rank,
decisive as it had been, did not save the unfortunate who
had no post from the unpleasing prospects of Half-Pay.
But now the sole fact that he has substantive *rank* will, for
the first time, save him.

Royal Highness the Lord
...l of the United Kingdom of
...and Ireland &c.

.......... hereby appointed
...s Ship the Royal Adelaide

...given I do hereby constitute and
.......... the Royal Adelaide
...d and take upon you the Charge
...rdingly. Strictly Charging and
...ging to the said Ship
...and severally in their respective
...e unto you their said Lieutenant
...the General printed Instructions
...time to time receive from your
...Majesty's service Hereof nor you
...ontrary at your peril And for
...der my hand and the Seal of
...day of September 1828
...sty's Reign.

...n" and "General Commission"

*By H[...]*
*High Adm[...]*
*Great Britai[...]*

*To Mr Michael*
*Lieutenant of His Maj[...]*

*By Virtue of the Power and Authority to [...]*
*appoint you Lieutenant of His Majesty's Sh[...]*
*Willing and requiring you forthwith to go on bo[...]*
*and Command of Lieutenant in her a[...]*

£ 1 : 12

*Commanding all the Officers and Company bel[...]*
*[...]ordinate to you to behave themselves jointly [...]*
*Employments with all due Respect and Obedi[...]*
*And you likewise to observe and execute as wel[...]*
*as what Orders and Directions you shall fr[...]*
*Captain or any other your superior Officers for [...]*
*nor any of you may fail as you will answer the [...]*
*so doing this shall be your Warrant Given [...]*
*the Office of Admiralty this [...]*
*in the [...] Year of His M[...]*

5

*By Command of His Royal Highness*

*[signature]*

*Seniority*
*18 Sep 1828*

A LIEUTENANT'S COMMISSION OF
Belonging to the intermediate period between "Ship Commiss[...]

This is not to say, let us emphasize for the last time, that the importance of "Post" is dead. It would be a bad day for any service in which it was. An officer will still suffer some financial loss from being without employment, in that he will be denied the not inconsiderable benefits of "allowances": and further, he will clearly be sadly obstructed on the promotion ladder if he fails to obtain a "post": in fact, he will, before very long, drop off it altogether. And the converse is equally clear. A good "job" will help his feet to twinkle up the ladder—hence the phrase, not uncommonly heard in Wardrooms, "a promotion billet". No, "Post" is far from dead; and it will only die when the Service does: for every Admiral in command of Fleets and Ports, every Captain of every ship, and every officer and man aboard them has a *post*, and always will so long as there are ships and fleets to commission.

# CHAPTER VI

## "SUPPLY"

### ENTRY AND TRAINING

THE beginnings of organized entry into the Navy date from the last quarter of the seventeenth century. Naturally officers *did* enter before that time, but the best way of describing the method of such entry is to emphasize the apparent *absence* of method. In each generation, the officers of the next just drifted in—and often out again before they had gone very far. This, in the days of part-timers like Drake, was of course only to be expected, but the absence of all method persisted for a good while after that. In these circumstances it is evidently hopeless to attempt the formulation of any *rules* governing entry. But some methods were commoner than others, and it may be worth while to sketch the early fortunes of a young gentleman who really intended to "follow the sea" in His Majesty's Ships in, say, the early seventeenth century, and who went about it in the most usual of the many possible ways.

He was first brought on board by one of the officers— usually, but not always, the Captain. That personage was allowed, by a custom at least as old as the Middle Ages, to take to sea with him his own "retinue". By Queen Elizabeth's time that elastic term had been crystallized into meaning a certain number of "servants", the number depending upon his social rank. If he were a plain commoner, he could have them at the rate of four per hundred of the Ship's

Company: if a knight, twice as many. This discrimination sounds odd at first, but becomes less so when we remember that social rank was still quite an important enough qualification to warrant a special rate of pay, and that this "Servant" system was, in effect, designed to supply that supplement.

As the ships were quite heavily manned, even in Elizabeth's reign, a commoner captain might thus obtain some twenty servants, and a knightly one as many as forty. This was clearly far too many to fill the menial office of domestic proper: some few were, no doubt, imported for that purpose, but the rest of the places were left at the Captain's disposal. Most of them he never filled; he merely pocketed the pay and the value of the victuals that went with it. Others—a few—he filled by importing his own sons or nephews, or the relatives of his friends, or of those to whom he owed an obligation. Such young gentlemen naturally drew their victuals, and sometimes—if the Captain was kind—might draw their pay, so that they did represent some pecuniary sacrifice to himself.

The lesser officers also were allowed servants, though in much smaller proportions; and so we occasionally find an officer beginning his naval career as Lieutenant's, or even Master's Servant. Or again, the lad might come on board rated to pretty nearly any minor post that was going— plain "seaman" even: the one essential was to scrape up sufficient interest to get himself rated at all. Or he might appear frankly as a volunteer, in a quite undefined position Indeed, if he were fortunate enough to know the *very* best people, he might dispense with all these stepping stones, and go direct to sea as a Lieutenant, or even as Captain. But we are following the career of one not quite so privileged as that. More often than not, he had to figure first in one of the categories mentioned above; and in these, whatever he was called, he was usually, in fact if not in name, a part of the Captain's "retinue".

Growing up as it did, long before the full amalgamation of Seaman and Fighter, this curious system approximates in many ways to that standard form of vocational training in the middle ages and early modern world—the system of Apprenticeship. There was the same kind of personal relationship between the apprentice and his Master: and, as elsewhere in the system, the Master was compensated in various ways for the instruction which he gave. But the parallel cannot be too closely pressed, for there are many obvious differences, arising out of such phenomena as the privileged position, in the Navy, of many of the parties concerned, and the constant, if gradual, growth of the "Service" idea, which is inimical to the principle of Apprenticeship in its true form. So, if we may venture to give this apparently methodless a name, we shall not be far out if we call it the "Captain's Servant" entry.

Once on board, our young man relied, perforce, on the patronage which he could command. If that were good, he would probably find himself made a Lieutenant at the first possible opportunity, and by the simple selection of the Captain himself. But he might have to wait a little longer, and fill the intermediate post, say, of Master's or Boatswain's Mate. It all depended on the Captain. For, incredible though it may appear to us of today, the latter appears to have had complete freedom in the choice, and the making, of his own lieutenant, as well as of his own servants, up to the beginning of the 1630's. In fact, until that date, the Authorities did not, in most cases, have anything to do with selecting any of their own future officers, except the Captain himself. But there existed an even stranger anomaly. We learn from the remarks of Edward Nicholas, who was the private secretary to the Lord High Admiral at that time, that Captains not infrequently did with their lieutenants what they were doing with their servants: viz. they left the place vacant, and diverted the financial proceeds into their own pockets!

This may be one reason for the almost total disappearance of lieutenants in James I's lists.

It was in those same dark days of the Navy, the 1630's, that the Government took its very first step to secure control of its future "commission" officers. It decided to appoint the lieutenants itself. The captains objected—naturally—but the Authorities held firm. This action of theirs did not, probably, spike the guns of the influential captain: that he continued to be able, as a rule, to "wangle" the appointment of his protégé is evident from the fact that lieutenants so often followed captains as they rose from small ships to larger ones. But one point was gained for ever; the Government controlled the "commission" officers, even though the men from whom they had to select were not usually of their own choosing.

As to training, in the modern sense, nothing whatever was done about that, either in Charles I's time or for a very long time after. Yet there were not wanting thoughtful writers connected with the sea who realized that it would be wise at least to make some attempt at training embryo officers. Nathaniel Boteler was one such, and the interesting solution of the problem which he suggested in 1634 will be discussed later.[1] There was evidently, too, quite a widespread, though vague, feeling abroad that some sort of "class" or "pool" of men qualified to be officers should be established, and some sort of effort was certainly made to secure the services of the same people again and again. This is not much advance, it is true, but it is something, because it shows that the desirability of a permanent personnel was beginning to enter men's heads.

The Commonwealth Government, in that they had more ships, used them more frequently, and therefore made more employment for their officers, undoubtedly helped on the cause. They also made the profession much more attractive, not only by raising the pay all round, but also by paying

[1] See below, p. 214.

it—a thing Charles I, with the best will in the world, could seldom afford to do. And they took one concrete step forward in the realms of both entry and training. They laid it down that the "office" of "midshipman" should only be filled with men who, at a pinch, could take on the duties of a "Quarterdeck" (i.e. Commission) officer.[1] It was an advance, perhaps, rather in Training than in "Entry", but it did have the effect of ensuring that candidates for lieutenants were at least capable men, with potential ability to command.

Here as elsewhere in the story of the Navy's transformation, the Restoration period is the era when matters really began to move. The new king had a very real love of the sea and ships—was he not, to all intents and purposes, the earliest English yachtsman?—and his Lord High Admiral and brother, James, Duke of York, had the good fortune, or the good sense, to pick up quite early on that lovable and gifted little man, Mr. Samuel Pepys, whose fame is world-wide because he made a diary. But this, of course, his own contemporaries did not know: they merely acclaimed him as the man who created at the Admiralty an office run on business lines, and with the weapon he had forged, brought order out of chaos for the whole Navy.

His contribution to the problem of "Entry" is soon told. It was complete as far as it went, though—numerically speaking—it did not go very far. There had been, in many ships, and dating back for many years, a class of person known as Volunteers. Thomas Doughty, we may remember, was an Elizabethan specimen of the breed—though not, we may hope, a typical one. They were not the same thing as the "Captain's Servants" just described. For one thing, they were usually older—young men rather than boys; for another, they were *always* "gentle", and for this latter reason, no doubt, were less restricted both in the matter of discipline and even as to numbers allowed on board.

[1] See below, under "Midshipmen."

Their numbers, in fact, varied with the fashion of the day. At the height of Elizabeth's Anglo-Spanish War, in Charles I's "Ship-money" days, and perhaps most of all at the time of the Second Dutch War, it was *la mode* for the young blood of the day to boast that he had been through the racket of a naval engagement, or at least had served a term in a sea-going ship. Sometimes, of course, these young men took to the sea, and as they were sure to have plenty of "interest", they would then secure lieutenancies, and perhaps turn ultimately into good officers. But more often they tired of a sea-life, which must have been hard even for men who could afford all available luxuries; and so just faded out. They were, it may well be believed, unpopular with the regular breed of sea-officers and men, and, on the whole perhaps, did as much harm as they did good.

It was this class upon which the far-seeing Pepys laid hold, and in 1676, by the simple process of limiting their age, on first entry as Volunteers, to sixteen, he weeded out most of those who entered merely because it was the thing to do, yet retained such as were genuinely anxious to embark on a naval career. They were, also, no longer to be "super-cargoes", but their numbers were limited to fixed figures, according to the rate of the ship which bore them, and they were woven into the structure of the crew by having special places assigned to them—as all other regular inhabitants had. These were the "16 and unders". Pepys had something to say, too, about the "17 and over.", but that we will discuss later.[1]

The official name of Pepys's new class of youngster was "Volunteer-per-Order". The "Order" mentioned in this title was His Majesty's own order, and the young gentleman was furnished with it before going on board. Further, so runs the command, the young gentleman in question is to be "preferred before any others who have not formerly served Us in that capacity". In other words, the Captain

[1] See below, p. 219.

is bound to take him on, even if it upset the rest of his
own "arrangements". This is why such lads were promptly
known as "King's Letter Boys", and why they were none
too popular with the Captains: who, no doubt, had their
own means of retaliation!

Yet these poor bullied little boys were, in the eyes of
History, very important people. The King, in this connection, is of course a euphemism for the Board of Admiralty.
These boys, to use a far more modern phrase "held Admiralty nominations". They were, in fact, though not in name,
the first Naval Cadets. And the Admiralty chose them.
Influence, of course, could still perform prodigies on the
strings which men pull, but the fact remains that, in the
last resort, the Authorities were at length to be able to
select some at any rate of their own officers from the very
start of their careers. This innovation contains the whole
kernel of the modern system of entry.

But—there is always a "but" in the story of any English
evolution—these gloriously sane rules, so far ahead of their
time, applied to a strictly limited number of boys: we may
guess—though accurate figures are impossible to obtain—
that they furnished not more than ten per cent of the
officers required. It was in Pepys's eyes, no doubt, largely
a question of expense. It obviously cost much more for the
Admiralty to bear the cost of training a youth from the
very start, than it did to let these expenses come entirely
out of the private Captain's perquisites—for that is the real
difference if we look closely at it. And, as we have already
seen, the Crown could not afford to be over-generous in
those days.

But what of the other ninety per cent? Well, they went
on exactly as before for another 118 years. They continued
to enter in the old haphazard way which, for lack of a
more comprehensive term, we have designated the "Captain's Servant" way. Knightly Captains, indeed, had lost
their double allowance, but right up to 1794 the ordinary

Captains retained their old privilege of taking four servants per hundred of the Ship's Company to sea with them: and other officers in the same proportions. Up to that date the Admiral and Commander-in-Chief was allowed as many as fifty; and, what is more, they were in the strictest old sense a "retinue", since they were borne over and above the ship's complement, which was not the case with the Captain's servants. It was from these sources that most of the "Ninety per cent" continued to come.

Before we condemn this "pitchfork" method out of hand, let us remember the old proverb about the "proof of the pudding". However much we may marvel at the incongruity of it, it is dangerous to deride a system which gave us an enormous majority of all our eighteenth-century officers, including such men as Rooke and Shovell, Anson and Hawke, Howe and Hood, Duncan and Collingwood, even Nelson himself. What the method did, in effect, was to put the onus of choice on to the captains; and since they tended to take with them, as we have noticed, either their own relatives or else the youth of their own class, it all depended in the end upon whether the captains themselves were of the right type. The character of the average sea-captain thus becomes a matter of double importance, and we shall discuss the question again when we deal with that officer personally. Much has been written from time to time to show that he fell sadly short of the required standard: but here, it would seem, is very strong proof that he did not. "Do men gather grapes of thorns, or figs of thistles?"

But though the Government continued for all that time to control only about ten per cent of the entry, Pepys himself had a good deal to say about the training: at any rate about the training as the word was then understood. Colleges, cruises and courses were unknown to him, but he did try to insist that all would-be "commission-officers" should serve a regular apprenticeship. In 1677 he laid it down that they were to have done at least three years at sea, of which one had been spent as Midshipman, or two as Volunteer-per-Order, before presenting themselves for promotion: and he inaugurated an examination which had to be passed and an age limit of twenty years which had to be reached before a candidate could receive a Lieutenancy. This ensured that each new lieutenant had received all the *practical* training which service on shipboard could provide: and that was something—indeed, a great deal: it was all the training, for instance, that Hawke or Nelson ever did receive. It was Pepys, in fact, who was really responsible for creating a professional *class* of Lieutenants which would infallibly turn into a *rank* as soon as the principle of seniority was established: and he did very nearly as much for the *rating* of Midshipman, which he turned officially into the jumping-off place for embryo officers: though here his action was not quite so decisive, for, as we shall see, it was still possible to obtain a commission without ever having been rated Midshipman, and it was still possible to be a Midshipman and yet never receive a commission. These rules remained henceforward in existence, with minor changes only, the most important of which was the pro-longation of a lieutenant's sea-apprenticeship from three to six years—a regulation broken or evaded during the whole of the eighteenth century to a degree which must astonish the modern mind.

The "Entry" situation, then, remains static during prac-tically the whole of the eighteenth century, some nine out of every ten officers continuing to be recruited, not by the Admiralty, but by the Captains. But the "training" side of the business cannot be so summarily dismissed, because it was in this century that men first saw the need for some form of vocational naval training. The "ninety per cent" who still drifted in unofficially could not very well be caught and practised upon, but the ten per cent could be —and were. It was, therefore, the "King's Letter Boy" who was first put to school.

Some vague idea of importing schoolmasters into ships is
discernible at the very end of the seventeenth century,[1]
but the earliest person to be struck by the idea that it
might be a good thing to make some attempt at training
would-be officers *before* they went to sea was a certain
philanthropic gentleman named Lewis Maidwell, who, in
the year of Blenheim and Gibraltar, not only made the
very modern-sounding suggestion that the Navy should
have its own Public School, but even offered to build and
endow it gratis. The Admiralty expressed their utmost
delight, and reported most favourably to the Lord High
Admiral, declaring that the project would be of inestimable
value to the Service. And there the matter unaccountably
ended. Nothing further was heard of the scheme. Did the
bursting of some forgotten financial bubble, perhaps, cause
the public-spirited Maidwell to count the cost before it was
too late? Or did the scheme wreck itself on the grandiosity
of his ideas? He certainly seems to have had very ambitious
notions about the capacities of budding officers, for he laid
it down, as part of the curriculum of his establishment,
that candidates should, among many other things, acquire
no less than six foreign languages! Yet this suggestion, sadly
over-sanguine though it was, is interesting because it seems
to give us a glimpse into a mind remarkably far ahead of
its time. It really looks as though Mr. Maidwell meant, not
only to train the young gentlemen, but even to educate
them.

Though the scheme came to nothing then, the authorities
did not, apparently, forget about it altogether. In 1729
we find them, rather suddenly, becoming dissatisfied with
the "King's Letter" system, and proposing to start a
"Naval Academy" in order to give the "Volunteer-per-
Order" some training before he went afloat. It was an
epoch-making moment, and it is strange how completely
it has been forgotten: so much so that many people—even

[1] See below, p. 275.

well-informed ones—take it for granted that naval colleges
on shore were a twentieth-century invention, having come
into existence as a result of the famous Selborne Scheme of
1903. Such folk are nearly a century and three-quarters out!

The plans were passed with wonderful promptitude—in
a week. But there was no Mr. Maidwell now to foot the bill;
and before the necessary buildings were finished in Portsmouth Dockyard, four years had elapsed, so that the first
consignment of "volunteers" only arrived in 1733. Had
they been just a shade quicker about it, the first batch
would have contained one George Brydges Rodney; but
as it was, that great man was the last of the old "King's
Letter Boys."

So the "Naval Academy" came into being. It was a
great experiment; but, let us recall once again, it was on
a very small scale. Forty students was the maximum number to be admitted: they were to be "sons of noblemen
and gentlemen", between the ages of 13 and 16, and they
were to pay £25 per annum for their keep.

We know all too little of the life at the Naval Academy.
If we may judge by the analogy of contemporary schools
it was a roughish one. Yet the students enjoyed one amenity
which we are accustomed to associate rather with Edward
Thring of Uppingham and Victorian England: everyone
had his own room. It was small, it is true—between six and
seven feet square—and it might not pass muster now,
especially as, sometimes, it had no window: but it must
have afforded a rather unlooked-for privacy two hundred
years ago.

In 1748—the year in which officers' uniforms were introduced—the scholars also went into uniform—"blue turned
up with white", like the rest of the Service. There was an
Entrance Examination too, conducted by the head mathematical master, but the "Passing Out" Examination, now
such an important hurdle in the race of the modern cadet,
was then a very different matter. It took place not, as

might be expected, when the candidate had studied for a fixed number of months or years, but when he had completed his "Plan of Learning". He began it upon joining, and worked solidly through it, copying the perfected sum of his labours into an exceedingly large and elaborately illuminated note book. When all the "Plan" was safely inscribed in the book, to everyone's satisfaction, and in a particularly fair round hand, then the student was considered to have digested all that the Academy had to offer, and departed for a ship, armed with a filled-in certificate of which this is a blank specimen:

Mr. ———— has, in ——— years, ——— months, and ——— days, finished the Plan of Mathematical Learning, and made a manuscript copy thereof: in consequence, he is judged qualified to serve in H.M. Navy.

He was not allowed to take more than three years, it seems, but might take less. A number of these relics of eighteenth-century scholarship still survive: several specimens may be seen at the National Maritime Museum. The illustration facing page 90 is taken from one of them. It is, in the original, a water-colour sketch of the Naval Academy itself, and it forms the frontispiece of one W. H. Burnaby's "Plan of Learning," completed in 1806. Such embellishments are very common in these books, and the meticulous care displayed in their compilation is remarkable. Another interesting Plan, now appropriately enough, at the Royal Naval College, Dartmouth, is that of the famous Captain Broke, of *Chesapeake* and *Shannon* fame. It, too, is a beautiful piece of work. He was no fool, as both his "Plan of Learning" and his subsequent career prove. Yet he took his full three years. We are not told what happened to those less talented boys who failed to do the work in the time, or otherwise "blotted their copy books". But we may suspect: unless the young gentlemen of the Academy were a great deal more honest than their elders (in all walks of eighteenth-century life) they paid some more skilful hand to complete their note books for them!

Within its limited scope the Naval Academy was perhaps a success. But the scope was *very* limited—even more so than the Authorities intended. By 1773 there were only fifteen students there, and the average over many preceding years had been only twenty. The Admiralty had evidently failed to attract the "nobility and gentry". And this meant that their scheme was failing, for it seems probable that one of the principal reasons for it, in the Admiralty's eyes, was to ensure some real training for those who would in any case reach the very top of the tree by reason of the extensive patronage which they commanded. But such people were, unfortunately, the very ones who received the swiftest advancement by entering the Service under the "patronage" system—i.e. as "ninety-per-centers". They seem to have preferred this latter, and less exacting, method, while the powerful patrons of the system did not relish the idea of losing their patronage. One important result of these things was to depress the reputation of the Academy.

In 1773 the Admiralty made a partial admission of defeat, by inviting fifteen "sons of officers" to be educated at the Academy, at public expense, though they left the twenty-five remaining places for the "nobility and gentry", if they would come. At the same time the establishment acquired the additional epithet of "Royal", perhaps in order to register the then Board's interest in it, and to advertise to the public that it was indeed part of the Royal Navy. The fact that George III inspected it during his visit to Portsmouth in 1773 seems to corroborate the "advertisement" theory.

But still the experiment did not prosper, for now yet another prejudice against it, always present, began to find more open expression. This was the latent scorn of "book-learning", embedded in Captains who had been brought up without it: and this, combined with the scarcely veiled

THE ROYAL NAVAL ACADEMY, PORTSMOUTH, ABOUT 1806

[W. H. Burnaby

hostility of the "privileged" classes, put the poor Academy and all its works into such ill odour afloat, that, at the dawn of the new century, a man like St. Vincent, at the very top of the profession, could write to the parent of a prospective Academy boy, "Are you so partial to that seminary as to hazard a son there?"

Yet the Admiralty still persisted, and even enlarged their scheme a little. In 1806 the Academy was completely overhauled, and given yet another name. From that ordeal it emerged with the more familiar title of "The Royal Naval College"—still of Portsmouth. The number of students was increased, and the old buildings at the south-east corner of the Dockyard were enlarged. It reached its zenith (numerically speaking) in 1816, when it was laid down that its establishment should be one hundred in war-time, and eighty in times of peace.

The Headmaster—or "Professor", as he was called—who was appointed in 1806, and held the post throughout the life of the College, was one of the most distinguished mathematicians of his day. His name was James Inman, and there can be few, if any, modern naval officers who have not, at one time or another, handled one of his works—*Inman's Tables*. He was very versatile in other ways as well: directed the construction of at least ten ships of the line, and wrote books on Gunnery, Ship-Construction and Haversines: he is even said to have given Captain Broke many valuable hints for improving the gunnery in H.M.S. *Shannon*.

Such a man might be expected to aim high where syllabuses were concerned, and a perusal of the work laid down—particularly for the senior "volunteers"—might well turn a modern cadet's hair grey. Here are the "Plans of Study" laid down for the two senior classes:

*Fifth half-year.*—Fortifications, doctrine of projectiles and its application to gunnery: principles of flexions and application to the measurements of surfaces and solids: generation of various curves, resistance of moving bodies: mechanics, hydro-statics, optics, naval history and nautical discoveries.

*Sixth half-year.*—More difficult problems in Astronomy, motions of heavenly bodies, tides, lunar irregularities: the "Principia" and other parts of Newton's Philosophy to those sufficiently advanced.

How did they do it? The age of the eldest scholar, we must remember, was somewhere between fourteen and a half and fifteen. So perhaps it would really be more apposite to ask, *Did* they do it? Was the history of Lewis Maidwell and his vaulting ambition perchance being repeated?

The story of the end of this first Naval College makes such a suspicion seem almost likely. In 1829, there began an innovation unusual in a boys' school. It was laid down that commission officers might come to the College on half-pay, and attend these same studies. They certainly seemed more of an age to do so with some chance of profit, though we must not forget that none of them perhaps had ever attended any academic studies anywhere since they were mere infants. But in the end they succeeded in outlasting the volunteers themselves, for in 1837 the College was closed down for the latter class. There had long been, as we have seen, a good deal of opposition to it among the higher officers, perhaps (as they said) because the training offered was too abstract for their taste; but even more because there still lingered much of their old antagonism to the "alternative method", in which pie they had no finger.

But, be that as it may, when the College reopened two years later, it had completely changed its nature, and had become a place of adult study, where courses were held for "mates", or, as we should now say, Sub-Lieutenants, and for groups of other senior officers. It became, in fact, the forerunner of the present Royal Naval College at Greenwich, to which its remaining activities were transferred in 1873, when the famous buildings at the latter place at length ceased to be used as the Pensioners' Hospital, and began, as they do today, to house the University of the Navy. These innovations are important in that they mark the beginning of those "Courses" both educational and technical, which are such a prominent feature of specialist and quasi-specialist training in our own time.

Now we might surely be entitled to expect, having reached the Victorian Era, that the question of Naval Training would be seriously tackled at last, and the "ninety per cent" of completely untrained First-class Volunteers at last brought into line with the "ten per cent" Volunteers-per-Order (by then usually known as "College Volunteers"). And Authority did tackle the question, but in rather an unexpected way. They took the opposite view, and ordained that one hundred per cent of the officers should go to sea untrained.

But that it not to say that the official aim was to *leave* them untrained. It was the Admiralty's intention, as explained by their Parliamentary Secretary in 1837, to have the training on board ship, instead of on shore: and to give it to all entrants. For this purpose the whole Schoolmaster branch was to be overhauled; the status of its members (as well as its numbers) raised, and a University man borne as Schoolmaster in every ship. We shall touch upon this subject again when we come to discuss the Naval Instructor, for this Admiralty resolution was the making of him.

The Admiralty had changed their tactics. Thwarted in their attempt to train the few for high command *before* they sent them to sea, they now bowed to privilege and prejudice, and sought to train all when they had got them on board.

How far the "schoolmaster-training-afloat" was effective is doubtful. The atmosphere of a ship at sea was not, perhaps, very conducive to intensive studies of an educational kind, and we are bound to suspect that the new schoolmaster often fought a losing fight with the executive officer

for the presence of his scholars in his "place of teaching".[1]
Still, this system lasted for twenty years, before the Admiralty made the great stride forward, and undertook, not only
to train all future officers, but to do so in an environment
set aside exclusively for that purpose.

This was all that Authority had done up to the middle
of last century. But, as in the days of Boteler, so in the
eighteenth century there were folk who were not satisfied
with what was being attempted officially, and who were
prepared to make suggestions and even experiments of
their own. There were several of these, of which space
allows us to name but two. One, Jonas Hanway's "Maritime
School at Chelsea", actually came into existence in 1779,
as a private concern, backed by interested naval officers,
and it may be regarded in some respects as an unofficial
eighteenth-century "Osborne", since it was intended to
provide their sons with a preliminary training for the Naval
Academy and for life at sea. It lasted, under one manage-
ment or another, up till 1830, when, by one of those ironical
turns of fortune's wheel, it became a School of Discipline
for Girls, under the watchful eye of the celebrated Mrs.
Elizabeth Fry. Three years then elapsed, and, Authority
still being quite unprepared to fill the gap, a very similar
private venture was launched called "the Royal Naval
School", which, after flourishing in turn at Camberwell,
New Cross, West Chislehurst, and finally, Eltham, survived
until 1910, by which time the Government had at length
taken the matter in hand, and the real Osborne was in
existence. But a relic of this venture exists to this day, for
the endowment of the Royal Naval School is now used for
the R.N. Scholarship Fund.

Another most interesting solution of both the "entry"
and "training" problems was also suggested by the ingenious
Mr. Hanway, of Marine Society fame. This was, indeed,
merely an offshoot of his much larger scheme for providing

[1] See below, p. 276.

the Service with a complete complement of men, by found-
ing "County Naval Free Schools on Waste Grounds", and
training boys to be at the same time seamen, agricultural,
and perhaps industrial labourers. In addition to the "boys"
there were to be housed in each establishment six "sons of
gentlemen", paying fees, who, under the quaint name of
"Artists" should act (to borrow the modern term) as "Cadet
Captains", receive a rather more elaborate training, and
ultimately enter the Service as Officers. As there were to be
fifty schools, the scheme would have provided for three
hundred young officers under training at any one time—a
number which would have gone far to cater for the whole
Navy's needs. But the scheme came to nought, even as
regards the "boys". The time was not yet ripe.

Occasionally, too, and in isolated instances, young officers
received some real schooling at rather unexpected moments
in their careers. Thus young Raigersfeld's father was advised
in 1786 by that very thoughtful officer, Lord Hood, to
remove his son from sea (where he had been for three and
a half years) and to send him to a private school on land
for a year. And this was done. We hear also, of a certain
number of even older officers who took advantage of "half-
pay" time in order to put themselves to school—thus
Dundonald attended Edinburgh University. But such action
was quite unofficial, and so rare as not to allow us to change
our ratio of nine "untrained" officers for every one "trained".
In any case, regular training (outside the College) was
quite unknown until the 1850's.

But now we have let the "Training" side of our story far
outrun the "Entry" side, for we have passed the two "key"
dates of 1794 and 1838. We must therefore return to see
how the Admiralty were entering their officers.

That absence of method which, for convenience, we have
labelled the "Captain's Servant" entry lasted, as we have
seen, up till the former date. Then the "Captain's Servant"
passed away—at least, officially, and in name. We make

these two qualifications with good reason. It is true that the young gentleman who used to bear this name now became "Volunteer of the First Class", or "First Class Volunteer"; while the other people who had also borne the name—for we must remember that it still was, and always had been, an ordinary rating on board—were divided up into three classes: (*a*) The adults—a small number—became *bona fide* "domestics" to Flag Officers; (*b*) Three-quarters of the boys who bore the title were turned into "Boy" (in the modern naval sense of "makee-learn" seaman) who had to be between 15 and 17 years old; and (*c*) the few remaining were allowed to be the *bona fide* servants of the other officers. Thirty years later—in 1824—a further distinction was made between "Volunteers of the First Class" and "Volunteers of the Second Class", the former being destined for executive rank (i.e. ultimately lieutenant), the latter for the Navigation Branch (i.e. ultimately Master).[1] So the old "office" of "Captain's Servant" finally split into five ratings of very different natures, namely:

(1) Volunteer of First Class—later Naval Cadet.
(2) Ditto of Second Class—an embryo Navigation Officer.
(3) "Boy"—embryo seaman.
(4) Admiral's Servant—real domestic.
(5) Officer's Servant—ditto.

It is the first of these groups which concerns us. He was now "First Class Volunteer", and his numbers were strictly limited—officially—as was his age of entry (over 13 unless the son of an officer, when he might be over 11).

---

[1] We see opposite specimens of these beautiful "young gentlemen". The Second-Class Volunteer is the one perched upon the gun. The First Class pair, whose uniforms can be examined back and front, are distinguishable by the wearing of dirks and by the white "twist" at the collar still characteristic of the Naval Cadet, R.N.

[*L. Mansion*

VOLUNTEERS OF THE FIRST CLASS, AND VOLUNTEER OF THE SECOND CLASS,
ABOUT 1835

But "graft" was far from dead in the 1790's and for some time afterwards, and many captains still contrived to take their protégés to sea, over and above the numbers allowed, as "seaman-boys" and "servant-boys".

The old abuse, too, of entering in the ship's books the names of boys far too young to be allowed on board by the Regulations still continued, though not perhaps so openly or in such extreme degrees as in earlier days. The "13–11 year" rule was, in fact, an old one, dating back (on paper) to at least as early as 1731: but that it was always "more honoured in the breach than the observance" a few cases will show. Two regulation-dodging methods were very commonly practised. In the one, the boy was not only entered in the ship's books, but actually taken to sea at a very tender age: for instance, one Edward Hamilton, who later rose to be an Admiral and a Knight, was taken on board his father's ship in 1779 when he was just seven years old, and "fought" in an action in the following year. In this particular case, a further breach of the rules was committed, for he was rated "midshipman"—a post he had no business to hold until he had served "four years at sea and was in all respects qualified for it"! It is significant, too, that even Nelson broke the rule, though not by nearly so much: he went to sea at the—for those days—mature age of twelve, and therefore, not being the son of a naval officer, went one year too soon.

The other—and even commoner—procedure was for the boy's name to be "entered" while the boy himself was elsewhere. Sometimes his name travelled from book to book for years on end, when his father (or patron) changed his ship. Two astonishing cases of this practice may be cited. A certain John Clavell, Collingwood's First Lieutenant at Trafalgar, was born in 1778, and began his "book" career in 1779, at the age of *one*, though he only put in an appearance on board in 1792, having reached the advanced age of fourteen. There was also another flagrant case as late as 1801, when one William Walker, a lieutenant, was court-martialled for entering his own son, aged one, in the books as an A.B., and for drawing, on his behalf, five pounds in "bounty-money", though the child was, needless to say, not there. He was convicted and dismissed the service; not for entering the baby's name, however, but for the far more heinous offence in contemporary eyes, of acquiring money with intent to defraud. But perhaps the best-known, or rather the most notorious, example of a process which would now be considered as rank fraud, is that of the famous Thomas Cochrane, Lord Dundonald. First entered in a ship's books at the age of five, his name passed on from ship to ship until he was eighteen: and in the meantime his father had procured for him a captaincy in the 79th Foot! It would indeed be hard to find any distinguished Admiral of the eighteenth century who was altogether guiltless of these practices, either in his own person, or in the abetting of others. This may perhaps furnish an extenuating circumstance, but it does not make the practices any the less fraudulent.

Things got a little better after 1794, but not much: for, still no adequate means existed whereby the Admiralty could control such anomalies. In short, they *still* had no say in the appointment of the "ninety per cent". The First Class Volunteers were no more their choice than the captain's servant had been. The chaotic state of "entry", even in the first decade of the nineteenth century, may be measured by the true story of the "Russian Midshipman". This "young gentleman" appears to have been admitted on board on English ship almost without question, on the recommendation of the Czar of Russia. It was only when the ship was captured by the French in 1806, and our men saw with astonishment that their midshipman was received by the victors with open arms, that the fraud was discovered. He was a French spy, sent by Napoleon, *via* the Czar. And he said, later, that there had been many

more like him in the Service who had not been de-
tected.

One of the immediate results of the peace of 1815 was
that the number of entrants required was radically reduced;
and so—naturally enough in peace-time—was the number
of aspirants. This enabled the Admiralty to make a drastic
cut in the numbers of First Class Volunteers to be entered
by the captains. This was done in a series of edicts during
the twenties and early thirties without much opposition:
for the captains, who would certainly have objected to any
curtailment in their ordinary privileges, could hardly complain at not being allowed to continue overloading an
already obviously overloaded profession. Thus by 1833,
although they were still doing the selecting, they were
entering comparatively few, and the Authorities had contrived to slip in a proviso—almost meaningless at first—
that the entrants were to be "approved by the Admiralty".

In 1837, as we have seen, the "College Volunteer" joined
the rest, and all were pitchforked straight to sea, as they
had been before the Naval Academy began. In February
1838, in fact, the term "College Volunteer" was officially
abolished. All were once more on a common footing. But
in the preceding month, and in that quiet, unobtrusive
way in which the major reforms in England always seem
to come about, it had been laid down that a "Volunteer
of the First Class must . . . be able to write English cor-
rectly from dictation, and be acquainted with the first four
rules of arithmetic, reduction and the rule of three". It
does not sound very epoch-making. Yet it was, because if
one lays down such rules for candidates, one must hold an
examination, if only to see that the aspirant conforms to
them. And with every examination there goes the automatic
right to plough a candidate. In a word, the Admiralty, in
this quite unostentatious manner, assumed, *for the first time*,
the choice of future officers—if they cared to do so: not
only the "Ten-per-cent"—they had examined them for

years—but *all* future officers. The date was January 20th,
1838.

Those who have followed this story so far will not, perhaps, think it altogether redundant if we add that this
examination was actually held. It *was* held, though it seems
to have been a complete farce. That sprightly nonagenarian,
Captain J. E. Hunter, who wrote his memoirs a few years
ago, and survived into the present decade, has left a vivid
picture of his own ordeal in 1848.

My father . . . took me to Woolwich, and my examination
was to write out the Lord's Prayer, which I did. Then: "Can
you drink a glass of sherry?" I said, "Just you try me." I was
taken to the Surgeon to be examined. He said, "strip." I took
off my coat. "Go on, strip." Then he examined me, and was
going to strike me a blow with his fist on my chest. I stepped
back and prepared to fight, and said: "Oh, I'm your man."
He at once said: "Take that boy away, he will do."

Young Hunter thus became a "Naval Cadet". Had he
joined five years earlier he would have been a "First Class
Volunteer", for it was only in 1843 that the name was
officially changed.

But though the introduction of the examination in 1838
was the thin end of the wedge—the moment, that is when
the Admiralty *began* to get control of Entry—the grotesque
nature of the test should be enough to warn us that only
the extreme tip of that wedge had been inserted. The mass
which it was attempting to dislodge was, in truth, an
exceedingly large and powerful vested interest—the age-old
custom whereby the senior officers of the Navy appointed
their successors. This vested interest was all that remained
of the captain's rights in the matter of "servants", and was
enshrined in what we have called, throughout, the "Captain's
Servant" Entry. In the nineteenth century it was dignified
with the polite name of the "Principle of Nomination", but
it is the same thing.

Like all vested interests—especially English ones—it died

very hard, and demands a long and complicated story. But we must attempt here to indicate briefly the chief stages in this great change from "Nomination" to "Competition".

In 1839 it was ordained that every Volunteer should take an examination before becoming a midshipman, and it seems to have been—unlike the corresponding "Volunteer" examination—a reality from the first. This brought the Admiralty's real control down to Midshipman. Thereafter, though they could not—or at any rate *did* not—select the majority of Volunteers, they could—and did—control the promoting of them to the next stage.

A further big step was taken in 1848, when they regulated exactly—and reduced the regulation to paper—the number of "nominations" which various officers might make. Every Commander-in-Chief, on appointment, might make two, and every Captain, on commissioning a ship, one. They further limited the nominators' freedom, in the following year, by declaring that the nominee must be between the ages of twelve and fourteen: before that, he only had to be over twelve. In 1851, they stiffened up the examination, and made it a reality. We can see this from the fact that now, for the first time, the orders visualize the possibility of failure, and decree that, in this event, the nomination is cancelled.

A further long stride was taken in 1870, when "Limited Competition" was introduced. Under this scheme nomination, either by the Admiralty or one of the privileged nominators, was still retained, but the number of young gentlemen nominated was to be twice as great as the number of vacancies. In that year, for instance, seventy-four were to be nominated, but only thirty-seven entered.

This system of competition—even in its limited form— raised a storm of protest in interested quarters, and the Authorities wavered once or twice. But they won in the end, for competition tended to become keener, and nominations to become rarer. Still, the double system lasted out the century, and even, in modified form, survived the great

changes of 1903.[1] By 1906 the number of nominees allowed
to Flag Officers and Captains had shrunk still further—a
Captain, for example, could now make his one nomination
once only during his full period as Captain, and not at the
beginning of each commission. By this time, in fact, a great
majority of the nominations were in the hands of the
Admiralty, and, by reason of the numerical competition
for cadetships, the choice lay, in practice, with them.

But the fight was not quite over. One more step was
taken in that year, when a subtle change appears in the
wording of the regulations. Thenceforward nobody "nomi-
nates" any more; instead, the Flag-Officers and Captains
"specially recommend".

In 1913 came the "Special Entry",[1] in which, from the
first, there was open competition; and in January 1914
comes the final blow. Then, for the first time, the public
are informed that no nomination whatever is required,
even the "special recommends" disappearing.

So, on the full tide of democracy, came Open Competition. But though, since 1914, any boy of the required age
may apply, he still has to pass through three grids (or sieves)
before he can enter—a personal interview, a medical test
and a written examination. There can be no doubt that the
Admiralty has secured complete control of "Entry" at last.

But now we have allowed this side of our story to outrun
the "Training". So we must return to that crucial year in
the latter's history—1857—when the great revolution
occurred. "Every cadet", it was then announced, "on
passing, will be appointed to a training ship."

So, when it came, it came suddenly. From "nought per
cent" to be given preliminary training, the proportion
sprang at a bound to "one hundred per cent". The Admiralty, already beginning to secure the right of choice, were
now undertaking to provide a specific training for all
executive officers, in a ship designed solely for that purpose.

[1] For these, see next chapter.

# CHAPTER VII

## "SUPPLY" (continued)

### ENTRY, TRAINING AND EDUCATION

MUCH was thus achieved: but not all. For though all cadets were now to be trained professionally, no one seems to have given a thought to their general education. It is hard in our day when the whole subject of Education is so much in the forefront of the national mind, to realize how very modern that phenomenon is. It is, indeed, probably true to say that, if the early Victorian Admiralty thought about the matter at all, they considered that the professional training they were offering was the only possible education that they could give to a boy who was to spend the best years of his life in the Navy. Professional training, to them, was the vital factor of Education. What they did not consider—what is, in fact, only the discovery of ourselves, or, at best, of our fathers—is the exact reverse—that Education is a vital factor in Professional Training: that a man, however expert in his own particular job, will be a much more effective entity in every way if the rest of his mental outfit is developed at least up to normal standards. And this, which is true of all professions and other walks of life, is particularly so in the case of a profession which is, by its very nature, active rather than sedentary, and demanding contacts with men as well as with machines.

The Training Ship did not, indeed, give a *wholly* professional training, and omit general education altogether. At the start, alternate days were devoted to "Seamanship", and "Studies", but the latter were almost exclusively studies with a highly professional trend, so that it would perhaps be fair to assess the "professional" time-factor at not less than 90 per cent of the whole, and the "general education" factor at a bare 10 per cent. The lads learnt a little French and Drawing, it is true: but, it seems, it was *very* little. And the older members of the present generation do not have to be so very old to recall how often the Drawing Master or the French Master, even in their own schooldays, was a joke, and rather a good one at that!

The story of the Training Ship era is too recent to demand much detail in the telling. It lasted from 1857 until 1903, so that all executive officers of flag rank now on the active list, and a large number of serving captains too, are personally familiar with its closing stages. The merest outline must here suffice.

Credit for the idea belongs very largely to one man, Captain Robert Harris; and it bears this resemblance to Hanway's "Naval Schools" project—it emanated from a scheme for training seaman-boys.

It was during the Crimean War that the then First Lord, Sir James Graham, had started the *Illustrious*, two-decker, as a training-ship for young seamen. Captain Harris had been put in command, and had quickly made such a success of it that *Illustrious* boys were in great demand throughout the fleet. Then it occurred to him that a process which made good seamen might reasonably be expected to make good officers too. It sounds obvious enough—most big inventions do, when invented. But perhaps it was not quite so obvious then: at any rate, the suggestion was strenuously opposed in high quarters, and nothing was done about it. But Harris was not the sort to give up without a struggle: he soon saw his chance of trying out his experiment on a very small scale, and took it. It happened that his own son—also Robert Harris—was about to enter the Service.

He applied for him—any Captain could still do that—and put him through the full *Illustrious* course with the seamen-boys.

Fortunately, the younger Robert, who was a bright boy, proved a great success. He ended his days, in fact, as Vice-Admiral, k.c.b., k.c.m.g., and his father was probably banking on his brightness. Anyway, it was only six weeks after he had finished his course that, opposition having melted away, the *Circular* of February 23rd, 1857, announced training for all Naval Cadets.

The *Illustrious* herself was used at first, and she received both seaman-boys and naval cadets. But clearly this could not last, and in 1858 the former were removed. But even then the ship was not big enough, and in 1859 the three-decker *Britannia* was taken over for the purpose.

At first the length of the course was very short—a maximum period of one year, and a minimum of a mere three months. But in 1860 the time was lengthened to four terms of three months for all: which, in practice, was actually five terms, since Authority, having ordained a three-months' cruise to follow the course, somewhat characteristically omitted to provide a ship to cruise in, and the cadets apparently stayed on in the *Britannia*.

The *Illustrious* lay all her "training" days in Haslar Creek, Portsmouth, and the *Britannia* did the same up till 1862. In a conservative institution like the Navy no one seems to have thought of putting a training-ship anywhere else. The late lamented R.N. College had been there for over a century, and that was good enough. But with a cadet training-ship there arrived also upon the scene another new—and very formidable—factor in the training problem —the British Parent. Haslar Creek was muddy and insanitary, and—at low tide—undeniably smelly: while Portsmouth Town was *not*, on moral grounds, quite a nice playground for the sons of Victorian gentlefolk. So the *Britannia* weighed anchor, and moved to Portland; possibly because Weymouth had been *very* genteel in the reign of

George III. But that did not really make the anchorage off the Bill, exposed to the full force of every easterly gale, any more desirable; and a further change was inevitable. So in the next year a fresh move was made, this time to more permanent moorings: for in 1863 the *Britannia* entered Dartmouth harbour. The cadets, if not the ship, have stayed there ever since.

In 1864 the *Hindustan*, an old two-decker, built of Indian teak, was added to cope with increasing numbers, and was moored in a permanent position ahead of the *Britannia*, with a bridge joining the two. Meantime, also, the establishment had spread on to the shore, where such amenities as a gymnasium and playing fields quickly sprang up. And, lastly, in 1869 the old *Britannia* gave place to the new one, a ship of much less historic interest, though of greater capacity, which had started life as the *Prince of Wales*. This ship remained at her moorings even after the cadets had moved out of her into the College on the hill above, and only left for the ship-breaker's yard in the year of Jutland.

By then the days of the Training Ship were over—at least, of the Training Ship alone. The "Naval College" system had been revived—this time for all "military" officers. The reasons for the change at the turn of the new century were many, and the problems tackled may be divided for convenience under three headings—"Naval Colleges", "Naval Education", and "Common Entry".

NAVAL COLLEGES

There was, first, that aspect of the whole affair which was at once the most superficially prominent yet really the least important—the actual change of quarters from sea to land. Our friend the British Parent took a leading part in this phase. He wrote to the newspapers that the accommodation in the *Britannia* was damp, inadequate and out-of-date, and he got his M.P. to ask the First Lord whether he was aware of the fact: he had, indeed, being doing so, on and off, for twenty years or more before he had his way. According to the standards of 1900, there was certainly something in what he said, and some change was due on these grounds alone. The result was the setting-up of the Junior and Senior Colleges of Osborne and Dartmouth, with two years to be spent at each. The scheme was put through at a very great speed, as such things go. This meant the provision of admittedly shake-down accommodation at Osborne, which, as the junior establishment, was due for occupation first. The buildings received their first inhabitants in September 1903. Dartmouth, with two years' grace before the first Osbornites were due to arrive, fared much better, and a commodious—indeed a handsome—series of buildings arose there.

The modest nature of the Osborne accommodation gave the British Parent his third big chance of entering the arena, and he (or she) was quick to respond. The poor dears' dormitories, it was asserted, were on the site of the Osborne House stables, and all the diseases that beasts are heir to were being transferred automatically to the future Naval Officer. In fact, in the words of a gifted local parodist,[1]

> He quickly acquires the most quaint of appendices
>   Varicose veins and a curvital spine,
> Ophthalmia, 'flu, scarlet fever and hen-disease,
>   Measles, mumps, whooping-cough, all in a line.

In reality, the dormitories were *not* on the site of the stables: yet there certainly were big epidemics of the "measles-and-mumps" order. And there was a much more rational explanation of them than that put forward by the British Parent—nowhere else in the country were quite so many twelve- to fourteen-year-olds, all just ripe for the delectation of such germs, congregated together in one place. So in 1921 Osborne, as a Naval College, disappeared,

[1] R. P. Keigwin, in *Lanyard Lyrics*.

though it is only fair to record, in passing, that it was not so much the breeze fanned by the British Parent which overwhelmed it, as the rather more devastating hurricane of the Great War. Both Colleges having been considerably enlarged, in order to house the greatly increased numbers which passed through them between 1914 and 1918, it was found, when retrenchment came and the post-war axe began to swing, that either set of buildings was quite large enough to hold the smaller numbers now required: and, very naturally, the permanent edifice was retained, and the temporary one relinquished. But though Osborne as a place of instruction for naval youth thus disappeared, the principle underlying it did not. Its occupants simply moved on to Dartmouth, and became the Junior College there. The course was, however, cut short by one term all told: so that now the Cadet, first Junior and then senior, remains there for eleven terms, or three and three-quarter years.

### NAVAL EDUCATION

But Naval Colleges were only the most superficial result of the famous Selborne Scheme. Much more important were the two radical changes of Admiralty policy which it inaugurated. Selborne was then the First Lord, but it was the dynamic personality of his First Sea Lord, Sir John Fisher, which furnished the main drive.

The first great change concerned Education. In 1903 that subject was a force to be reckoned with—Education with a capital E: and by that word we mean, both here and in all which follows, that more general "drawing-out" of all the latent abilities, in contradistinction to instruction in merely technical and professional subjects. Now Selborne and Fisher had to face the fact that, under the old scheme, the Naval Officer's "education" stopped, to all intents and purposes, the moment he entered the *Britannia*: that is, approximately, at the moment when, if still in civil life, he would have been entering his Public School. This had been good enough in Harris's time, but it was clearly out of date in Edwardian England. One of two alternatives alone remained. Either the aspirant must be allowed to acquire his education elsewhere, and be received into the Navy when he had done so—the entrance-age, that is, must be boldly and considerably raised: or else the State must itself undertake to provide the education as well as the training. That was the essence of the problem which had to be faced: and Selborne and Fisher plumped whole-heartedly for the latter alternative—Fisher, indeed, was a man who did not believe in doing anything by halves.

History and Tradition backed them in no uncertain way. We have already shown the chaos which had for centuries embraced the whole problem of "entry", but there was one principle which had been common to all previous methods: the principle of "Catch them Young"; sometimes, as we have seen, so very young as to be absurd and wasteful, but, in ninety-nine out of a hundred cases, *young*. Statistics are of course impossible, but we shall probably be right in assuming that Nelson's twelve years was just about the average age of entry, taken over the last two centuries. So it would have been an immense breach with a far from unsuccessful past, had they decided the other way. And further, there can be no doubt that Fisher was keenly conscious of the value —both to the officer and to the Navy—of those years of boyish enthusiasm, when the essential loyalties are almost unconsciously imbibed, and the age-old traditions of the Service acquired by the processes of Nature rather than by the efforts of the instructor. It was for this reason that the Colleges—or, rather, now, the College—of his making, was, and has always remained, a "Ship", with that strong naval flavour in the life, to be glimpsed a score of times in every day's routine, in its uniformed officers, its "divisions", its "watches", its "quarterdeck", Colours, Ship's Bells, bugles, Reveillé, Sunset and Last Post. Yet, with it all, it is, right enough, and always has been, what Fisher intended it to be—the Public School of the Navy, where the "General Education", now so universally accepted as a necessity, always has pride of place.

A story is told that would, we feel, have delighted the old Admiral's heart, for it shows up so clearly all that was very near to it. A deputation of officers from a friendly nation whose Navy is a far newer thing than ours, paid Dartmouth a visit not so long ago, with a view to discovering how they might improve their own training arrangements. They were taken the rounds by the Captain, and shown (as he thought) all that could possibly interest them. They attended closely to all he said, and narrowly watched all they saw, making copious notes. And yet they seemed to the Captain a thought distrait, like folk who, having come to see the Heavy-weight Boxing Championship of the World, are being treated to a preliminary bout by the local light-weight novices. At length, the round complete, the Captain, with an inward sigh of relief, suggested a glass of sherry before lunch. Thereupon his visitors' faces fell as far as Nature ever permits that particular type of countenance to fall, and their leader broke the uncomfortable silence. "And now", he said, "may we see the 'Esprit de Corps class', please?"

Upon the Captain's reply History is silent. But the true answer is the last word in Sir Christopher Wren's epitaph— "*Circumspice!*"

Later—just before the War—the Government reversed some parts of the full Selborne policy. Certain of these changes we shall notice shortly: but one aspect should be mentioned here. In 1913 the "Public School Entry" began to run concurrently with the "Dartmouth Entry". Thus the other alternative of 1903 was introduced, though sparingly. For, under this scheme, the cadet receives his general education *before* he enters the Service. Much ink has since been spilt by champions of these two methods, urging weighty arguments on either side; but into these we will not enter, save to observe that there seems to be a proper place for both in the scheme of things, and to give one very practical reason why this is so. The Public School (or "Special") Entry supplied—and supplies—both the Executive and the Engineering branches. To the latter we shall refer again shortly. Of the former, it may be said that the method furnishes a good, if not a necessary, aid to the Admiralty in the extraordinarily difficult task of assessing the correct number of entrants at any given moment. The nature of this difficulty may be most easily explained by observing that it takes a long time to make the complete Naval Officer. Between entry into Dartmouth and the end of the Sub-Lieutenants' courses there normally elapse eight years—a period which is a good deal longer than that required for building a ship to put him in; and incomparably longer than the time taken to scrap a ship. It follows, then, that there is grave danger of over-supply when the country's policy demands a sudden reduction of total naval force, and an even graver danger of shortage when the fleet is to be quickly expanded. The "Special Entry", which turns out an officer in but little over half the time, is clearly a very convenient safety valve, which may be all but closed when the Dartmouth flow is likely to prove large enough, or too large, and yet may be opened up indefinitely when it threatens to prove inadequate. This consideration, in fact, was an important one in 1913, when the Special Entry Scheme began, the intensive "naval race" with Germany, then in progress, creating an urgent demand for a bigger supply of officers.

"COMMON ENTRY"

But we have still to deal with the third set of problems confronting the sponsors of the Selborne Scheme—problems which, in many ways, involved even larger issues.

We have discussed, so far, only the entry and training of the "executive" branch of the Service—of those men, that.

is, who are primarily the "fighting-seamen-officers" and who, in all periods of our story, have held the commands of fleets and ships at sea. And we saw, in the opening chapters, how they evolved originally from the two distinct elements of "fighter" and "seaman". They are most important folk in our story—perhaps, even, we need not boggle over the definite article, but may call them *the* most important. But they are not the *only* people in it by any means. There are whole hosts of others without whom the Navy could not function for a week or a day. And all these others have this in common with the "executives"—they are all compounds of two distinct elements, one of which is always the same—"Naval Officer"—while the other is in each case different. Thus the Naval Engineer-Officer is Officer and Engineer; the Naval Chaplain, Officer and Priest; the Naval Instructor, Officer and Schoolmaster; the Naval Surgeon, Officer and Doctor; the Naval Paymaster, Officer and Accountant; the Marine, Officer and Infantryman or Artillerist. We cannot get away from it. Here, within the profession of Naval Officer, we have fully qualified members of at least six other primary professions—there are really a good many more than these, but we are only generalizing now: seven professions within one profession (for we may add here the "Fighter" himself).

Of these "inner-professions" we shall have more to say in due course. Here we are concerned only with the problems of "entry" and "training". Now there are three stages at which it is theoretically possible to "enter" any exponent of these seven. We may take him really young—say at twelve, thirteen or fourteen: but if we do, we shall be forced, as we saw in the case of the seventh, to "educate" him first, and then we shall have to "train" him, as well, to his "inner" profession. For instance, if we take our coming Surgeon at the age of thirteen, we shall have first to educate him, and then train him in medicine and surgery. Again, we may decide to dispense with the first stage, letting outside schools educate him in the wider sense up to the age, say, of eighteen, and only take him on to learn his profession. Lastly, we may not even be prepared—may not have the facilities—to teach him his profession either: we may take him on only when he is a fully-qualified Doctor, Accountant, Engineer, Schoolmaster, Priest or Soldier; which he will only become when he is somewhere in the twenties. Each case must doubtless be decided on its own merits. But, sometime or other, it must be decided.

In order to view in its right perspective the change intended in this matter by Selborne and Fisher, we must see what, roughly, was the usage of the past—say a century ago. In 1839, then, the Executives, or a vast majority of them, were entered at the twelve–fourteen mark. But none of the others were. At the eighteen mark—approximately—came the bulk of the Marines, a few of the (then newly formed) Corps of Engineers, and some of the junior members of the Purser's branch. The candidates for the other three "inner" professions were all taken in only when they were considered to be masters of their own particular job. In these three cases, this was the logical thing to do, and no change whatever has been made from that day to this. Obviously the Surgeon will receive better medical training in the properly constituted medical schools and hospitals: a School of Naval Medicine, to train medicos from scratch, would certainly be no more efficient, and yet incomparably more expensive. The same would apply to a Naval Theological College, while the Universities furnish the Naval Instructor with almost all the preliminary mental equipment he requires. At least, in all these cases, a short "course" is sufficient to turn a Doctor, a Parson and a University Honours man—into a very effective Surgeon, Chaplain and Naval Instructor.

But the other cases admit of some argument. Accountancy in the Navy, for instance, is a rather specialized branch of Accountancy in general, and a boy with a good general education will probably receive the best training in Naval Accountancy if he studies it under able Naval Accountants already fully qualified in this special branch of the profession: he has therefore come, in our day, to be "entered" at the eighteen-mark, when his general education is over, but before his special training has begun.

There remain the Executives, the Engineers, and the Marines. The first-named, as we have seen, were always on the twelve–fourteen mark, up to, and after, the Selborne Scheme. The Engineers—latest comers of all—proved, in this as in other respects, a difficult problem, which we shall have to discuss at a later point. Suffice it to say here that, by 1903, their numbers had multiplied enormously, their duties were becoming yearly more numerous, and infinitely more complex, and their responsibilities were ever increasing, as the days of sail receded once and for all into the dead past, and mechanical propulsion held the seas alone.

The view of them which the reformers took was that they had now become specialists, essential to the Service, essential even to the *military*—i.e. in the most direct sense, the "fighting"—efficiency of the Service, and therefore in no noticeable way distinguishable from the "executive" specialists already in existence: such people as specialist gunnery officers, or specialist torpedo-men. They therefore proposed boldly to wipe out the hard-and-fast line separating executives and engineers, and in future to recruit the two from exactly the same class, and educate them both together, from the start, in exactly the same way. All future executives and all future engineers would thus begin in one common "pool". They were all to start as Osborne Cadets, and all to pass on to Dartmouth.

Again, just as all "executives", whether destined to specialize or not, received the first stages of their training (as opposed to education) together, so was the new specialist —the Engineer—to be treated. All, therefore, were to go to sea together, there to be instructed in all the practical

subjects: all to become Midshipmen, and pass three years
in that capacity: all to become Acting-Sub-Lieutenants,
and go to the R.N. College, Greenwich, and to Portsmouth
afterwards for further courses. Then, and then only, would
their ways part. Those who wished to join the Executive
Branch as ordinary "deck" officers; those who wished
to specialize, while remaining "executives", in Gunnery,
Torpedoes, Signals and Navigation, *and* those who wished
to specialize in Engineering could now all take their choice.
All would equally become Sub-Lieutenants, and the initial
letter of their specialization would be tacked on after their
title. Thus, the Gunnery officer would become Sub-Lieutenant (G), and the Engineer would become Sub-Lieutenant
(E), instead of, as formerly, Engineer-Sub-Lieutenant. The
coloured band of distinction, too, worn between the gold
rings on the arm, would disappear from the new Engineer's
uniform. He would, henceforward, look—even as he would
be—indistinguishable from the executive officer. And, partly
in order to safeguard the vital subject of Engineering from
early neglect, and partly because it was deemed essential
that *all* officers should know at least a little about engines,
that subject was included, with the rest, at all stages of
training, as well at Osborne and Dartmouth as on board
ship.

For reasons which are hardly so clear-cut or obvious, the
Royal Marines were to be brought under exactly the same
régime. The principal one was that the young subaltern,
who came on board ship trained to land-service only, was
considered unfit to "pull his weight" when he got there.
Nor did it seem feasible, once he was on board, to give
him the necessary sea-instruction. "From lack of early sea-
training", says Lord Selborne, in his famous memorandum,
"the Marine Officer is compelled, sorely against his will, to
remain comparatively idle on board ship, when everyone
else is full of work". So, in future, he was to be trained,
from the start, like any other naval officer, and the Corps

was to be recruited exclusively from the "pool" of Acting-Sub-Lieutenants, who had thus yet another choice when their Portsmouth courses were done.

There can be no doubt that the real aim of the reformers was to amalgamate these three "fighting" branches, finally and completely; and it was in order to do this with true Fisheresque thoroughness that they determined to make them all start from exactly the same mark. Lord Selborne makes this perfectly clear. "The result arrived at is, to a certain point, community of knowledge, and life-long community of sentiment. The only machinery which can produce this result is early companionship and community of instruction. These opportunities will be secured by a policy of 'One system of Supply, one system of Entry, one system of Training'."

This represented, unquestionably, a fine ideal. But would it work? There were not wanting many gloomy prophets who foretold that it would not: and in this case the Jeremiahs were correct. The experiment was, in the case of the Engineers, only very partially successful from the start, while with the Marines it failed entirely.

Detailed reasons would lead to explanations rather outside the scope of this book. In the case of the Engineers, it is sufficient to say that the scheme was perhaps aiming too high. As the modern warship became, year by year, a more and more complicated "box of tricks", the demand for further and deeper specialization was unavoidable: and an arrangement based upon the principle that every officer should have at least a working knowledge of so many separate branches was doomed to be wrecked on this rock of ever-growing complexity. It soon began to dawn on people that the gunnery officer, say, who had to reach as well a certain proficiency in engineering, would be a less complete gunner in consequence: while the engineer, who knew a little about a very large number of naval subjects well outside his immediate province, would not be so efficient an engineer, nor so up-to-date in a constantly advancing science.

Here, too, Tradition doubtless helped to contribute to the failure. In all epochs of our Navy's history, as we have seen, the Executive Branch has, traditionally, held the leading position on board—even, up to less than a century ago, to the extent of being the only commissioned officers. That tradition could not be expected to die, as it were, in the night; and the result of its survival was very soon evident. Not enough—not nearly enough—volunteered from the "pool" for engineering duties: and, rightly chary of the results of using *force majeure*, the authorities had in the end to unlink the two careers, and, to a very considerable extent, to fall back on the Public School entry to fill the ranks of the Engineers. Yet to this day an appreciable proportion of Dartmouth cadets find their way into the Engineering branch: only the roads now part on leaving the training cruiser, instead of some four years later, as Lord Selborne intended.

The last—and perhaps the most certain—cause of failure lay in the fact that, from the very nature of the case, all the most obvious "plums" of the profession must go to that section of the "pool" which had decided on an "executive" career: to those, that is, who had been trained to command complete ships, and whole fleets, rather than a single—even though vital—*part* of ships and fleets. Quite early on the authorities realized that officers could not be allowed to flutter indefinitely between quarterdeck and engine-rooms, or the result might be that no officer would be fully qualified to adorn either. They were therefore forced to "make the division into the various branches definite and final". That meant, "once an Engineer, always an Engineer; and goodbye to high Fleet Command". It is true that Selborne also wrote that "every endeavour will be made to provide those who enter the Engineering branch with opportunities equal to those of the executive branch, including the same opportunity of rising to flag-rank". But this pious hope has never been realized, for the simple reason that, in the Navy as at present constituted, it is an impossibility. The Engineer has his compensations, it is true. He has, for instance, a better chance than the Executive of promotion in the middle ranks, and therefore of a longer term of employment: he has, too, in the nature of things, a better "second string to his bow"—he can find, far more readily than his Executive brother, a professional job on retirement. But a glance at the relative number of Executive and Engineer Flag Officers in the Navy List will show very clearly who has the overwhelming advantage there.

The Selborne Scheme for obtaining Royal Marine officers appears, from the first, to have appealed neither to the young officers of the "pool" nor to the Marines themselves. Promotion in the famous Corps, never remarkably fast, was, at the time, rather notoriously slow, and, for an ambitious boy at least, his chances of reaching the top were very small compared with his chances in the Executive branch. Nor was that summit either so broad or so high: in fact, the "plums" that could be offered him were hardly so attractive, even, as those reserved for the engineer. He was, it is true, to be allowed to keep watch at sea, and to do "general and executive duties on board ship up to and including the rank of Captain of Marines". But this sounded very much like saying, "you may do all the routine work of Lieutenants, R.N., but when it comes to the responsibilities of Commander, you will not be allowed to assume them". In these circumstances was it altogether surprising that singularly few from the "pool" of those who had all been so carefully trained together in "early companionship and community of instruction" were prepared to accept the implications of so insidious a distinction?

As for the Corps itself, its personnel, both of officers and men, has been, for a very long time, hereditary to an extraordinary degree. And this has tended to make the

officers of any one generation anxious to attend personally
to the training of their successors—a wish which the Selborne
system in no way assisted. Nor did these officers believe that
the "pool" education would cater adequately for the training of their youngsters in the very highly specialized functions expected of the Corps: in fact, that though the new
system might make them better *Naval* officers—in which
capacity, however, they were not to be employed after the
first few years—it would tend to make them less efficient
in their true rôle of *Marine* officers. So, as far as they were
concerned, the scheme remained all but still-born, and the
number of Dartmouth-trained cadets who have found their
way into the Royal Marines can almost be counted on the
fingers of one hand. The Subaltern, R.M., is now once
more on the "eighteen-year" mark.

Three small additional channels of entry to commissioned
rank, all of which belong to the present century, ought to
be mentioned in conclusion. There are, first, the "Mates"
—promising youngsters carefully selected from the Lower
Deck, who merge with other executives at the Sub-Lieutenant stage—are indeed, now called Sub-Lieutenants and
not Mates. We shall have occasion to mention these officers
again later. Next, there are a few entries annually from
the Nautical College, Pangbourne, and the training ships
*Conway* and *Worcester*—all three of which are, of course,
training establishments for officers of the Merchant Service.
The great usefulness of this link between the two Services
is too obvious to require enlargement here. Aspirants from
this source are also, mostly, on the "seventeen to eighteen"
mark at the moment of entry, since they join their Dartmouth colleagues in the training cruiser: though in this
case their education has been, in many respects, similar
to that of the Royal Naval College, Dartmouth, some, indeed, joining the latter for the last half of the course. And
lastly, since 1937, there has been forged yet another link with
the Merchant Service, a number of Royal Naval Reserve

officers being entered annually direct into the Royal Navy.[1]

Our English history has a curious way of repeating itself. The executive officers of our own day are thus drawn from four main sources—Dartmouth, the Public Schools, the Merchant Service, and the Lower Deck. All those same sources were available and were actually being tapped, during most of the periods covered by our story: though, of course, in other days, they had not these names, and were completely lacking in all the cut-and-dried regulations of the twentieth century.

The ancestors of the Dartmouth cadet—the old "catch-them-young" group—were always, as they are now, the most numerous. Most of the Volunteers, both "of the First Class", and "per Order", come in this group, as well as a big majority of those "young gentlemen" who first went to sea as Captain's, Lieutenant's or Master's servants, or as "Ordinary" or "Able" Seamen. But the ancestors of the Public School Entrants were there too; and, even though not very numerous, yet furnished some fine and well-known officers—Edward Vernon, for instance, of *Porto Bello* fame who was educated at Westminster and only went afloat at the age of seventeen: and Thomas Cochrane, the immortal Dundonald, who, as we have seen, only went to sea as an eighteen-year-old—and, incidentally, as a six-footer.

As for the Merchant Service Entry, there are many seventeenth-century cases on record, especially before the differentiation of the two Services was complete. There was also a steady trickle during the eighteenth century, but it was growing less, and almost dried up in the nineteenth. Shining examples of merchant-service seamen who reached the quarterdeck of a man-of-war and lived to adorn it, are found in such men as John Benbow, John Campbell, and

---

[1] Discontinued. There is now, however, an entry for the new Electrical Branch (denoted by the letter L after the officer's rank-name, and a green distinguishing band on the arm). The entrant's age is, approximately, that of the Special Entrant.

that prince of navigators, Captain Cook. Of those who
entered, as the sailors' saying went, "through the hawse-
hole"—that is, as the cables do, through the lower deck—
there was a persistent, if not voluminous flow right up to
the end of the eighteenth century. During all ages but the
present, however, the subject is not one that lends itself to the
formulation of rules, for such promotion always demanded
either exceptional ability or exceptional good fortune.
Usually, too, the officer was promoted too late in life to rise
very high—a handicap which the modern system is specially
designed to overcome.[1] Examples of men who rose superior
even to this obstacle are Sir David Mitchell, who was—
probably—"pressed" into the Service in the first place, and
rose—not without interest of course, for that was impossible,
yet mainly on sheer merit—to carry his flag afloat: and—a
late example—James Clephan, who was "pressed" in 1794
and promoted to Lieutenant in 1801: he was present at
Trafalgar, and died a captain in 1854.

Thus, within the duration of a long life, the Naval Officer
has acquired a modern system of training, and within the
memory of the middle-aged, a modern system of education.
The system of entry, too, has been completely regulated,
for the first time, well within the last hundred years. But
here the change is in organization rather than in principle.
The passage of a century has altered the fleets of England
beyond all recognition, so that Nelson himself would stand
agape, and utterly lost, on the quarterdeck of the ship
which now bears his name. But, save in technical knowledge
and education, and, of course, in the skin-deep changes of
dress and living that the lapse of a century must bring, he
would find no radical alterations in the officers themselves.
Most of them would have entered the Service at much the
same age as he did: and in almost any one of them he
would be able to recognize, and greet, some type who had
served with him, long ago, in the *Agamemnon*, or the *Victory*.

[1] See below, p. 212.

# CHAPTER VIII

## "RETIREMENT"

### SUPERANNUATION AND AFTER-CARE

THAT "Service" came before "Supply" is not surprising. That "After-care" came late in the day is even less so. Such a "humane" conception is comparatively modern. It was not only in the Navy that it was long delayed, but in nearly every other profession and walk of life. Such a thing was, indeed, almost unknown so long as the great principle of *laissez faire* held sway in the economic field, and the Government's very last duty in its own eyes—was to be "paternal".

But this applies to only one—the humanitarian—side of "Retirement". What of the practical side? Retirement thus considered is, or ought to be, an essential adjunct of any fighting profession, since the machinery will not work properly until it is introduced. If we look at the matter in this light, we shall find the long delay in regulating Retirement a most surprising circumstance: no less so than the equally long delay in regulating Supply. In a word, that the *heart* of eighteenth-century Authority was not stirred is what the historian would expect: but it is strange that its rather hard head failed to grasp the necessity. Yet such is the case: so much so that some small beginnings of "After-care" actually appear first, and so render it necessary for us to begin with that, rather than with Naval Retirement proper. The latter, in anything like its modern form, is a strictly nineteenth-century phenomenon. "After-care" began—on paper—in 1700.

It could not very well begin much earlier, for one very good reason. So long as the Navy was a "jobbing" affair, and not a whole-time profession, there was no particular call for any such thing. In most ages of man's long history there seems to have existed a sort of natural charity—an innate feeling that an employer is only "doing the right thing" if he rewards the long and faithful services of his dependents by making some provision for their declining years. So, no doubt, the medieval baron would reward a trusted steward with a cottage and a strip or two of land: so would a modern employer "pension off" an old nurse or gardener, even though the State itself make provision for them: and more certainly still if it did not. But we do not normally feel any particular obligation to pension off our window-cleaner, and still less our solicitor. And why? Because the people in the first group have rendered a life-time of service to us personally, and have not distributed their labour among a number of clients, as have the second. They are, in fact, "whole-timers", where the others are "jobbers".

The story of After-care in the Navy follows exactly—though slowly—this same general course. The first people to obtain "Retired Pay"—or, as they then called it, a "pension on superannuation"—were the first people to be anything like "whole-timers"—the Navy's earliest "permanent staff", known as the Warrant or "Standing" officers. We have been introduced to this class in the opening chapters of this book, and we shall obtain later a closer acquaintance with them. Here let us merely add that they may be divided into two distinct groups for purposes of "After-care": those in "constant employ", to use the seventeenth-century phrase, and those in "inconstant employ". These are, of course, merely degrees of continuity of service. The Boatswain, the Gunner, the Purser, and the Carpenter form the "constant employ" group. They were, we must remember, the original "standing" officers, the Gunner and Purser not appearing quite so early as the other two, but very old-established none the less. They made their homes in the ship, whether she was in commission or "in ordinary", and normally had no job elsewhere. By the ruling of December 11th, 1700, all these were to become eligible for "superannuation allowance" when they had fulfilled the twin conditions of (a) being old and worn-out in service, and (b) having completed fifteen years in "constant employ". These conditions having been proved before a competent commission, they were—very generously, it seems—to be allowed "an annual pension equal to their pay in the ship of the highest rate they have served in".

The second group which became entitled at the same time to the allowance, comprised the Master and the Surgeon —both familiar figures on shipboard for many years, yet not to the same extent in "constant employ". For they were not "standing" officers in quite the same sense as the others. They did not always live on board, even when the ship was "in ordinary". There was no reason why they should. The Master, the navigation expert, would have no work to do while the ship lay in harbour, dismantled and at her moorings. The Surgeon would be idle, since there was, at such times, practically no crew on board: the most that was allowed in the medical line was a single dockyard- or port-surgeon, and he was very often only the local practitioner taken on for the occasion. Further, Masters and Surgeons were both (nominally at any rate) skilled men, and therefore able to earn a living outside the Navy betweenwhiles. And this they normally did, the Master mainly in the Merchant Service, the Surgeon either there, or wherever an opening presented itself ashore. So they were bracketed together as being of "inconstant employ", and were eligible for "superannuation allowance" (a) when grown old and worn-out, and (b) after *eight* years of service in the Navy; the allowances to be at the rate of *half* the best pay they had ever received.

Even this sounds fairly generous—especially in the case of the Master, whose half-pay was appreciably higher than the "standing" officers' full pay: and particularly so when we consider that it was awarded at a moment when the Government could still not afford much liberality. It may even be asked, why did they give Masters and Surgeons any pension at all? Why did they not treat them just like the "commission" officers of the day, who got nothing? The answer lies in the problem of supply and demand, and is rather different in each case. The Master was not only a skilled man: he was one of rather a rare class. There were never more than enough of them for the requirements of the Navy *and* the Merchant Service. So there was a certain competition between the two, with the Merchants, as a rule, in a position to offer the better wages. The Government was compelled, therefore, by sheer force of competition, to make the post of Master as attractive as possible. They did so in several ways which will appear later, and this was one of them. They wanted to regard him—and they wanted him to regard himself—as primarily a naval man. The Surgeon, on the other hand, though not so rare a bird, had plenty of opportunities of earning a living on shore, and, once he was settled down there, might decide not to face again the rigours of a sea-life. He too needed encouragement if he was to accede to the Admiralty's desires, and come to sea whenever they wanted him.

In this bestowal of Superannuation Allowances, the Chaplain—that other officer who was, superficially, in much the same case as the Surgeon—received no benefit at all. We shall discuss the reasons for this when we come to deal personally with him.

But though the "Standing" Officers obtained thus early a certain after-security (on paper) which they have never since lost, it is quite possible, we believe, to over-estimate the generosity of the donors. We must not forget the first of the two qualifications for pension mentioned above. Not only did they have to serve their period: they also had to be "old and worn-out in the service". And it was the prerogative of the Donor to decide when this latter condition was fulfilled. Such figures as are available seem to show one of two things. Either the Warrant officer was an astonishingly "tough life", who could stand up to the wear and tear of his exacting profession for an incredibly long time, or else the Authorities were the very reverse of liberal, and postponed the pension up to the very last moment. For it was always possible, apparently, just to leave the man on the half-pay list, on the assumption that, some time or other, he *might* be employed again. This, as we shall see, is what happened to a great majority of the "Commission" officers, up till well on in the nineteenth century. There are many reasons for thinking that it happened to the Warrant officer as well.

Some examples, culled from so late a date as 1840, will help to illustrate this. It should be mentioned that at this particular period there was a very serious overcrowding throughout the entire Navy; but that fact should not have affected the one section of it in which orderly retirement (with pension) was already possible. Yet, in the lists for that year we find there are only eight superannuated Masters all told. The senior among them has sixty-two years' seniority in that rank to his credit, and the junior as much as forty-six. The names of all the rest are in one list, but have, over against them, one of three descriptions: "Half-pay, unfit for service"; "Half-pay, fit for service", and "Employed". The senior man in this list has been a Master for sixty years: he is on half-pay, but is also scheduled "for active service", and so *might*, we suppose, be called up: in theory, that is, but hardly in practice, for he must have been well over eighty. At any rate he was not getting his superannuation allowance.

The seniors in the corresponding lists of Surgeons and Pursers are equally remarkable for their length of service, and their inability to obtain complete superannuation. The man at the top of the former list, one Thomas Seeds, has been a Surgeon for sixty-three years, though they have had the charity to label the old gentleman as "unfit for service". The senior "fit" Surgeon is a mere youngster of fifty years' standing.

The doyen of the Pursers in this list, however, takes the palm for long service. Mr. Rothery is on half-pay, though not "retired". His seniority as Purser dates from 1777—just before the War of American Independence broke out. He lasted until 1843, when at length he was really retired; but only after sixty-six years of "Pursery", when fifteen years might have got him his pension.

Now these curious figures, occurring at so late a date as 1840, and in a part of the Service where—ostensibly—superannuation allowances had existed for 140 years, will serve to warn us that we shall meet with a state of things even stranger and more chaotic when we come to the "Commission" officers, in whose case no such provision had ever been made.

The key to the situation lies in the fact that, until well on in the nineteenth century, the vast majority of "Commission" officers simply did not retire. There was no such possibility for them. Indeed, before 1737, *none* retired. They were either employed, or they were not employed. In the former case they had their full pay; in the latter—after it was instituted—their half-pay. There was nothing else to have. This state of things we must regard as inevitable, considering the way in which half-pay came in. It was introduced, let us recall, because the Government decided to retain the officers' services *for next time*. Then, perhaps, came Peace, with a smaller number of posts to be filled; so that, for many officers, there *was* no next time. Sometimes, again, the deciding factor was Inefficiency, or—more often—lack of influence: but in either case, the result was the same—no next time. In all such cases "half-pay while

unemployed" changed gradually and imperceptibly into
hopelessly *permanent* half-pay, with no prospect of anything
else to follow.

It was little enough. A lieutenant, for instance, up to
1737, received five shillings a day in full-pay: and, when on
board, he also received his lodging and victuals. But his half-
pay was half a crown with no board and lodging. It was not
so bad, perhaps, while he was still hale and hearty, because he
might well be able to find another job. But when he became
"old and worn-out", he was inevitably reduced to penury,
unless he had money of his own. No wonder that eighteenth-
century literature makes such play with the "half-pay
officer"—Army as well as Navy, for the former were but
little better off.

Early in the eighteenth century there was started a
system of gratuities for Commission Officers hurt in action.
The earliest set of rules governing them appeared in the
first *Regulations and Instructions* of 1731. But these were
gratutities, not pensions, and the payment of the former
rather than the latter is quite in keeping with those general
dictates of mankind's conscience mentioned above. Even
apart from Insurance, and Employers' Liability Acts, any
employer might feel it a moral duty to compensate, at
least temporarily, a man who got hurt in carrying out his
orders, especially if they were dangerous ones. The *least* he
could do, we should think, would be to give him a gratuity
which would last him until he was cured. Well, here in the
Navy we have the Employer doing just this minimum and
nothing more. But it is only fair to remember, both here
and in almost all matters where the issue involved the
disbursement of public funds, that it was the ultimate
employer—the State, represented here by the Treasury—
who dictated the policy. The Admiralty, the officer's
immediate employer, should not be required to shoulder
the blame. At the same time a gratuity began to be paid
to the widow, or other relative, of a "commission" officer

killed on active service. Again there was no pension. In
this case, not only were the amounts payable particularly
mean, but also, with the wage-earner permanently removed,
the moral right of his dependents to some form of permanent
pension was more obvious than in the case of wounds. These
facts were probably realized, or at least it was feared that
the absence of such compensation might tend to discourage
officers: It would be very awkward, for instance, if it made
them unduly shy of dying for their country! So there was
passed in 1733 the Act of Parliament which led to the
appearance of the famous "Widows' Men".

Few phenomena in our story can better illustrate the
workings of the official eighteenth-century mind than these
curious phantoms. The idea was praiseworthy enough: it
was decided to create a fund for "the relief of poor widows
of Commission and Warrant Officers". It is the clumsiness
of the method that is so typical. For the creation of the fund,
"there shall be allowed upon the books of every ship of war
in sea-pay, one seaman in every hundred men". In 1751,
the law was extended to allow "one other seaman in every
hundred men", whenever the total number in the Navy
exceeded 20,000. The money thus collected was to go towards
the purpose stated: but, since the Authorities were determined to respect the age-old rule about no one drawing pay
unless he had a post on board, and his name actually
appeared in the Pay-book of the ship, all captains were
instructed to order their pursers to enter fictitious names
therein, in the above proportions, as Able Seamen, and to
go through the whole accounting process, even down to
filling in the normal pay-tickets in their names, and "mus-
tering" them solemnly once every ten days to see whether
these wraiths were still there, or whether they were "dead"
or "run". This farce is really, of course, just one more
symptom of "Post's" stubborn rearguard action: but the
principal result was, probably, to give the self-seeking purser
yet one more opportunity of increasing his perquisites. The

I

practice continued beyond the end of the century: up to 1808 the whole performance is still being enacted in full.

There is, too, right through the seventeen-hundreds, a paragraph which appears unchanged in the various editions of *Regulations and Instructions*, beginning in the first edition (of 1731) and appearing for the last time in 1790. Many a generation of aged and poverty-stricken officers, with nothing between themselves and starvation but their miserable pittance of half-pay, must have read it, as it appeared and reappeared, with a rather bitter smile.

"His Majesty," it reads, "is pleased to reserve to himself to consider the Merits and Pretensions of Commission Officers who shall be worn out or disabled in His Service . . . and to settle such Allowances or Pensions upon them as His Majesty shall think fit."

"Put not your trust in princes", we can almost hear them say. "This is what comes of not having things down in black and white!"

But gratuities for wounds and death, and even royal promises, are not pensions, and still less do they constitute Retirement in the modern sense. This came in the end, but like most naval changes, it came very slowly and gradually. Authority's first move in the matter was so beggarly that it must almost have seemed a studied insult to well over 90 per cent of commission officers. In 1737, the half-pay of the thirty Lieutenants who headed that list was raised from 2s. 6d. per diem to 4s. Since they were all (as well as very many below them in the list) already "retired" in the modern sense of "never-to-be-employed again", this order may be said to amount to a sort of "retired pay" for the lucky ones. Let us follow for a moment, this cheese-paring method of doling out favours. The 4s. was increased to 6s. in 1776, and in 1796 the number of recipients was brought up to 50, when the fortunate ones were also allowed to assume Commander's rank, and so make their half-pay a trifle bigger. In 1814 the number was increased to 80. But even then none of them was regarded as being "retired", for the whole idea of such a thing was still quite foreign to the system. Indeed, up till 1846 the only *truly* "retired" commission-officers were the few "retired Captains" of whom we shall take notice shortly: and, added in 1816, a *very* few "retired Commanders" who were really those same senior Lieutenants. How generous was the largesse poured out by the Treasury the Lieutenants' figures of 1816 reveal. In that year, there were no less than 3,350 unemployed: and 80 of them—rather more than 2 per cent—received the benefit! And further, the benefit, when received, was not exactly dazzling. It was 7s. a day instead of 5s. Nearly 98 per cent still received the latter, which was the old half of the ordinary pay, itself raised owing to the immense increase in prices. Truly the cornucopia of a grateful country was being poured forth—through a fountain-pen filler!

But this drip-drip of benefits, this snail-like progress, would not even now have given their deserts to one half of the officers concerned had not something else occurred to precipitate the whole process. That something, it is regrettable to have to admit, was not the awakening in Authority's mind of a sense of individual injustice: but rather a sense of ever-growing collective inconvenience. In the 1740's the Admiralty first began to realize that the whole officer-system was failing to work. The reason was that the channel was blocked, and the flow interrupted. It is a well-known phenomenon in nature that, if a man dams a stream at the bottom of a valley, the waters will collect dangerously about his dam, especially if he continues to allow the water to flow from higher up the stream in the same quantities as before. That is what had been happening in the Navy. The flow from the source had to be allowed to continue, or there would have been no junior officers, so that the remedy did not lie in diverting the stream higher up. No, the only cure was to allow water to escape through the dam, and thus ease the pressure. This, in the Navy, means *Retirement*. But, once again, nothing sudden or revolutionary followed the Admiralty's discovery.

It is very noticeable that the regulations governing this side of naval life belong almost exclusively to two periods in our history—the last decade of the first half of the eighteenth, and the two middle decades of the nineteenth century. The reason is not far to seek. In the whole two hundred years which separate the First Dutch War from the Crimean War there have been only two stretches at all worthy of the name "Peace Periods". The first lasted from Utrecht to Jenkins' much-advertised ear—1713 to 1739: the second from Waterloo to Sebastopol—1815 to 1854. It was towards the end of each that the inconveniences of a "block" were most marked, because, in each case, the period of peace began with a very large officer personnel, recruited for the late war: in each case the normal practice was followed of laying up, or even scrapping, many units of the war-time fleets: which led, of course, in each case, to a great diminution in the amount of employment available, and also—an important factor—to far lower casualties and therefore to a far slower "flow" of officers from the junior to the senior end.

In the first of the two periods there was no elasticity in the system at all. In fact, as we have seen, the strict idea of "rank", as opposed to "post" was even then only forcing its slow way into men's minds. It was not until 1718, for instance, that it was first formally ordered that Captains should be promoted to flag-rank by strict seniority, and that flag-officers should pass up through the many grades of Admiral in the same way. This was, incidentally, one of the great victories of "Rank" over "Post", but here it concerns us in a rather different way. It really ensured that the "flow" *must* go wrong in the near future, unless—and this was not likely to happen—all remnants of "Post" should be cast boldly to the winds.

This needs some explanation. Up till that time the titles of Admiral, Vice-Admiral and Rear-Admiral had signified posts, and posts only: so much so, indeed, that, as there were nine flag-officers' posts, so there were nine flag-officers, and no more. This is logical enough, so long as we are prepared to make everything dependent upon "post". But when, by creating an order of seniority among our captains and our lieutenants we have established a definite conception of "rank", and when we have, further, ordered that seniority shall be the sole qualification for promotion; when we have refused to let any officer leave his place in the lists for any reason, save only death, and when, finally, we refuse to increase the number of flag-officers, we are obviously playing impossible pranks with our flow, and are asking our stream to do something which Nature cannot possibly permit it to do. We are, in fact, inviting a volume of water which would normally have filled a pipe some hundreds of inches in diameter to flow smoothly through the "Admirals' " bottleneck of nine inches: and we are still damming the stream further down yet, by not allowing even the admirals to pass out into retirement.

All this the Authorities did, with the foregone result that the flow very nearly stopped altogether. What made things so congested was not only that the flag-officers were so few in number: almost worse, there was only one thing that could force any of the incumbents to "move along". For the only way through the dam was Death: just that, and nothing more. No commission officer could retire from the Service without also retiring from the Earth. The result was ever-increasing and alarming Age in all holders of high places, and a stagnation all the way down which simply had to be faced. On the outbreak of the wars the two principal figures in the Navy were Sir Charles Wager and Sir John Norris. Both were veterans of the Louis Quatorze wars, with a big margin to spare. Both had been present at Barfleur in 1692, and both had reached flag-rank before the Spanish Succession War was half over. Both had been slowly working up the list ever since, and, in 1739, Sir Charles, as First

Lord of the Admiralty, was controlling the destinies of the Navy, while Sir John was Admiral of the Fleet: that is, the senior executive officer afloat. Sir Charles was seventy-three when the war broke out, and resigned from the Admiralty at the age of seventy-six. But did he retire altogether? Not a bit of it! He went on to the Navy Board, holding the more restful, but still highly responsible position of Treasurer, and dying in that office in the following year. That Sir John was a considerably older man is certain: how much so is not quite clear, but Sir John Laughton thought he was born in 1660. He would therefore be seventy-nine, or thereabouts, in 1739, and he was still commanding the main fleet of England in the Channel in 1744, when only a gale prevented a full-dress battle with the French. He was then, probably, eighty-four years old. Soon afterwards he resigned—in a huff. He was not retired, but went on filling one of the precious posts until his death in 1749. Sir Charles, it is true, was past his best, but it is only fair to record—and marvel in recording—that for all the early mortality of that port-swilling, disease-ridden age, Sir John was a thoroughly capable officer to the last.

It was in 1743, when face to face at last with a really major war, that the Government was forced to take action. The step was characteristic. Quietly, and without any unnecessary advertisement, they began to increase the flag list. How surreptitious it really was it is hard to say now. But this fact remains. The old Government rule that the established number of Flag-officers should be nine only (adding, even, to make quite sure that nobody stole a march on them, "and no 'Brevet Commissions' shall be allowed") remains unchanged in all the eighteenth century issues of the *Regulations and Instructions*—the latest is dated 1790. By then, of course, it was very far removed from the true facts of the case, for there had long been *scores* of flag-officers. It has always been one of our favourite ways of dealing with apparently insuperable difficulties to pretend that they are not there: years pass, and—lo and behold—they are not!

This simple solution widened the bottle-neck a trifle, but it did not remedy the evil, for it did not hit on the true solution: which was, of course, "Retirement". That soon began, however. In 1747 it was found that the Captains at the head of the waiting list had been made so in 1713—the year of the Peace! Several setbacks, too, in the war now fast drawing to a close might well be attributed to the advanced age of officers. On June 3rd, therefore, a big step forward was taken. It was laid down that Captains who, when their turn came for promotion to flag-rank, were not considered suitable for employment, should be promoted Rear-Admirals "without specifying any squadron or division of colour used in the Fleet," but that they should be allotted the half-pay of Rear-Admiral. As there was to be no post for them, they were, essentially, being "retired", though even then the naughty word is not mentioned. Their official tally was "Superannuated Rear-Admirals". But the Public soon found a word for it, as we have seen. The mythical squadron became "the Yellow". So the poor senior Captains who had been cooling their heels as best they might for thirty-four years, while their superiors were making up their minds to "send in their papers", were disappointed after all. Yet the gain to the Navy was great: and a measure of it is that both Hawke and Boscawen figure among the names of the younger men thus surprisingly promoted.

This was as far as things went during that Peace Period. There was a definite and lasting relief of pressure at the top end. But nothing had been done further down. Still there was the same wearisome wait in all grades until a position near the head of the Captain's list was reached. The long series of wars which followed, it is true, prevented so complete a stagnation as the earlier one, but even so promotion was never brisk, especially from the bottom to the top of the Captain's list. Thus an officer of the calibre, and with the influence, of the Hon. Samuel Barrington took thirty-one years to work through it: and that the most talented naval officer of all time—and one almost constantly employed—should have had to spend eighteen years of his forty-seven on earth as a captain, shows that promotion was not exactly brisk even in Nelson's time.

The curious controversy in Parliament in 1788 throws a good deal of light on the attitude towards "retirement" both of the Admiralty and of the officers concerned. In some big promotions of the preceding year, the former had advanced sixteen captains, and passed over forty. It is significant to note that they had *offered* superannuation to the unlucky ones, but most of them had refused. This was quite in order, if they cared to do so. They simply remained on the Captain's list, hoping (we must presume), that next time the Admiralty would recognize their claims, if not their merits. All this shows quite clearly that there was no official machinery for enforcing retirement; and, even that among the officers themselves, there was no idea that anybody had the right to make them go.

In fact, the sequel seems to show that no one had: that the Admiralty itself claimed no such right. The captains did not raise the point themselves, but they had political champions in both Houses of Parliament who did. The Admiralty, in the person of the great Lord Howe, then First Lord, defended its conduct with vigour, and the Earl of Sandwich, who had had a longer experience of that office than any other man then living, supported him. Yet none of their arguments are based on the legality of their action. Howe made a strong and practical case for "selection", as opposed to "seniority": the best men must be found to fill the high commands: old-age in such posts must be avoided —all the common-*sense* arguments, in fact, which are now common-*place*. Sandwich's argument is more legal in one sense, but less so in another. Far from asserting that the Admiralty were acting on the basis of law, he argued simply on precedent. What his plea amounts to is simply this. "We did much the same thing in 1747, because we had to, and nobody, in Parliament or out, said us nay. We've only done the same thing again now." It is quite clear that "Retirement" was still, in everybody's eyes, a voluntary thing. Even the Admiralty could only say, "Stay if you like, but we've given you a hint not to expect anything if you do." And even so they sometimes weakened their own position by promoting captains who, having been passed over, had refused to go.

The Admiralty won the day in both Houses, though barely in the House of Commons, where their majority was only sixteen. Had they been defeated, the modern idea of "retirement" might have been postponed to the Greek Kalends. Even as it was, it took another Peace Period, of still more formidable dimensions than the last, and another terrible "block", before the solution was reached. And as late as 1847—exactly one century after the first widening of the bottle-neck—we find the Admiralty actually circularizing the **two** hundred senior captains to discover how many of them will graciously consent to retire—with compensations of course.

The Revolutionary and Napoleonic Wars were on a much bigger scale than any previous encounter in which the British Navy had taken part. So, as they drew to a close, the officer-personnel of the Service was very much larger than it had ever been before. Peace was always a gloomy prospect for the old Sea-Officer, and, on this occasion at least, the Authorities themselves sensed trouble in advance. In June 1814, when Napoleon was safely dethroned, they ordained a rise of half-pay all round. It was then that the ordinary, unprivileged lieutenant reached the princely figure of 5s. a day, while an Admiral of the Fleet's half-pay soared to three guineas. This was to prepare for the evil, and there was not much more that they could do, since, even now, there was no thought of giving retired pay to anyone but a few ageing captains, and yet more ancient warrant officers.

So once more the block of the century before repeated itself, and once more the situation was exacerbated by a long period of peace. Indeed, the period was longer, and the numbers of officers involved greater, than last time; so that the halt in promotion was worse than in the century before, especially at the point where there was no way round —that is, in the lower ranks. And even in the upper ones, things were really rather grim. By 1840, when the chaos was perhaps at its height, the first twenty captains on the list (which was, actually as well as nominally, the *Active* List) had all been captains since the year after Trafalgar. They were all on half-pay—for them, 14s. 6d. per diem— but they were not "retired". There are in the Navy List of that year, a number of "Retired Rear-Admirals", who are, of course, the "yellowed" officers of their day; and there is one insignificant group of eight Captains on Retired Half-Pay, who represent a forlorn little effort, made in 1830, to relieve the congestion. At the head of this miniature band is Captain John Rodney, disappointing son of a great father. This man's naval record is probably unique for all time, and is worth a word in passing, since it shows both what influence could do in the eighteenth century, and what stagnation could achieve in the nineteenth. He was (quite illegally) made a lieutenant in 1780, at the age of fifteen, and—equally illegally—*a full-blown Post-Captain five weeks later*, also in 1780. Sixty years after, he was still a captain. Nelson's record is also interesting, and his potential record, had he lived, more interesting still. He became a lieutenant at seventeen—also too young to comply with the regulations: at twenty he became Captain of a small ship, or—in rank— Commander: at twenty-one full Captain, and at thirty-nine Rear-Admiral. Laymen often make the not unpardonable assumption that Nelson reached the top of his profession. In rank, of course, he did no such thing. He attained a place exactly half-way up the flag-list. Further—and this may surprise many even better-informed people—had he lived, he would only have reached the rank of Admiral of the Fleet *nearly forty years after Trafalgar*—in 1844, to be exact, when Admiral Nugent, who had always been just above him in the list, passed away, still unretired.

Once more, of course, all these senior people were very old. Some of the 1806 captains were septuagenarians, and they were, of necessity, the next Admirals to be advanced, though they might then be "yellowed". Yet so little had this useful device been employed, even in 1840, that the Admirals themselves were far too old. No one on this occasion quite equals Sir John Norris's record, but Admiral Bowles and Sir David Milne took up the commands at Portsmouth and Plymouth respectively at the age of seventy-nine, and were octogenarians before they hauled down their flags: while, even in fleet commands, Stopford was engaged in active service at seventy-three, and Lord Dundonald flew his flag at sea for the last time at seventy-five.

But things were at their worst in the lower ranks. This same 1840 list shows that the Senior Commander, who is not even on half-pay, let alone "retired", had served as such for forty-six years. The few "Commanders on retired half-pay" who do appear, are the lucky few from the Lieutenants' list, whose numbers have been slightly increased in 1830 by a further frugal squeeze of the Treasury's fountain-pen filler.

The number of Lieutenants, either retired, or on any *permanent* form of half-pay, in 1840 is *nil*. The Senior Lieutenant, who, so far as the list shows, may be called upon at any moment to take up his duties on the quarterdeck is James Roberts. He was created Lieutenant in 1778, and died —still a Lieutenant—in 1841, with sixty-three years in.

What might happen lower down still is eloquently shown in Hunt's beautiful engraving reproduced facing page 140, where the unfortunate "reefer" of 1825, his professional instruments in pawn, is revealed in very reduced and humble circumstances.

The remedy came when the disease began to grow intolerable. But, when it did come, it was at last the right one. By a series of steps, which it would be tedious to detail, Retirement in the modern sense, accompanied by Retired Pay, was introduced. The principal landmarks are 1847, 1851 and 1864.

In the first of these years (after obtaining their "victims'" consent) the Admiralty got rid of two hundred captains by quite a generous increase in their "half-pay" and by allowing them the rank of Rear-Admiral. At the same time, in order to insure that a similar deadlock should be avoided in future, they put a strict limit on the number to be allowed to be "serving". One hundred and fifty flag-officers (of whom thirty were Admirals, forty-five Vice-Admirals and seventy-five Rear-Admirals) were to be the maximum: and not more than five hundred Captains were to be sanctioned.

Four years later an even bigger move was made. The number of serving flag-officers was reduced to ninety-nine, (twenty-one, twenty-seven and fifty-one respectively). This reduction was obtained by removing to what they now called "reserve half-pay" such officers who had not served at sea in their present rank. Captains were further reduced to three hundred and fifty, and in this case the object was achieved, for the first time, by the method of promoting, on the average, only one in every three eligible. They now tackled the Commanders as well, and even the grotesquely swollen Lieutenants' list. Fifty selected commanders were promoted to captains, and so straight on to "Reserve half-pay"—the promotion being, of course, a bribe or a sop, however we like to look at it, which enabled the officer to draw more half-pay. One hundred more were promoted to "Retired Captain"—a category which, as we have seen, existed in 1840, but only contained eight names. All other commanders who had not been employed for the last twenty

A MID_on            HALF PAY.

TOWER                HILL.

[C. Hunt

years were removed to the "reserve-half-pay" list. The idea
of twenty years' "unemployed time" in one rank would, by
itself, make the modern officer smile!

As for the Lieutenants' list, that Augean stable took some
cleansing. In 1851, a further fifty were promoted by selection
to Commander, and put at once on "reserve half-pay"—a
mere continuation of the process begun in 1816, and still
a mere drop in the bucket. But now they went further, and
of the rest, all who had not served for twenty years, or who
were unfit—a very large number—were put into a new
category of "Lieutenant, Reserve Half-Pay"—rather a
shabby piece of treatment. As for the remainder—and this
too was large—one in every two was to be promoted, as
vacancies occurred, until the total reached twelve hundred.

The last big step was taken in 1864 when the Lieutenants'
list was at last really cleared. This time the Admiralty were
more generous, and all who wished to do so were promoted
to Commander "for purposes of reserved half-pay". In spite
of previous efforts—there had been yet another in 1856—a
prodigious number of "promotions" followed. In the *Navy
List* of 1864 there are actually sixteen double-column pages
of Commanders promoted from various categories of Reserve
Half-Pay Lieutenants. It was only then that they really passed
out into what was, at last, real retirement: which merely
serves to show how incredible the blockage had been. The
senior man advanced to Commander in 1864 had last known
the thrill of promotion fifty-nine years before, when he had
been made a Lieutenant just before Trafalgar. Nor was his
case markedly unfortunate. He was merely, as it were,
*primus inter pares*. The officer, for instance, whose commission is
reproduced between pages 76 and 77, who had thus served as
Lieutenant for thirty-six years and who had seen much service, was still only one hundred and sixty-seventh on the list.

With this really thorough clearance of the lower grades
in 1864 our story of "Retirement" may close. Six more years
were to elapse before the *Navy List* showed the "Active"

and the "Retired" officers in quite separate categories, but in essentials, the process was complete by 1864. For though there have since been an infinity of minor changes, the Admiralty had acquired by then, as it was ultimately bound to do, not only the full powers of "posting", "promoting", "entering" and "training", but also of "retiring": while Public Opinion and the officers themselves had at the same time secured a reasonable, if not over-generous, measure of "after-care". The whole of the essential machinery of the modern Navy was at length in working order.

The test of its efficacy came when the Great War ended, with an officer personnel of immense and unprecedented proportions to be regulated to a peace establishment. And, as far as Retirement was concerned, the system may be said to have proved its worth. There were, of course, inevitable cases of personal hardship: and some minor cogs in the machinery showed themselves to be not exactly perfect. The Axe was wielded boldly, and—or so it seemed at the time— even brutally. But it did its work, and that without mass injustice. It was unquestionably, in the main, cruel only to be kind. Had the reforms described above not materialized in the nineteenth century, the state of the *Navy List* in this year of grace 1939 would have been too chaotic to contemplate. The senior Admiral of the Fleet at present on the Active List would still have been a Captain, and the senior active Lieutenant might have been last promoted in 1880!

## BOOK THREE

# Some "Old" Officers

# CHAPTER IX

# THE LORD HIGH ADMIRAL AND HIS DEPUTIES

WE have seen that every modern Naval Officer who is "employed" at this instant is also an officer in the *old* sense—an Office-*Holder*. Captain X, for instance, who is in command of H.M.S. *Y* is an officer both by rank and by post. But there are—and have always been—a number of most important "posts" which are essentially "naval" posts, and yet do not bear very much relation to "rank". Thus there are some naval office-holders who have a naval rank which seems at first sight disproportionately low for the post they hold: or they may have no naval rank at all, but only a military one; or they may hold no rank at all in any of the fighting services. The most obvious modern examples of these phenomena are those members of the Board of Admiralty who are not "active" officers. The present First Lord, for instance, holds no naval rank; another member of the Board is a Colonel, and a recent First Lord was a Commander (Retired). Even among the members who are serving naval officers the same thing is noticeable in a lesser degree. Though on the Active List, they are by no means the Senior ones on it, and may hold any rank from Admiral of the Fleet down to Captain.

It is with the story of these office-holders that this and the ensuing chapter deal. We must not omit them, not only on account of their obvious importance, but also because—whatever modern usage may dictate—they are really "naval" officers, even though they are not all "naval officers". Oddly enough, until fairly recently, the names were in some measure reversed. The man we now call a "Naval Officer" was almost always called a "Sea-officer" up till 1800, and often so named for a good long time after that; while the term "Naval Officer" was almost always reserved for officers in administrative posts (such as the Navy Board and the Dockyards) whom we should now call "Civilian Officers". Thus we find Pepys recording in his diary that "W. Coventry"—essentially a civilian in the modern sense—"told me he must now take leave of us as a naval man", i.e. as a member of the Navy Board: while in all the Regulations, from 1731 up to at least as late as 1858, the "Naval Officer" was the correct title of the Admiralty official in minor naval establishments and dockyards overseas. Nelson might perhaps have called a man like Sir Charles Middleton, the head of the Navy Board, a "naval officer": but he called himself a "Sea-officer". We may recall, too, that the *List of Sea-Officers* was the title of that important annual compilation right up to 1846: and we may notice that, to this day, the active-service, executive officers on the Board of Admiralty are always "*Sea*-Lords", not "*Naval* Lords".

We must confine ourselves here to the most important "Office-holders" only, and we will group them under three heads:

1. The Lord High Admiral of England.
2. The Vice-Admiral and Rear-Admiral of England: or—later, of the United Kingdom.
3. The Principal Officers of the Navy, commonly called, collectively, "The Navy Board".

The offices filled by these people were always offices; never ranks; and the holders of them to-day—or of the posts which correspond with them—hold no rank by reason of their tenure of office.

## THE LORD HIGH ADMIRAL

There was once a time—very long ago now—when the whole Government of England was really quite a simple affair. That, needless to say, is so no longer. Set the breath-taking machine which produces *The Times* against the first English printing press: think of the former as the England we know, and Caxton's primitive little apparatus will typify the England of long ago.

One man could work that early apparatus, and one man generally did—the King. If he were a capable man he could even work it fairly competently. But such a delightful state of things could not last. The work became too complex for one man and in the end he had to engage help. He still remained the "boss", of course, and kept a tight hand—when he could—on his assistants; but he could not check the ever-growing complexity without wrecking the machine; and this, for obvious reasons, he was unwilling to do.

So that great decentralization started—slowly, and, as usual, a trifle blindly—which we may call the "putting of the Crown into commission". One by one there grew up about the King those indispensable officials whom we may safely name—for so they often named themselves—the "Nine great officers of the Crown".

The ninth of these, in time, if not in importance, was the officer destined later to become the Lord High Admiral, responsible to the King for all the maritime activities of England. But at first he had neither the power nor the title of the later holders of that exalted post. In other words he did not spring into existence all at once.

Someone who begins to look like him emerges in the reign of Edward I. In 1297 that particularly enlightened and far-sighted monarch sent a certain William de Leyburn, who was "Captain of the King's Mariners", to represent him at a conference which was being held at Bruges on maritime matters. Leyburn is not entitled to be regarded as the fore-

runner of the Lord High Admiral simply because he was
Captain of the King's Mariners. The nearest approach in
our own day to that title would be, perhaps, "Commander-
in-Chief, Home Fleet". For in that age, and for some
time afterwards, the ordinary title of the man commanding
the fleet at sea was "Captain"; and "Sea-Command" was
actually the last big function which the Lord High Admiral
acquired. Leyburn's claim rests on two things: first, as
representing the Crown in the sphere of naval affairs, he
was—for the time being—a great officer of the Crown: and
second, he was granted the very special, and—as far as
England is concerned—the *new* title of Admiral—"Admirallus
Maris Angliae". Thus this title, when first granted, denoted
an administrative post pure and simple, and not an executive
one.

Six years later, one Gervase Allard, a famous seaman of
the Cinque Ports—those medieval purveyors to the Crown
of a quasi-public naval force—had his authority enormously
widened. The Crown conferred on him the snappy little
title of "Captain and Admiral of the Fleet of the Cinque
Ports and of all other ports from Dover by the Sea Coast
westwards as far as Cornwall, and the whole of Cornwall".
It was the most important part of the coast then, and he was
to be responsible to the King for all matters maritime which
arose thereon. He also—since he was "Captain"—was to
exercise the actual command at sea in those parts. He therefore held the most important *half* of the powers of later Lord
High Admirals.

But there was more coast-line than this, and something
had to be done about the rest. So, soon afterwards, another
"Admiral" was appointed for "the north of the mouth of
the Thames". These posts grew rapidly in importance,
partly, indeed, owing to the growth of man's traffic on the
seas, but mainly because of the powers and rights which
were added: powers in the matter of discipline, the suppres-
sion of pirates, and the jurisdiction over all sea-causes: and

rights—pecuniary for the most part—in the matter of prizes, fines and dues of various sorts. Herein lie the germs of two out of the three great powers of Admiralty ultimately possessed by the Lord High Admirals—Power of Administration and Power of Jurisdiction. But they were not yet collected under one hand. There were two Admirals. They could also appoint "Lieutenants", or "Vice-Admirals", and they did so freely, until there were almost as many of these lesser luminaries as there were sea-shires.

A curious echo of these dim and far-off functionaries resounded in the papers a few years ago. In 1928, when the Mayor of Southampton visited New York, *The Times* informed the public that that civic official was entitled to be greeted on arrival with a full Admiral's salute, because the Mayor of Southampton was still the medieval Admiral of those parts. And what made this such a good "story" was the fact that the Mayor in question happened to be a lady. It did indeed give promise for a little fun, reminiscent of the pleasantries of musical comedy. But, sad to relate, *The Times* was misinformed—not, we believe, in affirming that the Mayor *was* the local "Admiral," but in supposing that she still retained her rights in respect of salutes; or, for that matter, in any other respects, even the legal ones. She never had any of the former, while the latter had been abolished by a far-seeing Parliament nearly a century earlier.

But, to return to our medieval "Admirals". The immediate effect of the great increase in the scope of their power, and, more particularly in their emoluments, was to make the posts what we should now call "plums" of the first order. In fact, if all the powers were collected together again under one man, the resulting post would be important enough, both in dignity and in monetary value, to be very useful to the Crown for bestowal upon some really highly placed personage whom it might be politic to woo. And this is what happened. The powers were collected into the hands, and the fees into the pocket, of a single Admiral: his name was changed to "Admiral of England", and he became a "great officer of the Crown". The first man thus to obtain what was really the full status of the Lord Admiral of England—though not yet the title—was John de Beauchamp, brother of the Earl of Warwick, whose patent is dated 1360.

But the immediate practical result was that the Admiral ceased to be the *executive* head—the Commander, that is, of the King's Fleet at sea. Nobody efficient in the practical command of ships could hope in those days to be allowed to swallow the great new plum; and the kind of person who did swallow it would not have dreamed of going to sea himself. Such a one would be a great nobleman, with an immense position to keep up, and, be it added, with immensely wide responsibilities. We still have to deal, we must remember, with the days when the whole shipping of England was England's national fleet, and one of the most important of the Admiral's many duties was to see to the collection—or the collectability—of that scratch force; or, if the fleet required were on a smaller scale than a full rally, it was for him to procure that smaller collection. Such duties are not, in any age, the duties of the Commander-in-Chief, and the medieval Admiral had no hesitation in leaving the particular job of Command to a deputy.

The first man actually granted the title "Admiral of England", in 1391, was Edward of York—very high and mighty: as was Henry IV's own son, Thomas of Lancaster, appointed in 1405. Among the later holders in the fifteenth century were Warwick the King-maker, and—on and off for twenty years—the Duke of Gloucester, better known to history as Richard Crookback, who only dropped the Admiralty of England in order to snatch the Crown. We cannot be surprised to hear that personages such as these did not normally regard it as part of their duty to command at sea.

It was that dynamic personality Henry VIII who suddenly changed the whole place of the Admiral in the scheme of things. Like his father, he had no love for the old baronage, and he recognized the danger of having as Admiral a great nobleman who was not completely under his control: and, since he had a very big fleet of his own and loved efficiency, he meant to be sure that the man who pocketed the emoluments—and they were still enormous—also pulled his weight in the boat of State. In a word, he re-harnessed his Admiral in a tighter set of reins and sent him to sea. And this is the first time, oddly enough, that an English Admiral ever did go to sea as Admiral. At the same time Henry changed the title of the post to "High Admiral", or sometimes, "Lord Admiral". Not even yet do we find the famous combination of the two.

But Henry did much more for his navy than this. He was the first king who had, in his own ships, a force which could shoulder any appreciable percentage of the kingdom's defence: and so it was he who first gave it a set of administrative officers of its own. These officers we shall discuss in the next chapter: they are the future "Navy Board". Here we need only mention that they were all—in theory—subordinate to the High Admiral, who thus at length exercised—or was supposed to exercise—complete control of all things maritime, under the King alone: for in him resided at last the three great functions, Military Command at Sea, Admiralty Jurisdiction and Control of the whole Administration.

It was, even in Henry VIII's time, an enormous task, probably too big for any one man. But the King clearly intended one man to tackle it, so that it had to be attempted. The obvious way out was the way employed by all the High Admiral's predecessors. A "Lieutenant of the Admiralty" or "Vice-Admiral" was appointed, the words to be taken at their face value. The High Admiral, great though he was, could not be in two or more places at once. He could not, for instance, command the fleet against the French, and at the same time remain in London, collecting more ships from far and wide, supervising the Navy Board, deciding "causes" and collecting dues. So the "Man-holding-the-place-of", or the "Man-acting-instead of" the Admiral had to come into existence. He came, and he survives in name to this day under the title of "Vice-Admiral of the United Kingdom and Lieutenant of the Admiralty". He does not do any of the things for which the office was created, it is true; in fact, *qua* Vice-Admiral and Lieutenant, he does not do anything at all; but he is a fine example of how unwilling we are to drop a good title when we invent one.

His principal duty at first was to form a link between the High Admiral and the "administrative" officers of the King's own ships, the Navy Board. To an efficiency-worshipping age like our own this might seem the most important branch of the Admiral's threefold duties, and therefore the last which ought to be left to a substitute. But it did not seem so to our early sixteenth century Admiral. He would acquire most honour from the command afloat, and most prestige—as well as the great bulk of his emoluments—from his Admiralty Jurisdiction. The hard, and highly technical, work of preparing the ships and looking after them was evidently the task for lesser men. Besides, we must still keep ever before our eyes that other "fleet of England", and remember that—even in Henry VIII's day—the Navy Board was the King's private organization, and only existed in order to administer the King's ships; while the Admiral's purview extended to *all* the ships of England—the potential, full-strength fleet—not to mention all other "sea-causes" whatsoever. These were far larger and higher charges: even as late as 1588, let us not forget, some 80 per cent of the Anti-Armada Fleet were not "Queen's ships" at all. The administration of the Royal Fleet was in *fact* an affair of smaller import to the Admiral than many of his other duties. And this is true certainly up to the close of the sixteenth century, and probably up to the Commonwealth period.

The Lord Admiral had, in Henry's time, a badge of office,

or—to be exact—*two* badges of office, which strike the modern mind as distinctly quaint. They were whistles. One—a very large, ornate and heavy affair, made of gold—was his "whistle of office". It was a point of honour with him that he should never lose it. Thus when Sir Edward Howard was unfortunately cut off and surrounded on the deck of his enemy's flagship in 1513, his last thought before he was struck down was to hurl the precious thing into the sea. The second was his "whistle of command"—a less expensive instrument which no doubt had a real and practical use in the days of galley-fighting. Almost the only known illustration of this curious symbol is reproduced here. The wearer is Lord Howard of Effingham's predecessor as Lord Admiral, Lord Clinton—afterwards Earl of Lincoln. The whistle is that of "command". No representation of the Whistle of Honour survives. It is significant to notice that there is never any mention of an "Administrative Whistle", nor of any insignia to remind folk of that side of the Admiral's functions.

Very soon, too, another factor conspired to weaken the Admiral's hold on this, the least attractive of his duties. The building and maintenance of the King's ships cost money, and, from the first, the High Admiral was only indirectly concerned with the King's Purse. Yet there was another "great officer of the Crown" who was very intimately concerned with it: who existed, in fact—and had existed for some time longer than the High Admiral—simply and solely in order to look after it. That was the Lord Treasurer, obviously a very important officer. He was the man who would certainly have to pay the piper, and he very quickly showed his determination to call the tune.

He won—the first game at any rate—because he held all the trumps: he controlled the money, and he was vitally interested in the way in which it was spent, when his high-born Admiralty colleague was, on the whole, indifferent. The results of his victory appear in two stages: first, at the close of Mary's reign, he was empowered—with, however,

the *advice* of the High Admiral—to decide on the amount
of the annual expenditure on the Navy: and second, in
1564, he was enabled, on the score of economy, to abolish
the post of Lieutenant of the Admiralty—the Admiral's link
man—and to set at the head of the Navy Board its *financial*
member, the Treasurer of the Navy, who was already, as
we have seen, firmly tied to the Lord Treasurer's apron-
strings in the matter of finance.

Thus, the administration of the "Royal" ships came to
be separated from the other activities of Admiralty. That
separation remained after the National Fleet had made its
appearance, and for nearly three centuries caused many
curious anomalies in the naval service. The Navy Board,
only too often, found it had two masters—nominally the
Lord High Admiral, but, in reality, the man who held the
purse strings—the Lord Treasurer.

This division did not matter a great deal at first, perhaps,
because, when the call came later on in Elizabeth's reign
—when the hard test, that is, of War had to be applied—
the Queen happened to be lucky in her Lord Admiral and
her Lord Treasurer, but *very* lucky in her Treasurer of the
Navy, by then the real creator and sustainer of the Queen's
fleet. The first-named was, of course, Lord Howard of
Effingham, a nobleman of sterling worth rather than of
genius. The second was the great Lord Burghley himself:
while the third was John Hawkins, who proved himself,
over and above his other talents, a naval administrator of
the very first order. It was the Queen's ships built and con-
ditioned by Hawkins, fought by Drake, Frobisher and
himself, and supported by the collective contribution of
maritime England, which overthrew the might of Spain.
It was Burghley's job to find the money for them, and
it was Howard's job to oversee them all as they did it;
and, by his nobility and tact, to see that no unseemly
squabbles broke out among those high-spirited and sometimes overbearing personalities—that Frobisher, for instance,

EDWARD FIENNES, LORD CLINTON, LORD ADMIRAL OF ENGLAND, 1550–1585

did not fire his guns at Drake instead of at the Spaniard: to preside over the whole effort, throwing over all the mantle of his vast authority, and the tremendous prestige which his title, no less than his personality, gave him, and very well he did it. In the Armada fights, let us notice in passing, Drake was Howard's "Vice-Admiral"—the Second-in-Command, that is, of the anti-Armada fleet: not the Vice-Admiral of England, and still less the Lieutenant of the Admiralty. His was a local executive command afloat, for just that one occasion.

But Drake and Hawkins unfortunately died, as men will, and Lord Howard, who did not, grew old instead: and, while clinging still to his great office, which was a life-tenancy, came more and more under the influence of his time-serving relations and followers. Worse still, Hawkins's next successor but one, Sir Robert Mansell, proved venal to a degree, and corruption of all kinds became rampant. Also, in James I's time, money was notoriously scarce, the great constitutional quarrel of "King and Parliament" happening to be fought out on that very issue. The King's Navy went to the dogs, and with it the Merchant Marine as well.

At length, in 1618, there came on the naval scene George Villiers, Duke of Buckingham, James's notorious favourite. This man has received, in his time, the sneers and abuses of many generations of historians. Many he deserved: but we must not overlook his merits. He had the making of a fair administrator, and in his dealings with the King's Navy deserves even stronger praise. He bought out old Howard, he sacked not only Mansell but—for the moment—the whole Navy Board, and, as Lord High Admiral himself, he bravely set about retrieving the situation.

When the Duke has thus reassembled his powers, he was actually back again in the position of Henry VIII's Lord Admiral. He had full control of all three branches, since he had recovered the Administrative side. Indeed, it was only in this department that he shone. His efforts at commanding afloat were quite exceptionally bad, though this was not entirely his fault, since he lacked even Howard's stand-by—an efficient set of real seamen to advise him. As a statesman, too, he left a great deal to be desired, and invariably contrived to use the instrument which he had in some degree revived by his administrative ability for the furtherance of an undesirable policy. Still, with all his faults, he was the first whose patent was made out to the Lord High Admiral of England.

He met his death in 1628, stabbed by a disgruntled lieutenant—a military one this time. And at once a great revolution took place—the greatest, as it turned out, that was ever to happen to the Lord High Admiral. His office was "put into Commission", and for the first time a "Board of Admiralty" appeared—one man no longer, but a collection of men, whose united energies were to "execute the office".

Now this, as is well known, is the procedure of our own day; and taking it all in all, it is—and has been—a remarkably successful one: typical, in fact, of our happy knack of using committees to execute harmoniously what was once one man's job. It would be pleasant to be able to report that King Charles I, for all his shortcomings, showed amazing foresight in this one particular. But, alas, such was not the case. The ultimate results were admirable, the immediate motives not so good. The principal aim, in fact, was simply to provide for poor "Geordie's" widow. The perquisites of Admiralty must somehow be allowed to remain with her. So, while the Judge of the Admiralty did the work of Jurisdiction, he did it in the name of the King, who thus got control of the emoluments, which he passed on to her. Nor did he hand all the rest of the powers of Admiralty over to his Commissioners. He kept the important one of Sea Command in his own gift, to be bestowed by a separate patent. In fact, practically all the commissioners obtained in practice was the old, and not too popular, administrative job.

Still, it was something. The Commissioners appointed were a "Committee of the Council"; that is, to all intents, the other great officers of Crown. And here was my Lord Treasurer's chance. Ousted from his control of naval finance during the régime of the omnipotent Buckingham, he instantly returned to the attack, and had no difficulty in appointing himself First Commissioner of the new Board. We may even go further, and suspect that the Lord Treasurer's advocacy of the scheme, when it came up for discussion, was not altogether born of pity for the poor widow!

It was this Commission which was functioning when the great question of Ship-money came up, and, this time, we may find something good to say about poor King Charles. He insisted on the building of the fleet in spite of a rain of criticism and even obstruction from the Treasury-controlled Board of Admiralty; though, since there really was no money available in the middle of the "Eleven Years' Tyranny", the equipment of the ships was shocking, and the payment of the personnel almost non-existent.

In our own days of "water-tight compartments" we should open our eyes in wonder if we read in our morning paper that the posts held by the Bishop of London, the Chancellor of the Exchequer, and the First Lord of the Admiralty had all been entrusted to one man. But that is just what happened. a bare three hundred years ago. Neither the Treasury nor the Admiralty could storm the Church's defences, of course. It was the other way about: a clergyman was Lord Treasurer and First Lord. He was Juxon, Bishop of London. This will perhaps help to explain why the Puritan champions of Parliamentarianism were more than a little suspicious over this Ship-money business. What, they naturally asked, is to prevent our doctrinal foe, the Bishop of London, from persuading the Lord Treasurer to persuade the First Commissioner to hand over the Ship-money for purely anti-parliament purposes? What indeed! The answer—if there is one—was difficult for the opposition to believe; namely, that the King was preventing it.

From Buckingham's death up to 1709, the Navy's head was sometimes an exalted individual and sometimes a Board. The most exalted of such personages was James, Duke of York, and, later, King of England. He was ear-marked for the office at the rather startling age of five; for it was then that his father publicly declared his intention of creating him Lord High Admiral as soon as he was old enough. Circumstances quite unforeseen by the Royal Martyr caused the Duke to be kept out of office until 1660; but he succeeded to it at last on his brother's restoration: and he made a great success of it, thanks partly to his own natural enthusiasm for the sea and the sea-service, but mainly, perhaps, to the quite exceptional organizing genius of Samuel Pepys. This brilliant team, with one rather lengthy interruption, lasted up to 1688, when James went into exile and Pepys into retirement.

The Revolution marks, for all practical purposes, the end of the individual office of Lord High Admiral. In the last year of his life, it is true, William III elevated Lord Pembroke to the post for purely political reasons: and Marlborough, because he wanted the direction of the Navy in his own safe-keeping, obtained the titular position for the Queen's Consort, a well-meaning prince with, even in his own day, an unenviable reputation for dullness. But both were little more than puppets, worked on strings by more powerful and abler men. On Prince George's death, Pembroke succeeded once more, only to resign almost at once. From 1709 to 1827 the Board held the field. In the latter year the old office was revived for the benefit of William, Duke of Clarence; but only, as a very famous member of the Board[1] recently described it, "for ornamental purposes",

---

[1] The late Sir Oswyn Murray, Secretary of the Admiralty, to whose work the author is indebted for much of the contents of this chapter.

and after legislation had been passed to make quite sure that
the Royal office-holder could do no mischief. It is interesting to notice that the commission reproduced between pages
76 and 77 was issued during the brief term of this last Lord
High Admiral, as the heading and the signature reveal. For
though he became king two years later, William IV (who
has signed it) was, in 1828, still Duke of Clarence. Since
then the Board has reigned—and reigns. We must not say
"will always reign", because there is no reason—in theory—
why the Sovereign should not issue Letters Patent to an
individual instead of to a number of individuals whenever
he likes. But the chances that he will ever do so may be
regarded as negligible.

With the story of the development and growth of the
Board of Admiralty we do not propose to deal. What we
should remember here is that all the members of it were
always—and are always—"Officers" in the old sense of
"office-holders", but were not—and are not—by any means
always naval officers in the modern sense of "Rank". In
fact, in the lists of the earlier Boards the names of sea-officers
of experience are few and far between. In Commonwealth
times Blake and Monck were commissioners, but after that
we must travel almost to the end of the century before we
find the really leading lights among professional officers
beginning to appear at the board-table, to become the true
forerunners of the modern "Sea-Lords". After that a compromise was reached, and during the eighteenth century
the First Lord was, quite as often as not, a professional
"Sea-Officer", and often at the very head of the profession.
Such names as Anson, Hawke, Keppel, Howe and St. Vincent
leap to the mind. They were all First Lords in their day.

In the nineteenth and twentieth centuries the pendulum
has swung very markedly in the other direction as far as
First Lords are concerned, and W. S. Gilbert, with his Sir
Joseph Porter, was neither the first nor the last man to
comment upon the apparent paradox of having a civilian

minister at the head of the Senior Fighting Service. The key to that paradox really lies in the word "Minister". In Queen Anne's reign, the Board became a purely political body, and its head became, very rightly when one comes to think about it, a member of the Cabinet, which was just then in process of evolving. Exclusion of the Navy from representation in the highest executive Committee in the land would have been inviting disaster, for there would have been no one with sufficient authority—above all in time of war—to inform that committee of the Navy's potentialities and limitations, or to make a stand against impossible demands upon it. This strong political complexion of the eighteenth century Boards did not cut out the leading Admirals from participation, as it would now, because the higher naval officers of that time, more often than not, dabbled—and dabbled deeply—in politics: not always to the ultimate advantage of the Service, yet enabling them to compete in *both* walks of life, Politics and the Navy. But the inevitable specialization of the nineteenth century—that same phenomenon which was changing Caxton's press into *The Times* printing machine—soon made this impossible. Long before the middle of the century a man had to choose finally, and while he was still young—which profession he would make his career. But the need for a Minister at the head of the Navy still remained: and hence the possibility of a Sir Joseph Porter. But though the First Lord is now always a civilian, and to all intents and purposes must be, it does not follow that the whole Board need be political. And our own fathers were wise enough to see that this was so. That is why, in 1886, the Board *ceased* to be political: ceased, that is, to change when the Government did. The First Lord changes, of course, but the Board as a whole does not. It was a great triumph for common sense, but it was also a complete recognition of the fact that the age of Specialization had come.

The "Commissioners for executing the Office of Lord

High Admiral of the United Kingdom, etc.", appear, after the King and his staff, at the head of the modern *Navy List*. Their numbers—especially in war-time—vary from time to time. At present they comprise six "active" naval officers and four non-naval officers, of which latter group three are members of Parliament, and one is a Civil Servant. The last-named is the Permanent Secretary, and the most permanent member of them all: for though the political members go with a change of Government, and the naval members after serving in that post for variable terms of years, the Permanent Secretary outlasts both groups, and only retires on reaching an age-limit.

So we end the story of our Lord High Admiral. He was created, as one of nine, to shoulder a portion of the King's burden. He is still there in name, and perhaps in spirit, though, now, ten highly qualified men execute his office: and not only execute it incomparably more efficiently than he ever did, or could, but also find that it takes them all their time: and this in spite of the fact that the process of decentralization has made further gigantic strides, so that the department for which each member is individually responsible, has been "put into commission" again and again, until the number of people in whole-time "posts" created for the running of the Navy amounts, in our own day, to very many hundreds. And much the same process has happened in all other departments of the State: for it is not only in the production of the written word that Caxton's simple little machine has grown into the modern printing press.

### THE VICE-ADMIRAL AND REAR-ADMIRAL OF ENGLAND

Immediately below the "Board" in the modern *Navy List* appear the names of two distinguished officers who bear these exalted titles. They need not delay us long, but they deserve a word of explanation.

We have already seen how the Vice-Admiral of England

(with his alternative title, Lieutenant of the Admiralty, still
to be seen in the *Navy List*), was created for the purposes
described in 1546, and was squeezed out of existence again
by the Treasury in 1564. There had been vicarious officials
bearing one or other of his titles, or something very like
them, in even earlier times, but we may ignore them here,
since, when they existed, they were probably nothing more
than legal assistants to the Lord High Admiral in his
"juridical" function. Traces of these people survive still in
the pages of the modern *Navy List* devoted to the Judicial
Department of the Navy, where we find Vice-Admirals of
the Coast of Great Britain, and of Ireland. The office with
which we are now concerned has nothing to do with the
Lord High Admiral's legal functions, but rather with his
duties of "Sea-Command".

The post was revived again in 1604 under the second
title "Lieutenant of the Admiralty" in favour of Sir Richard
Leveson, an officer who had distinguished himself as a sea-
commander at the end of Elizabeth's reign. He died in the
following year, and the office was not filled again until 1618,
when Sir Robert Mansell was appointed, apparently as a
sop to him for being thrown out of the Treasurership of the
Navy by Buckingham. Once in office, he was immovable—
for it was a life-appointment. We all have a tendency to
fit our history into water-tight compartments: so this man's
biography is worthy of mention if only to show how dangerous that process may be. As a young man he commanded
Elizabeth's Fleets in the old Spanish War—the war of
Hawkins and Drake: in his middle age he earned himself
the reputation of being one of the most corrupt of naval
administrators: a little later he commanded the first Royal
English fleet that ever entered the Mediterranean: in his
old age Charles I wanted to put him in command of his
"Ship-money" fleet when he feared, in 1642, that the
Parliament was going to try and filch it from him. In the
end it was decided that he was too old; but that did not

prevent him from holding on to his office—and his life—
for another fourteen years. He died at last in June 1656, only
just a year before Robert Blake himself, having lived to see
the conclusion of the First Dutch War.

The next two holders of the office were both eminent
naval commanders—the Earl of Sandwich (Pepys's "My
Lord") and Prince Rupert, the King's cousin; and both,
as one would expect, commanded afloat during their tenure
of office. The place was not yet a sinecure.

After Rupert's death, the old practice of "honorary"
appointments began to creep in again. The next holder
was the Duke of Grafton, a natural son of Charles II, very
young and quite inexperienced. This is the more strange
when we learn that the place was not a particularly profitable one, the emoluments being worth only about £400 a
year.

The young Duke obviously could not shoulder any responsibility. His father therefore created a new post which should,
logically, have been called "Vice-vice-Admiral", for its
holder was expected to act for the Vice-Admiral. But,
instead, it was called "Rear-Admiral of England"—the
second under discussion here—and that rising officer Arthur
Herbert, afterwards Earl of Torrington, was put into it.
His appointment, unlike Grafton's, was not by any means a
sinecure.

But already both posts were doomed to become "honorary"
if they were to survive at all, for already the grades of sea-
going admirals had been established for commands at sea,[1]
so that there was no longer any room for these two as
substitutes for the Lord High Admiral in his "executive"
capacity: nor, whenever he was "put into commission",
and there came into existence a whole-time group of men to
carry out his other functions, was there any real point in
giving him a "man to act for him" or a "man to take his
place". The Board of Admiralty was in fact doing that.

[1] See below, p. 183.

Thus there were no real functions left for them to perform, so soon as the Board came to stay.

Yet, as honours, the posts remained. The titles of both officers were changed in 1707 to Vice- and Rear-Admiral of Great Britain, and in 1801 (on the Union with Ireland) "Great Britain" became the "United Kingdom". And so the offices continue to this day. There have been only two gaps in the sequence of Vice-Admirals (1709–1717, and 1887–1901), and four in the case of Rear-Admirals (the last, 1885–1901). Both have been filled from the ranks of senior and distinguished officers—usually, but not always, "retired" —who have quite often been "promoted" from the junior post to the senior one, on the death of the latter's holder. Some of them, however—and especially the earlier ones— have held commands of various kinds while holding the posts. But the offices themselves have carried no commands with them, and—since 1870—no pay. Like the Lords Commissioners, the Vice-Admiral and Rear-Admiral of the United Kingdom are office-holders; but, unlike them, they do no work as such. The posts are, in fact, honourable sinecures, denoting social status and naval prestige, but neither Command nor Rank. Indeed, they could hardly denote the latter, for the holders of the offices are invariably, upon appointment, full Admirals at least: and, even in England, it might be thought a little strange to promote a man from Admiral to Rear-Admiral.

CHAPTER X

# THE "PRINCIPAL OFFICERS OF THE NAVY"

IF the old names really meant anything—and they always did—no excuse is needed for telling briefly the story of the Navy Board. No one attempting the history of the officers of the Navy could very well omit a group of men who were called by their creator the "Four Principal Officers of the Navy". These were, the Treasurer, the Controller, the Surveyor, and the Clerk of the Acts—the men who were jointly responsible for the whole administration of the King's Ships.

What has become of them today? If we search the *Navy List*, and try to discover them as a body, we shall be disappointed. They are not there. In fact, only one of the four titles survives—that of Controller, the alternative (and, in naval circles, perhaps the most usual) title of the Third Sea Lord. The Navy Board, as a separate body, disappeared over a century ago, and the duties of its Principal Officers were taken over by the Board of Admiralty.

Until that time, however, they were of prime importance. They were, indeed, the principal "naval officers" (as opposed to the "Sea-Officers"),[1] and as typical "office-holders" as we shall find anywhere.

Let us pick up their story where we left it. We saw how Henry VIII created them, though we did not then specify their names, nor their functions. It is sufficiently clear what,

[1] See above, p. 146.

in broad outline, their respective duties were intended to be, both by Henry VIII and subsequent authorities. They are, after all, the four officials whom one might expect to find in any business created for ship-building purposes. Such a concern would require a Secretary, a Treasurer, a Designer, and an Inspector—or, perhaps, General Manager; and this is what, in effect, were the Clerk of the Acts, the Treasurer, the Surveyor and the Controller respectively.

But it is not by any means easy to see this in the early stages of the Board's life, because Henry's Principal Officers seem from the first to have formed an interdependent group organized on an elaborate system of safeguards. It is hard to decide whether to call them a "mutual admiration society"—for they usually clung together—or a "mutual suspicion society"—because their duties, when first we obtain a clear view of them in Elizabeth's time, seem to have been designed deliberately to make independent and individual action impossible. Elizabeth's instructions to her Principal Officers may be paraphrased, almost without exaggeration, as follows: "No one officer shall do anything without telling all (or nearly all) the other officers what he is doing, how he is doing it, why he is doing it, and (above all) exactly how much it will cost." The Treasurer, it is true, handles the money and (after 1564) is the titular "boss": but the Surveyor's principal duty appears to be surveying the Treasurer, and the Controller's main task is to control them both, while the Clerk of the Acts warns all three that anything they may do or decide will be set down and used in evidence against them.

In practice, all depended upon the ability, the personal strength of character and, above all, the honesty of the "boss"; for, as we have seen, the real control of Administration left the hands of the Lord High Admiral at a very early date, and, save for short periods, never returned to him: nor, until 1832, to the Board of Admiralty after him. John Hawkins was such a great Treasurer because he had all three qualities in abundance. He did a dangerous thing, such as only a man both courageous and honest could do. He proposed to the Queen, who was poor (as Sovereigns go) and always short of funds, to carry on the whole administration of the Navy by contract, for a "sum down". What a target poor Hawkins presented to the jealous, the petty-minded, the "Paul Pry" of his own day. They accused him of every villainy under the sun, and their accusations have been renewed, not infrequently, in succeeding ages. And no wonder. Judged by the current morality, it was *most* unlikely that such a scheme would work. But it did, because John Hawkins was as honest as he was competent, and went on manufacturing the maximum number of bricks with the minimum expenditure of straw, until the test came, and the Queen's Ships astonished friend and foe alike by their excellence in action.

This curious and, by the very nature of things, unique way of conducting state business had a double effect on the subsequent history of naval administration. For while it automatically kept the Lord Treasurer at arm's length, so long as it lasted, it also further divorced the Navy Board from the Lord High Admiral, still nominally responsible for it.

Another secret of the success of the Principal Officers in Tudor times lay in the fact that they were all—or almost all—practical seamen, and therefore knew just what they wanted. Like Hawkins himself, a great majority of the Board went off to take command of squadrons or ships when war came, and thus perhaps found another and more personal sort of inducement not to "let the side down".

But with the Stuarts all this was changed. The morale of the Officers, and especially of the Treasurer, declined seriously. It became increasingly common for persons with no knowledge of the sea to be "jobbed" into office; and, finally, as we have seen, the Lord Treasurer recaptured the fort.

The most immediate result of this last event was that the
"Treasurer of the Navy" lost his influence, and rapidly
degenerated into a purely financial official; becoming little
more than a go-between from Admiralty to Treasury, and
back. His appointment became, largely, a political matter,
and, from the end of the seventeenth century onwards, he
seldom even attended the meetings of the Board; when the
latter's duties were merged into those of the Admiralty in
1832, his functions passed, for the most part, to the
Accountant General of the Navy.

The Comptroller took his place as the most important of
the "Principal Officers". We may regard him, perhaps, as
being promoted now from the post of "Inspector" to that
of "General Manager". At any rate, during the eighteenth
century he was practically responsible for the administration
of the whole Navy. He was, it is true, still nominally subservient to the Board of Admiralty but, as in earlier days—
and even more so—his work was of far too specialized a
nature to enable the Lords Commissioners to exercise any
sort of effective control. In fact, they did not often try to do
so, but usually adopted a critical, if not actively hostile
attitude towards the Navy Board; and, when things went
wrong there, assumed the slightly smug attitude of "What
did I tell you?" They had, apparently, forgotten completely
that they were still *supposed* to be responsible for naval
administration themselves.

It was in this century, too, that there took place that
extraordinary multiplication of sub-departments of the Navy
Office which, in the matter of control, were to the Navy
Board itself much as the Navy Board was to the Admiralty.
There were, for instance, by 1782, no less than thirteen
different offices, scattered in or around the City of London,
from Whitehall to Greenwich, with far-flung outposts at
Woolwich and Chatham, in all of which some aspect of
naval business was transacted, often with little or no
liaison-work between the offices, but rather a spirit of petty

jealousy, secretiveness and mutual obstruction. It all sounds very confusing, and it was: and there was undoubtedly, first and last, an enormous loss of efficiency, not to mention an enormous leakage of more tangible things.

But what really prevented the system from being quite hopeless was this. With our innate common sense, and without perhaps being quite conscious of how we did it, or why, we did maintain just one safeguard throughout. Somehow or other we always contrived to have a Controller who was also a naval officer—often one of considerable distinction—who thus could keep in touch with realities even better, perhaps, than the highly "politicized" Board of Admiralty. Treasurers, Surveyors and Clerks of the Acts might be civilians—after the end of the sixteenth century they practically always were—but the record of the Controllers is exactly the reverse. Since the foundation of the office there have only been two Controllers who were civilians—one in the sixteenth century, and another in the seventeenth. Not that all eighteenth-century Controllers were good men, or perfectly suited to the post. Some were frankly political appointments: one at least—Captain Richard Haddock—was so old and decrepit that he could not visit the yards, and had to have a substitute appointed to do his work. But efficient and even brilliant administrators like Anson's nominee, Captain George Cockburne and, still more, Sir Charles Middleton, appeared sufficiently often, and lasted sufficiently long, to save the Navy from utter shipwreck. It is to such men, hampered at every turn by a chaotic state of decentralization, that we owe those fleets which brought us triumphantly—if sometimes barely—through the long series of Anglo-French Wars.

On the amalgamation of the Navy Board with the Board of Admiralty in 1832 this all-important naval "office" disappeared for a time, to reappear, as we shall shortly see, thirty-four years later.

The Surveyor, whose original duties, in so far as he had

any really independent ones, had been the provision and
upkeep of material, degenerated towards the end of the
seventeenth century, like the Treasurer, into a comparatively minor official, selected, for the most part, from the
Master Shipwrights at the dockyards. The general eighteenth century standard of efficiency in those who held the
office was clearly far from high; which was a very serious
matter, since the Surveyor was still nominally responsible
for both ship-design and ship-building, at any rate from
1672 to 1810, when the functions were definitely separated.
This helps to explain the undoubted inferiority of British
eighteenth-century ship-design to that of the French:
though, perhaps because so many of the Surveyors had once
been Shipwrights themselves, the same inferiority did not
exist on the building side.

To illustrate this sad falling off in the Surveyor's office,
we may cite one particularly limpet-like performance.
Jacob Acworth, having entered the service in Charles II's
reign—1682—was still Surveyor when the Jenkins's Ear
War of 1739 broke out. He could not walk, it is true, and
there is no evidence that his talents had ever been anything
but ordinary: still, they appointed another man to do his
work, and he lasted out the nine-years' war in full possession,
if not of his faculties, at least of his post.

This sort of thing mattered less if there was a good Controller in office. From 1739 to 1748 there was not, and
the situation was very serious. But that Providence, which
has been kind to the British Navy both before and since,
once more came to our rescue, and we were saved, this
time, by outstanding abilities in the *other* camp—the Board
of Admiralty, where the naval representative was George
Anson. In Middleton's day, on the other hand, the century's
peak of efficiency in naval administration was reached
because that amazingly industrious Controller took over
practically all the duties of all his colleagues.

The Surveyor actually survived the amalgamation of

1832, but in 1866, when the office of Controller was re-established he disappeared. His duties, by then mainly confined to "design", went to the Chief Constructor, a fairly new official with a scientific training far better than that which the ordinary Surveyor had ever received. It was the realization, at last, of the true importance of such higher training which really finished the Surveyor. This discovery had not eluded the logical eyes of the French, who, by creating a proper profession of trained ship-designers, had long since filched from us our once overwhelming pre-dominance in ship-construction. It was only towards the end of our long wars with them that our Authorities awoke fully to the dangers of such a state of things, and determined to make up leeway. But even then they moved slowly: and though, in 1810, Naval Construction, as a profession in itself, began with the opening of the School of Naval Archi-tecture at Portsmouth, this admirable establishment was abolished in 1832. After 1839, though higher training of a general kind was now obtainable in the newly reopened Royal Naval College, Portsmouth, the progress was still slow, and another abortive school was founded in the late 'forties, and scrapped in the early 'fifties, before success at length crowned the efforts of common sense, and a more lasting establishment appeared in 1864 as the Royal School of Naval Architecture and Marine Engineering at South Kensington. Already, too, the Institute of Naval Architects had been founded in 1860. In 1873 the Naval Architecture portion of the Royal School was transferred to the new Uni-versity of the Navy at Greenwich, where it came entirely under Admiralty control, and in 1883 the Royal Corps of Naval Constructors was formed under the old Chief Con-structor of the Navy, whose title had been changed, in 1875, to the modern one of Director of Naval Construction. It is this most responsible officer who has inherited the "design" side of the old Surveyor's duties.

The Clerk of the Acts, or, to give him his earlier names,

the Clerk of the Ships, or Records, was actually by far the oldest of the "principal Four", since he was there, all by himself, long before King Henry's day. Under the title of "Keeper" or "Clerk of the King's Ships" he may trace his ancestry back to a medieval Archdeacon of Taunton, one William de Wrotham, who was appointed to this post by King John in 1214. But he was none the less much the least important of the four from the moment when the other three appeared on the scene. In fact, he only thrust himself into the picture on those rare occasions when a big personality happened to hold the office *en passant*. He was usually selected from among the Clerks at the Navy Office or the Dockyards, but on one exceptional occasion, a newly appointed Lieutenant of the Admiralty, in a moment of brilliant inspiration, appointed his poor cousin to the job— and "job" may have been the right word in more senses than one. But if it was nepotism, it must be about the happiest example of that vice on record. For that is how Samuel Pepys set his foot on the first rung of the administrative ladder, the top step of which was the first Secretaryship of the Admiralty, a post created expressly for him by Charles II.

The Controller of the Navy reassumed in 1866 the greater part of his duties of Navy Board days, and now sits on the Board of Admiralty as the member responsible for the material of the Service. He has not sat there continuously since 1866, it is true: more than once he has been deprived of his seat, only to find his way back again when emergency arose. But modern opinion, borne out by the experience of the Great War, has now crystallized to the conclusion that the officer responsible to the First Lord, and so to the Cabinet and Parliament, for all the Navy's material needs, should be permanently seated at the Navy's supreme council-board.

Having seen the last survivor safely ensconced there, we may leave the famous Four, only remarking that we seem to have returned once more to a point not so very far removed from that reached more than two and a half centuries ago, when the Controller first emerged as the principal of the Principal Officers, and assumed, in practice, the responsibility for naval material. He has had his vicissitudes—including even temporary dissolution: he has outlived all his fellows, and he is now a member of that other Board which, once, grandly regarded itself as his master. But he still is the Controller, and he is still responsible for naval material.

## BOOK FOUR

*The New Officers*

# CHAPTER XI

# THE FLAG-OFFICERS

## INTRODUCTORY

THE first name in the 1939 *Navy List* is that of His Majesty the King, who is, of course, the Head of the British Navy, by reason both of post and of rank. There follows a list of his personal staff. Next comes a short list of "Honorary Officers in His Majesty's Fleet"—all of them foreign sovereigns or princes, whose presence does not concern us here. Then come the "Commissioners for executing the Office of Lord High Admiral of the United Kingdom, etc.", and then the "Vice-Admiral and Rear-Admiral of the United Kingdom". Down to this point all—save the foreign royalties —are office-*holders*, each labelled with the name of his office, as well as with the name of his naval rank (if he has one).

But thereafter begins the "List of Officers on the Active List of the Royal Navy with the dates of their seniority". In this list appears the name of every active commissioned and warrant officer, each appearing in his correct seniority in his particular rank.

It is with these various ranks that the last section of this book will deal. An attempt will be made to show, in rather greater detail than hitherto, how the most important among them have come into existence, and developed into what they now are. But we cannot keep altogether to the order of the *Navy List*, because our examination is to be primarily an historical one, and the years have brought quite spectacular rises or falls to the various categories of the Service. Some, like the Boatswain and the Carpenter, started in high places on shipboard and are now fallen to a lower sphere of usefulness : others, like the Purser and the Surgeon started life as Warrant Officers, and are now always of "Commission" rank, and sometimes even of "Flag" rank. Some, again, like the Master and the Mate, have disappeared altogether, while others, like the Sub-Lieutenant and all Engineer ranks, are comparatively new-comers.

In our own day the Flag-Officer, the Commissioned Officer, and the Warrant Officer are in three fairly water-tight compartments. A band of gold lace, one and three-quarter inches thick is the most conspicuous outward sign of the first group: one (or more) of half-inch[1] thickness denotes the second, and one of one-quarter inch the third. But this method of division will not take us very far back in time, and we cannot use it for our arrangement here. Historical treatment demands, rather, the following classification:

(1) Flag-Officers: that is, men who command a unit which is greater than a single ship.

(2) Ship-Officers of Commissioned Rank: that is, all the officers who have executive posts in ships of war, and who are appointed by the Commission of the King or of the Lord High Admiral. Until about a century ago the only "commission" officers in ships were the ordinary "executives"—Captain, Commander and Lieutenant.

(3) Ship-Officers of Warrant Rank and Executive duties: that is, the old "Standing" officers—the Master, the Boatswain, the Gunner, the Carpenter and—once upon a time—the Cook.

(4) "Civilian" Officers of Warrant Rank: that is, the "non-fighters"—the Purser, the Surgeon, the Chaplain, and the Schoolmaster. The first two were,

---

[1] Or, since 1930, nine-sixteenths of an inch.

strictly, "standing" officers, but they are more conveniently discussed along with the "non-military" group. All these are now Commissioned Officers.
(5) The Engineer—the "Cuckoo in the Nest".

There are many more, such as the Master-at-Arms, the Sailmaker, the Ropemaker, the Armourer, the Caulker, as well as the "mates" of all the standing officers, who were, called, in the old days, the "Inferior Officers": men whose importance was, and often *is*, very great, and whose history well repays the study. But here lack of space will compel us to deal more summarily with them than we should wish.

## FLAG-OFFICERS

### ADMIRAL OF THE FLEET

We are concerned here with one, and one only, of the three great functions of the Lord High Admiral—the Command at Sea. So long as a single Lord High Admiral existed there always remained the theory that he was to assume this post when the main fleet put out. The very last Lord High Admiral—not counting the "ornamental" nineteenth-century representative—the Earl of Pembroke, even caused anxiety amounting to dismay in high quarters when he was thought to be intending to exercise this prerogative. But when the office was "in commission", it was, of course, a different matter. In the first Board, as we have seen, the other great officers of the Crown were the people executing the office, and clearly none of them ever had the slightest intention of going to sea at all. Nor would Charles I allow any such experiment, for he was careful to keep the bestowal of the place in his own hands. So the command at sea came to be divorced from the other functions of the Lord High Admiral.

We have already explained how, in Blake's time, other "powers of Admiralty" were transferred to the Com-

mander at sea; and that is how his name came to be changed
from "General" to "Admiral". Once this was accomplished,
the rest was simple. So-and-so was appointed by the King
to be "Admiral of the Fleet" for a certain specific
occasion. The first to bear the actual name, was the Earl
of Dartmouth, so appointed by James II in 1688: while
Torrington, Rooke, Shovell and Leake each held it in turn
during the last two wars with Louis XIV. They were all,
still, strictly office-*holders*. Yet the office soon fell a victim
to the process which was outlined in the chapter on
"Service", and became a *rank*. The key year was 1718,
when, it will be recalled, the principle was inaugurated of
promotion by strict seniority, upwards from Captain to the
very top. In the "peaceful" years between 1718 and 1739
it became customary to give the senior Admiral on the list
the title of "Admiral of the Fleet", even when there was no
visible fleet, for the time being, to be Admiral of. This
happened fairly frequently during those years, and it
practically completed the process.

Yet, it must always be remembered, in spite of the emphasis
laid on seniority after 1718, "Rank" never entirely slew
"Post", neither here nor anywhere else. If it had, it would
always have been the man at the top of the Seniority List
who commanded the most important fleet, and the second
on the List who commanded the second most important.
In other words, seniority would have prevailed over selection.
But this has never happened—it would be a bad day for the
Navy if it did. Though it has sometimes fallen out that the
"Admiral of the Fleet" commanded the main fleet (as in the
case of Sir John Norris), it has much more frequently
happened that a more junior officer has been *selected* for the
highest command. Thus, Admiral Cornwallis, commanding
England's main fleet during the long blockade of Brest
from 1803 to 1805 was, at the moment of appointment, only
an Admiral of the Blue, and twenty-seventh from the top
of the list: Nelson, put at the same time in command of the

Mediterranean Fleet, was only a Vice-Admiral of the Blue, with five distinct grades of Admiral above him, and seventy-fourth on the seniority list: while, in the twentieth century, Jellicoe, on his appointment to the command of the Grand Fleet in 1914, was also only a Vice-Admiral, and twentieth from the top of the Active List. Nor did any of these famous men receive special promotion as a result of their important appointments. Jellicoe was appointed *acting* Admiral, it is true, but did not attain the substantive rank until 1915.

From the 1740's to the 1860's there was no change in what had now become the *rank* of Admiral of the Fleet. There was never more than one of them, and not quite always that: in 1857, for instance, the rank was empty, though it has never been so since. In 1862 the innovation began of appointing a second, and in the following year came a third. The maximum remained at three until 1898 when a fourth was appointed. Since then, the Crown, while promoting the senior Admiral, has exercised a right of selection among other Admirals. At the present moment there are four—about the average number, though one— the Duke of Windsor—is obviously an exceptional creation.

Two other points may finally be made. First, the rank is the only one in which the name of the original office has been retained in full. It is the only rank which has kept the all-important "of" in it. And second, so completely has it become a rank that, nowadays, the man who is, in fact, the Admiral of a Fleet is never—well, *hardly* ever—an "Admiral of the Fleet".

## THE ADMIRAL, VICE-ADMIRAL AND REAR-ADMIRAL

The medieval commander afloat was, as we have seen, called "Captain", and not "Admiral". The military commanders of the ships composing the fleet, however, were also usually called "Captains", which may occasionally have caused confusion. Sometimes, however, the latter were called "Under Captain", by way of distinguishing them.

But this too was crude and unsatisfactory, and was sure, sooner or later, to be remedied. The change was begun by Henry VIII's action in sending his High Admiral to sea; and, on those occasions when he did *not* go, by calling the Commanding Officer the "General". In Blake's time the term "Admiral" sometimes appeared in the title of a sea-commander, but only if he was at the time a Commissioner of the Admiralty. It is not until the Restoration Period that the "Flag-men", as Pepys calls them, included the word as a regular part of their title, even when they were not Commissioners. And even then—for as long as it remained a "post", and for many years afterwards—it was always followed by the qualifying words "of the", and often preceded by the words "Vice" or "Rear".

The etymology of the famous term itself has caused some discussion. There is little doubt that it is derived from the arabic "emir" or "ameer", a chief, and that the word made its way westward *via* France, where it assumed the form of "Amiral". The intrusive "d" is probably the outcome of a blunder on the part of contemporary Englishmen, who wrongly connected the unfamiliar word with their own words "admire" and "admirable". A further theory, which is at least picturesque, if not true, is that the original form was "Amir al Bahr"—that is, "Chief of the Sea"—and that the really crucial part of the phrase fell away in transit, as terminations will; so that what we are really saying when we use the word "Admiral" is simply "Chief of the".

Enough has already been said to show that, up to the Commonwealth times, the English Leader-at-Sea, by whatever name he was called, was almost invariably a gentleman, usually a nobleman, often a soldier, sometimes sufficiently adaptable to convert himself into a reasonable seaman, but practically never a seaman by profession. Exceptions of course there were, as Drake and his colleagues, and a few earlier examples like William FitzWilliam.[1] But these men

[1] See p. 32.

serve merely to emphasize the wellnigh universal rule. The chief command at sea must be held by "blue blood", with sea-experience if possible, but without it if necessary.

This idea held the field right up to Commonwealth days. But the "Generals-at-Sea" opened a new era. "Nobility" gave place to "Efficiency", and that ideal was never entirely lost again. After the Restoration, sometimes one principle was followed, sometimes another. The Duke of York alternates with Albemarle (now ennobled, but once plain George Monck). Prince Rupert is very "blue-blooded", but pressing close on his heels are Admirals of the White and the Blue (not to mention Vice-Admirals) who ranged all down the social scale—Edward Montagu, now Earl of Sandwich, Sir Edward Spragge, Sir George Ayscue, Sir William Penn, Sir John Lawson and Sir Christopher Myngs. But the general tendency is plain enough. The new type of sea-officer—the whole-time professional, born under the Commonwealth and legitimatized under the second Charles —took some years to grow to manhood, but, when he did, he became the universal rule, and nobility *per se* was no longer good enough to keep him down. The century closes on men like Russell and Herbert, of high birth; on Rooke and Shovell, of gentle birth; and on Leake, the ex-gunner, and Benbow, the tanner's son.

All three distinctive ranks—Admiral, Vice-Admiral and Rear-Admiral—arose directly out of posts, which, in their turn were the direct outcome of fleet organization. There are signs of a division of the whole fleet into Squadrons in very early times. But we need not concern ourselves here with galley tactics, and so need look no further back than the Armada fight—the first full-dress and purely sailing-ship battle in which the English navy took part. Some such division may have existed in our fleet from the beginning of the fight, but it was certainly there after the second big encounter, off Portland.

It was not, however, until 1620 that a fleet was distributed

into organized squadrons before ever it set out. But in
Sir Robert Mansell's Mediterranean expedition of that year
this was done. Red was the colour allotted to the senior
squadron, which Mansell himself commanded. He was
actually, we may recall, Vice-Admiral of England at the
time; but, though not then called it in so many words, he
was really the "Admiral of the Fleet". Sir Richard Hawkins
was the Vice-Admiral of the Fleet—of that particular fleet,
of course—and had blue flags for his squadron, while Sir
Thomas Button was Rear-Admiral of it, and had white
flags. A further innovation which, as it happened, came to
stay, was that Mansell carried his flag at the main, Hawkins
at the fore, and Button at the mizzen. It was a pretty
arrangement, and, when each squadron was further split
into three divisions—a thing which happened in the big
fleets of the Commonwealth period—the arrangement was
even neater. The main-mast—the most important and
highest "stick" in the ship, was used for the flags of the
most important and highest officers in the fleet—the
Admirals: the next most important—the fore-mast—was
used for the flags of the Vice-Admirals, while the Rear-
Admirals had to be content with the humbler mizzen.
The three colours, too, were now woven into the scheme,
and used to denote the squadrons, as before: only, now,
there were *nine* "flag-men" altogether, one for each division,
and therefore three in each squadron—three Admirals, in
command of squadrons: three Vice-Admirals, each commanding the second most important division of their respective squadrons; and three Rear-Admirals commanding
the least important divisions. By the end of the First Dutch
War, when the "close hauled line ahead" had been established as the normal battle formation, it had been discovered
that the Commanding Officer's best place was in the
middle of his command, whether squadronal or divisional:
the next most important place was obviously the van:
so there was placed the second most important man in each

squadron—the Vice-Admiral; and the least important flagman in each squadron—the Rear-Admiral—brought up the rear.

The Restoration arrangement, which was the one destined to last, retained the whole system intact, save that the order of merit of "White" and "Blue" was reversed, the Van squadron becoming the "White", and the Rear Squadron the "Blue".

Thus a full-dress English fleet of Pepys's day was commanded, and flagged, as follows:

| Post | Squadron | Flag, and Where Flown |
|---|---|---|
| 1. Vice-Admiral of the White | VAN | White at Fore. |
| 2. Admiral of the White | White Ensign | White at Main. |
| 3. Rear-Admiral of the White | (all ships) | White at Mizzen. |
| | | |
| 4. Vice-Admiral of the Red | CENTRE | Red at Fore. |
| 5. Lord High Admiral _or_ Admiral of the Fleet | Red Ensign (all ships) | Royal Standard at Main. _or_ Union at Main. |
| 6. Rear-Admiral of the Red | | Red at Mizzen. |
| | | |
| 7. Vice-Admiral of the Blue | REAR | Blue at Fore. |
| 8. Admiral of the Blue | Blue Ensign | Blue at Main. |
| 9. Rear-Admiral of the Blue | (all ships) | Blue at Mizzen. |

We notice that all Admirals' flags fly at the mainmast head, all Vice-Admirals' at the foremast, and all Rear-Admirals' at the mizzen; also each Admiral is in the centre of his own squadron, each Vice-Admiral in the van of his, and each Rear-Admiral is in the Rear. The supreme commander, too, is dead central.

It will also be observed that no place is left for an Admiral of the Red, since his natural position is filled by the Lord High Admiral, if he be present, or, if not, by the Admiral of the Fleet. There was never, therefore, such a _post_ as Admiral of the Red.

Now we have explained this squadronal arrangement at some length because things were exactly in this state when the Post-Rank revolution came along. And the result was that the nine "Flag-Posts" faithfully turned into nine "Flag-Ranks". It was through all these that a senior captain was condemned to plod when the "Seniority" ruling of 1718 came in. But it was not the Seniority Rule alone which brought about the change. Another important factor contributed at this point to the defeat of "Post". Though, as we have seen, the flag-list was actually kept down to nine men up to 1743, the posts which gave them their names were really things of the past some time before that. The day of England's one enormous fleet, with its three squadrons each sub-divided into three divisions, had gone, and was not to return. Now we had commitments, not only in the Channel, but in many other places as well—the Mediterranean, the New World, and Indian Waters. The result was that individual fleets were numerically smaller, and though the three squadrons were usually retained, they lost their distinctive colours, and—still more important from our point of view—they were too small to be worth cutting up into divisions. Thus, even before reduplication of Admirals of the Blue, Rear-Admirals of the White, etc., began, these titles had ceased to denote posts, for the posts themselves had ceased to exist.

Again, as soon as more than one officer holds any one of these titles, it is clear that the title itself must be conferring rank, if it is conferring anything. And this was so: yet once again we may notice the curious reluctance of the Authorities to admit it. In all the eighteenth-century Regulations and Instructions, the same rule, entirely divorced—after 1743—from the facts, is repeated with parrot-like reiteration: "The established number of Flag Officers shall be as follows: One Admiral and Commander-in-Chief of the Fleet: one Admiral of the White and one of the Blue," etc., etc.—nine in all. Only in the 1808 edition are the words changed. Then we have, "The Flag Officers are divided into three Ranks, viz. Admirals, Vice-Admirals, and Rear-Admirals. Each Rank is divided into three Squadrons." It was high time to make the admission that there were more than one of each, for the end of the war then raging saw a flag-list which contained seventy Admirals, seventy-three Vice-Admirals, and seventy-six Rear-Admirals! 

But still nothing was done about limiting the number of Flag-ranks. The only change, in fact, was in the opposite direction; for in November 1805 his advisers appear to have allowed King George III to be guilty of a slight historical mistake. As a reward to the Service for its glorious work in that year, His Majesty "restored" the rank of Admiral of the Red—a title which, as we have seen, had never existed before, even as a post, still less as a rank. The ladder from Captain to Admiral of the Fleet thus came to have ten rungs instead of nine. Can we wonder that Nelson, who was only forty-seven when he died, had merely got as far as Vice-Admiral of the White?

In the central figure facing page 188 we see how a Flag-Officer looked soon after the Service went into trousers. Though this Admiral may well have fought at Trafalgar, there is little left of the familiar style which we associate with Nelson. Cocked hat, knee breeches and silk stockings are all gone, and for the first time we catch something of the modern "dress" uniform in the flat peaked cap and frock-coat.

The system of ranking by squadronal colours, as well as by grade of Admiral, continued up till 1864, when the three old colours were distributed among the most important groups of British seafarers. The White was retained for the Royal Navy, the Red was given to the Merchant Service, and the Blue to the Royal Naval Reserve. The "Flagman's" ladder of promotion was thus drastically cut down from ten steps to four—the ranks which remain unchanged to this day.

### THE COMMODORE

Last among the "Flag-men"—and wearing only *half* a flag at that—comes the Commodore, that most anomalous of Naval Officers, beloved of the novelists and playwrights as well as of those naval annalists who delight especially in the picturesque. For apart from fictitious friends like Commodores Flip and Hawser Trunnion, some of the most stirring events in the lives of such flesh-and-blood heroes as Rooke, Anson, Byron and Nelson belong to their Commodore days.

This officer is unique in one respect. Of the old naval "offices" all the others ultimately turned into ranks: but this never did, though many an attempt has been made so to turn it. It is sometimes called a "Temporary Rank", which is the nearest it has ever reached to being a full rank: but that, when we come to consider it, is really only another name for a "Post". It has even been granted "equivalent rank" with an Army title which *was* a rank, without being such itself. But that is all; and to this day, though the fact that a Captain holds the temporary place of "Commodore" is duly chronicled in the *Navy List* alongside his name, that name is not removed from its proper "seniority" place in the List, and there is no separate list of Commodores.

Yet he certainly comes within the scope of our "Flag-Officer" definition, since the essence of his existence is the command of more than one ship. He also bears in our own day, the distinctive "Flag Officer" hall-mark in the shape of the one and three-quarter-inch ring; though, when or if he vacates his commodore's command, he reverts, without any thought or feeling of lost prestige, to the four half-inch stripes of the ordinary captain.

No "post" has changed less than this since its inception. Its story dates back to July 1652, when, on the outbreak of the First Dutch War, the States-General and Zealand Admiralty found themselves short of flag-officers. Unwilling to create more Admirals, they appointed a number of Captains to a new office called "Commandeur", and placed them in temporary charge of squadrons, either when detached from, or when serving with, the main fleet. One

CAPTAIN, FLAG-OFFICER AND COMMANDER, ABOUT 1835

of the originals was none other than the great De Ruyter himself, and we find that he actually divided his squadron into three parts under Commodore, Vice-Commodore and Rear-Commodore—a process exactly analogous to that in England which gave us the three "Admiral" titles. Thus the original Dutch Commodore was extraordinarily similar in every way to his modern English compeer. Even the famous "Burgee" or "Broad Pendant", so intimately associated with the Commodore through all his history, was originated on the same occasion.

England, however, had nothing to do with the new officer then. It was not until 1688, when Dutch William came to England that the "Commandeur" accompanied him. The word was then pronounced *à la française*: that is, with all three syllables equally stressed. But no Englishmen could ever bring himself to stress *all* the syllables of any word, and our forefathers singled out the first and the last for emphasis. The name was thus anglicized to Còmm-a-dòre, and so it was invariably spelt during its early sojourn in England.

In 1690, the Admiralty gave the title of "Commadore" to the senior Captain of a small squadron, or to a Commander-in-Chief of a small station, when no flag-officer was present. The Crown did not approve the step, though it seems to have made no move to stop the proceeding.

This was the beginning of a curious struggle between the Admiralty and the Government. In 1731, when the former, under Lord Torrington, drew up the original "Regulations and Instructions", they inserted in the first draft an order for the creation of three Commodores (so spelt for the first time). They were to be "of the Red", "of the White", and "of the Blue": so that it is evident the Board wanted to *add* them to the existing provision of Flag-Officers, already in the process of turning from "posts" to "ranks". Perhaps they saw more clearly than the Government the necessity of widening the "bottle-neck". But whether this was the case or no, the Lords of the Council, though they passed practically all the rest of the Regulations, pointedly rejected the Commodores.

In the next key-year, 1747, the Admiralty returned to the charge, but, this time, more insidiously. The first "equivalent rank" list, as between Navy and Army, was being prepared, and they proposed that "Commodores" should rank with "Brigadiers". The latter was an Army rank recognized by the Crown, and the Lords of the Council appear to have fallen into the Admiralty's little trap. They sanctioned the whole list. Thus it came about that for nearly sixty years a naval personage who had no legal existence whatsoever "ranked with" a perfectly legal soldier. This "order of precedence" appears in all subsequent editions of the Regulations till the end of the century. Byron and Nelson were commodores of this kind, and it was partly owing to this lack of legal definition as to their exact status which made possible such curious incidents as the Nelson-Moultrie dispute.

After Trafalgar the same Authority which had perpetrated the blunder about the Admiral of the Red made amends, in some degree, by regularizing the "Commodore" anomaly. It created the "temporary ranks" of Red, White and Blue Commodore, and made two classes of them:—First Class: a commodore was to be ranked and paid as a Rear-Admiral if he were of sufficient importance to be allowed a separate Captain under him. Second Class: if he commanded the ship himself "he shall have a large white ball near the staff (of his broad pendant), and he shall not rank as Rear-Admiral". And, as an assurance that even now the title shall not become a permanent rank, it is laid down that "if two or more Commodores serve together, they shall take precedence and command according to the *dates of their Commissions as Captains*"—not according to the date when they were given the *post* of Commodore.

In the redistribution of colours, in 1864, the number of

grades was reduced to the present level of two—Commodore, First and Second Class—and no important changes have since taken place.

There was perhaps more reason in the Crown's curious obstruction of Admiralty policy than is superficially apparent. Somebody whose honesty was above the average of the time, or who could probe more deeply than most into the less creditable subterfuges of the eighteenth century, perhaps feared that the Admiralty, in making Commodore a permanent rank, was attempting to create a by-pass through which favoured juniors might be promoted over the heads of their less fortunate seniors—a very likely contingency in those golden days of "jobbery" under Walpole and the Pelhams. Or we may look at it from the other point of view, and assume that it was a legitimate effort on the part of the Admiralty to overcome the Crown's aversion to the creation of more Flag-Officers, and thus to ease the block in promotion.

CHAPTER XII

## "COMMISSION" SHIP-OFFICERS

WE pass next to the officers of the individual ship of war, and, for historical treatment, must make at once a clear-cut division of them—the "Commission" Ship-Officer, and the "Warrant" Ship-Officer. To the first, up to comparatively recent times, belong only the "military" or fighting group, descended as we have seen from the medieval soldiers who came on board when the ship was commissioned for war. These men came to take command of the whole ship, although in certain particulars connected with navigation their authority was curtailed both by order and by custom. So it came about that, once accepted as an integral part of the ship's complement, they became, as it were by right, the men who gave the orders, who had the "command"—the general control of the ship. In fact, to use the modern term, they became the *executive* officers.

It is with these Executive "Commission" Officers that this chapter deals—the Captain, the Commander and the Lieutenant: and, added in the nineteenth and twentieth centuries respectively, the Sub-Lieutenant and the Lieutenant-Commander. All the other "Commissioned" officers of our own day, members of the "Civilian", "Non-military" and "Non-executive" branches, are the products of this later period. Their forefathers were on shipboard, of course, but they were there by virtue of Warrants issued by the Navy Board or the Admiralty, and not of Commissions from the Lord High Admiral or the King.

### THE CAPTAIN

The name, as used in the English Navy, is military in origin and of Latin-French extraction. From the root word *Caput*, *Capitanus* led to *Capitaine*, and so to the most familiar of all naval titles. We have noted the early association of the name with *fleet*-command, but once it had disassociated itself from that, and had linked itself with *ship*-command, its bearer had become what he has been, in essence, ever since—the Officer Commanding, with very far-reaching powers: powers which at once set him, and kept him, in a class by himself, and high over the heads of all other ship-officers.

When exactly it became the settled practice to have a Captain in every ship fitted out for war-purposes, we cannot say. Probably it was not *very* early. There survives an "Ordinance of the Commons for the Safeguard of the Sea", dating from 1442, and its authors think it worth while to remark, when eight merchant ships are to be sent out for eight months, "thereof the King our Sovereign Lord choose such of them as him liketh to be the Chief Capytayne, and other seven as the King liketh of the saide eight for to attend the saide Chief Capytayne: *so that every grete shippe have a Capytayne within borde*". Were the principle of "one ship, one Captain" already completely established, such detail would seem redundant. The "Chief Capytayne" was, of course, the man whom we should call the Admiral, and it is significant to note that all the "Capytaynes" are to be "Knights and worthy Squires of the West, South and North, so that no County should be dispised."

But, whatever the date may be, we can safely say that the principle was firmly established by Henry VIII's time, and that his Captain had reached that particular eminence on ship-board described above. Originally imported merely to *fight* the ship, he was at once given command of it, as befitted his "class", over the heads of the old ship-officers, the Master and the Boatswain. And, as he gradually lost his purely

N

military character, so he gradually assumed a more strictly naval one. The process was not completed without heart-burnings, especially in the breasts of the displaced ship-officers. Loud—and very human—were the complaints of the old and experienced Master when some raw, ignorant, and—sometimes—vicious young captain was pushed over his head. There survive complaints on the other side too. "These Masters," says Nathaniel Boteler's Captain, "being blown up on this fashion of late, undergo the Command of a Captain over them with a great deal of grudging and sullenness."

The powers of the Captain have naturally varied in detail in the last four centuries, but his general status on board has remained so much the same that further comment in this direction is not necessary. We have seen, too, in sufficient detail how this title, which was at first a post, was the first of the "commission" offices to become a rank: it is indeed actually called by that name in the *Regulations* of 1731, where it lays down that "none shall have the *Rank* of Captain", etc. What we have not yet seen—and this remains to tell a little later—is how it came about that the post of Captain turned into *two* ranks—Captain and Commander.

But first let us see if we can estimate what manner of man this potentate was—the personage sometimes nicknamed "the Owner" to this day: the man upon whom rested the unexpected responsibility of selecting the next generation's officers. General rules are not easy to formulate: much—but not all—depended on the times. In all those early periods when it chanced to be fashionable for a section of the gentry to "follow the sea", there tended to be a very hard-and-fast distinction between the two classes of "Gentle-man" or "Fairweather" Captain, and the "Tarpaulin"—names which sufficiently explain themselves. These names date from the Restoration days, and it is to this period that Macaulay's famous epigram refers. "There were gentlemen", he writes, "and there were seamen in the navy of Charles II.

But the seamen were not gentlemen : and the gentlemen were not seamen"—a half-truth, truer perhaps of the Tudor age than of the Restoration, and truer still of the "lean" period in the first half of the seventeenth century. The decade which saw the beginning of the real fashion of gentlemen-captains was the 1630's, and Clarendon makes it quite clear that the majority of the captains in the fleet which poor Charles loved and lost were gentlemen ; though, as it happens, the most vigorous of them, Captain William Batten, was not. But the very hard-and-fast line soon begins to become blurred, and a close examination of all available material leads rather to the conclusion that, though types of both extremes existed, in varying quantities, at least up to the end of the eighteenth century, the generality of captains through-out were of middle-class extraction, especially after the Midshipmen and Lieutenants of Pepys's creation grew up to that rank. Indeed, if English sea-captains had any common factor at all, we should be tempted to say that it was Poverty. For whether "needy hangers-on at Court", impecunious younger sons to whom the estate would not pass, or merely seamen who had entered "through the hawse-hole", they mostly had their careers to carve out for themselves, and their own fortunes to make. Some made them no doubt—with the Purser's aid : or, up to 1686, when the practice was officially forbidden, by turning His Majesty's ship into a good imitation of a merchantman. But there is no reason to suppose that the majority were anything but honest, if rough, servants of the State.

Some, of course, abused their very great powers, and, like Captain Oakum in *Roderick Random*, and Captain Pigot in real life, were tyrants and bullies in a community where no single individual could safely answer back. Some again, especially in the earlier days—men like Shadwell's Captain Mizzen or Smollett's Captain Whiffle—stirred the deepest scorn in the breasts of the horny-handed tar by carrying a natural leaning for elegance to the verge of effeminacy.

Some, like Commodore Flip, went to the opposite extreme, and did their best to merit the classic reproach in the *Fair Quaker of Deal*:

Why, Lord, Commodore, won't you give a man leave to be decent and clean? Will nothing please you but what stinks of tobacco? . . . Do you think because we *gentlemen* put on clean shirts every day that we can't understand the affairs of the Navy as well as those who wear their shirts till they are lousy? Do you think that nastiness gives you a title to knowledge?

And, lastly, some were rapacious, and used their power to make their pile, like the Captain in Ned Ward's scurrilous *Wooden World*. "Tho' he have not one Hand in the taking, he will be sure to have both in the disposing of a Prize. The King allots him three parts in eight for his singular Hazards, and he grants himself the other five, to prevent foolish Fractions and Divisions."

But all these are the extremes: and it is of extremes that we almost always hear. The pamphleteer, the novelist and the playwright have their grievances and their publics to consider, and both considerations combine to drive them to exaggeration. Everyone knows, too, how much easier it is to portray the extreme than to catch a passable likeness of the mean. Even the artist tends to depict the extreme, as Hogarth's picture shows. Though no caricature, it does depict one sort of extreme—that of birth. It shows very well the pomp and circumstance with which an aristocratic captain could contrive to surround himself even at sea, and even so late as the 1740's, when all—or almost all—officers were already "professionals".

Captain Lord George Graham was no Captain Whiffle, for all his performing dogs and adulatory "following" of Chaplain, Secretary and servants: but he was hardly "average". So let us balance him with one picture more—this time a pen-portrait of one who was an extreme only in ability and achievement. John Leake was certainly not a "gentleman Captain" by extraction, being the son of a

SON to 1sᵗ D. of MONTROSE

F⁊. HOGARTH.

[*William Hogarth*

CAPTAIN LORD GEORGE GRAHAM IN HIS CABIN, ABOUT 1745

master-gunner—albeit an exceptional one—and the grandson of another.

He was of middle stature, well-set and strong, a little inclined to corpulency, but not so as to incommode him in the least. His complexion was florid, his countenance open, his eyes sharp and piercing, and his address both graceful and manly, denoting both the military man and the gentleman. As he had a good person, he had also a good constitution, hardly ever knowing what it was to be sick: and though he took his bottle freely, as was the custom in his time in the fleet, yet he was never disgraced or impaired his health by it. . . . He was certainly one of the best seamen the island has produced.

But, when all is said, the commonest accusation against the English Sea-Captain is that he was a bully. This is the criticism *par excellence* of the eighteenth-century captain. With the rise of the new officer, he shed much of the rapacity and the foppishness sometimes found in his forebears, and some at least of the uncouthness. But the charge of cruelty remains, and cannot be altogether disproved. Yet the fault, where it existed, was the fault rather of the age than of the individual. The Governments which allowed such a tightening up of the Penal Code that it became at once criminal in its extent and farcical in its operation were much more to blame. For the attitude of the little king in his own ship-domain was inevitably influenced by that dark phenomenon which pervaded all walks of life. It is no part of our duty to explain here the reasons for the new views on Crime and Punishment. It is enough to place their existence on record, and to recall that the ordinary Captain perforce accepted them as his natural background.

Remembering this, are we going to brand the eighteenth-century Sea-officers, as a race, with the indelible mark of brutality and tyranny? The answer is, we are very sure, "we cannot". Let us, in common fairness, judge them by the standards of their own century, not by the "enlightenment" of ours. Their discipline was harsh to the verge of tyranny,

we are told. It was—or rather, if so enforced now it would
be. But then we do not kidnap our seamen by knocking
them on the head in the streets and in home-coming ships:
we do not keep them prisoners in dank and evil-smelling
dungeons, in which the Board of Agriculture would not now
allow us to keep our cattle. Nor do we, when we fail to
persuade enough of them of the joys of such a life, import all
the sweepings of the countryside, the riff-raff of the towns—
paupers, beggars, debtors and petty miscreants, and, even,
on occasions, full-blown criminals. It was not the sea-officer's
fault that such a crowd needed a tight hand, nor that he had
been taught to believe the only way to deal with them was
to flog them: he had certainly been brought up on corporal
punishment himself. Little wonder, too, if such a system
brought out in him any tendency to sadism which might
exist in his nature. It did that. Even allowing for the
exaggerations of the sensation-mongers, we have yet to face
the fact that there were undoubted sadists among the
eighteenth-century Captains, men who virtually murdered
their best hands by threats to flog the last down from the
yards, or who caused the last half of a flogging to be inflicted
upon an unfortunate whom the first half had killed. But
these creatures—and they really existed—are, again, the
extremes, whose very vileness has assured for themselves an
unenviable immortality.

What of the "means"—the thousand upon thousand of
ordinary good-hearted, god-fearing folk from country house
or parsonage—who have penetrated neither to the history
book or on to the films? In education neglected, by
upbringing rough, they were the products of a dark age of
materialism: they were born into a bad system, and they
died in it. But these men were our own forefathers: class for
class, as we have seen, they were branches of the very same
trees. Are we going to believe that they were, in their inmost
natures, so much more degraded than ourselves? If we have
any pride, if we have any of that mental balance which our

vaunted education should surely have given us, we shall, without any hesitation, answer, "No!".

## THE COMMANDER

This officer has a history neither so long nor so picturesque as his senior. As his name implies, so long as his job was still a "post" he was always in command of a ship: was, in fact, nothing more than an inferior sort of captain, who commanded a ship—at first a merchantman—too small to warrant the inclusion of both a Captain for fighting and a Master for navigation.

On the outbreak of the Civil War, the Parliament lost so many officers that they had to import extensively from the Merchant Service. Some such importees, like Lawson and Badiley, rose to the top because they were, in every sense, good material. But others were not so good; and in 1652 we find Penn writing to Cromwell and recommending that it would be advisable to place real fighting men in command of hired merchant ships, since their own Masters, if left in charge, showed little inclination to risk their ships in action. This was but natural: the Merchant Skipper, the world over, is nurtured on the principle that his first duty is to his owners, to bring their ships home safely. But that principle is not so good in war, and after the Battle of the Ness, when Penn's worst fears were realized, his advice was taken, and the officers thus put into hired ships were the prototypes of all subsequent Commanders.

At first the usual title was "Commander and Master", which is logically the more correct order, since command was, and always has been, considered a more important function than the mere control of the navigation. Indeed, "Commander" implied, even then, a Commission, while the Master was appointed by Warrant. But, for some reason by no means clear, custom crystallized the phrase the other way about, and the post was always known as "Master and Commander". When, in common with all the rest, the post merged into substantive rank, it remained "Master and Commander".

The actual name dates from 1674, when it was laid down that no officer should command a Sixth-rate—the smallest type of Royal Navy ship—unless he had passed the examination for Master at the Trinity House. Thus the title, clumsy though it is, is exactly descriptive of the facts. The officer concerned was actually both Master *and* Commander of his ship. Fifth-rates and above were "Post-Ships"—that is, ships entitled to carry both a Captain and a Master: and this classification remains substantially true throughout the eighteenth century, though slight changes occur from time to time as to which ships were "post", and which were not.

This brings us to that interesting, if somewhat anachronistic modern term—"Post-Captain". The present writer, on hearing the words used by a naval officer of the present day— and its use is very common—has frequently enquired of the speaker what precisely he means by it. The answers which he has received vary rather widely. Some have said, "Beyond all doubt a naval captain", or "not just a courtesy Captain, such as Commander, whose friends will introduce him in society as 'Captain X'; nor a merchant captain." Others again have answered, "A pretty senior captain"; or, "One who holds, or has held, command of a big ship." Or, lastly, some have said, after a moment's thought, "I suppose I mean it as just a synonym for 'Captain' ."

They are, all of them, right: or, perhaps it would be truer to say that, at one time or another, all these answers have been right. The origin of the term is easily grasped once we know what a Post-Ship was. In the days before Rank, a man who commanded a Post-Ship was a Post-Captain: while a man who commanded a *non*-Post-Ship— i.e. a man who was also his own Master—was only a Captain: a Captain that is, who, by virtue of commanding a ship, held the *office* of captain, but who, when Rank came in, found himself relegated to the *rank* of Commander. Thus "Post-

Captain" never became a rank: there was no need for it: it always remained a "post", the equivalent *rank* to Post-Captain—when Rank appeared—being, from the first, plain "Captain". And as Rank gradually overwhelmed Post, the term in its original sense, fell out of use in official circles, to remain only in naval parlance. Yet it survived for a long time even in official circles. In the first order of relative rank, as well as in the first uniform regulations (1748), the line of demarcation runs clear through the middle of the Post-Captains. "Officers who have taken Post three years" rank as Colonels, and have one sort of distinctive uniform: "all other Post-Captains" rank as Lieutenant-Colonels and have another sort of uniform. Rank is obviously ignoring the Post-Captain altogether. And, later in the eighteenth century, we find the term put to quite another use. It is sometimes employed to mark the distinction between "Flag"-Captains —the specialist understudies, or, later, advisers, to Flag-Officers, who have no ship of their own—and Post-Captains (i.e. Captains actually in command of Post-Ships). But the modern naval officer seldom, if ever, has this distinction in mind when he uses the term. So the modern (and collo-quial) usage would appear to be a survival from the days of "Post" when the term had a definite meaning, since taken from it by the victory of "Rank". Yet those officers are the most in the right who feel instinctively that "Post-Captain" should refer only to a man who commands a fairly large ship.

But, whatever be the rights in this matter, there is at least no question about it that the "Master and Commander" was the man who commanded a *non*-Post-Ship, and that "Master and Commander" became a definitive rank in the same way, and at much the same time, as the rest. It was the effective establishment of the hitherto nebulous rank of Second Master, and the order for his appointment, in the year 1746, to non-Post-Ships that first made the words "Master and" really redundant, in all but the very smallest ships. For henceforward even the Commander was to have a specialized member of the navigation branch in his ship, and so ceased to need a Master's qualification—indeed, ceased to be a Master. Yet the rank being already formed, and our natural conservatism still being in evidence, it was not until 1794 that the superfluous words were dropped from the official name of the rank, and it became for the first time, just "Commander".[1]

Even then, the Commander was never charged with the principal duty with which his name is associated today; he was not Second-in-Command, and general executive manager, of a big ship. He was still First-in-Command of a very small ship, and nothing more. It was as late as 1827 before those duties, hitherto invariably carried out by the First Lieutenant, became the Commander's birth-right. And when the change *was* made, it took the form of promoting the First Lieutenants who were doing the job to the rank of Commander, rather than of transferring Commanders into the post of Second-in-Command. The move was actually rather unpopular in naval circles until most of the First Lieutenants in the ships of the Navarino fleet were so promoted as a reward for their services.

Rank by then had clearly won the day, for, under a system of "Post" no authority could possibly have chosen such a contradictory name for a ship's Second-in-Command. And even as it is, polite foreigners sometimes lift their eyebrows in surprise when they learn that, in an English ship of a certain size, the Commander does not command her.

The fact is that here, and here only in the Service, two distinct ranks have emerged out of one office—the Command of a ship: for the only real difference between Captain and Commander, from the date of inception of the latter up to

---

[1] The title "Master and Commander" survives up to 1820 to denote certain officers in charge of packet-ships. But this is not the same thing, for these men were really Masters, appointed by warrant, as all Masters then were. They were not "Commission" Officers at all.

1827, lay in the size of the ship commanded—in the importance, that is, of the *post*. Indeed the French, who are justly
described as a logical people, have preserved throughout—
though at the expense of brevity—a nomenclature which
retains much of the original distinction. To this day their
*Capitaine de Vaisseau* is our "Captain", while our "Commander" is their *Capitaine de Frégate*.

### THE LIEUTENANT-COMMANDER

Just as the Commander slipped in between the Captain
and the Lieutenant, so, some two centuries later, as the
complexity of the naval machine continued to grow, there
gradually appeared a necessity for an intermediate step
between Commander and Lieutenant. But this did not
happen in the old "post" days. "Lieutenant", which originally implied "Lieutenant-Captain"—i.e. "the man who
takes the place of the Captain"—was sufficient for all needs.
Even when a small "post" of Captain might be filled by a
man with the new rank of Commander, the Lieutenant was
still a "Lieutenant-Captain" in the old sense, since, in that
sense, the Commander himself was Captain of the ship.
After 1827, it is true, a Lieutenant in a big ship might
well be called upon to take the place of a Commander in the
latter's capacity of Second-in-Command and, when he did
so, he became a lieutenant-commander even in the old
"post" sense. But by then all these titles were really ranks, so
that this is not the true reason for his appearance.

What actually happened was that the First Lieutenant, for
so long an outstanding individual among the rest of the
lieutenants, did contrive, at long last, to receive recognition
in the shape of a distinctive title and uniform. This set him
visibly, and in status, above his fellow lieutenants: in a word,
a new rank was created for him. But it was not under the
old name: it was just too late in the day for that. The real
glory of the old First Lieutenant departed when his principal
*post* went to the Commander: so that promotion, when it

came, came not to Lieutenants with important *posts*, but to Lieutenants with much *seniority*: Rank had won once again.

All through the nineteenth century, though he did not achieve a separate section for himself in the *Navy List*, the Senior Lieutenant did acquire most of the pleasanter perquisites of a new and more senior rank. Several times between 1830 and 1888 he received slight accretions of pay, and in the regulating 'seventies the Lieutenant of eight years' standing began to be distinguishable to the naked eye from his more junior brother. In 1875 he was allowed to add to his full-dress uniform the well-known "half-stripe" of quarter-inch gold lace between the two distinctive rings of half-inch braid which the ordinary lieutenant wore, and by 1877 he could wear it in undress uniform too. "Senior Lieutenant" had thus become a rank in all but name.

It was not, however, until March 1914 that the title as well as the perquisites came to him. In that year the substantive rank of Lieutenant-Commander was established, all Lieutenants of eight years' standing to be automatically promoted to it.

### THE LIEUTENANT

This famous sea-officer appeared on the naval stage later than the Captain, but earlier than the Commander. Like the former his name is of French and military origin.

We first find him appearing on shipboard in anything like his modern capacity about the year 1580, and his *raison d'être* in the general scheme of things is both clear and simple. He is to "understudy" the Captain, so that, in case of accident or illness, the ship may not be unprovided with a commanding officer. It would still have seemed a terrible thing in the 1580's if a *fighting* ship had been left in command of the Master and his ship-officers, with no "gentleman" on board. Further, there is already some vague idea about that he and his fellows are to provide a new series of captains when the present set fades out. For both these reasons he was, nominally, regarded as "gentle": though whether he always was so in practice is quite another matter.

But what he was *not*, in the sixteenth century, was the important ship-officer with a job of his own to do. That aspect came later, and its absence may account for a curious feature about these Elizabethan Lieutenants. They were not universally supplied to all ships—very far from it. An examination of the lists of officers serving in the anti-Armada fleet does not show very many of them—to be exact, five among the Queen's own ships (that is, about one in every seven ships) and *one* in all the rest. And even these scanty numbers diminish in the ensuing years, until in early Stuart times, they disappear almost completely. But the cause of this may be that, in that sad period of naval eclipse, the Captains were taking advantage of their right of appointment and not producing them in the flesh.[1]

Then, as we have seen, the authorities began to assert themselves, and the lieutenants quickly reappeared. In fact, in 1626, one lieutenant was to be allowed for in ships of the first three rates, while by 1635 there exists an embryonic list of them. But even then they do not seem very permanently established—there is a world of difference, in the seventeenth century, between what is laid down and what is done. Sir William Monson informs us that they have only recently been allowed in ships. This veteran of the Spanish War has a good deal of interest to say on the subject of Lieutenants, some of which is worth quoting, since it shows how little developed their functions still were.

"A Captain is to make choice of his lieutenant, and it is as necessary that he be a man of experience as himself." Here Sir William seems to side with the captains against the Admiralty on the question of selection. Nor, it may be noted, is there much trace of "training up the young officer". The Lieutenant was evidently, somehow or other, to be the ready-made article when appointed to his post.

[1] See above, p. 80.

Again, "the Master repines to have a Lieutenant above him, yet do I hold it fit to have a lieutenant". This is history repeating itself, the Master once more finding himself passed over, and relegated to third place.

After this, beyond saying that "a lieutenant is an employ-ment for a gentleman well-bred", and that he is "to be sent ashore on a message", Monson assigns no specific duty what-ever to him, where the work of every other officer on board is most succinctly defined. He ends with a little moral homily on the lieutenant's deportment to Masters, in which he lays it down that the former must never interfere with the navi-gation of the ship—a precept which became a rule that was still the ordinary procedure two centuries later.

Boteler treats his lieutenant in very much the same way: assigns him no work whatsoever, except in the case of the Captain's absence or death, and closes with another homily almost identical with Monson's. But he does at least imply that the Lieutenant is normally a young man. And even if he was not necessarily so in earlier days, there is consider-able evidence that, by 1642, his position was not only thoroughly established, but was regarded as the ordinary stepping-stone whereby a promising or well-backed young officer might attain to a Captain's post. Ships which had "gentlemen captains", both before and after the Great Rebellion, were usually the ones who had "gentlemen lieutenants" too; and, in these cases, probably, neither of the "Commission" officers knew much about ships. But this was not always the case. Sometimes—if the Captain were modest enough to know his own limitations and their dan-gers—he would be only too pleased to secure the services of a "tarpaulin" lieutenant, if only to relieve him of some of his less pleasant responsibilities.

After the Restoration, the energetic Mr. Pepys, becoming dissatisfied with the professional attainments, as well as the "dullness and heaviness" of the lieutenants as a body, got an examination instituted to test their qualifications, and in 1678 he "thanks God we have not half the throng of those of the bastard breed pressing for employment . . . they being conscious of their inability to pass their examination". What Pepys was doing, in fact, was—as usual—taking a vital step: he was transforming their office from that of Captain's understudy, pure and simple, into a post with a full job of independent work attached. Henceforth the Lieutenant, while still fulfilling his old function of replenishing the Captains' List, added to it a set of whole-time duties of his own.

By the end of the century, the number of lieutenants carried in the larger ships had increased to two, and, occasionally, three. The senior was already the "organizer and administrator in chief of the internal economy of the vessel": that is, the First Lieutenant of the eighteenth century and the Commander of our own day. The junior was already the officer who "is to have the particular Care of the seamen in the Exercise of the Small Arm": that is, the musketry officer.

Ned Ward, in 1707, has three of them in his *Wooden World*, the middle one being "a kind of spare top-mast that lies idle while the first is standing"—in which definition we still see lurking the old *locum-tenens* view of this officer. The other two are given ludicrously dreadful characters. The senior is an ambitious, swaggering coward who bullies all beneath him, but fawns on the Captain (whose death, however, he hopes for at an early date). The third is a "Hobbledehoy", or "Boy in Man's Cloaths", who suffers especially from the bullying of the Captain, leads the Press Gangs—their commander always had to hold a commission—beats "the poor Tars . . . like Dogs in a Church", and boasts loudly, yet falsely, of his feminine conquests.

Then, suddenly and rather unaccountably, Ned's vicious tongue relents. He concludes: "Now, after all that has been said, it must be owned you shall sometimes stumble upon a Lieutenant . . . of a very different make to what you find here, who, as they have been born to, and bred up in the Principles of Honour and Virtue, so they would not, for all the plunder of Alicant, stoop to any thing beneath their Birth and Character"; which description, from so acidulated a pen, along with the Lieutenant Bowling of the scarcely less venomous Smollett, gives us a welcome hint that the right breed was about.

As more lieutenants appeared on board, they simply fell in between the senior and the junior, keeping watch and taking charge of divisions very much as they do today. Their number quickly grew until by the middle of the century the Regulations allowed six in First and Second Rates, and proportionately fewer in smaller ships. By 1815 the maximum had increased to eight.

In these latter days we still find a sprinkling of rather "rough" lieutenants, like J. A. Gardner's[1] comically dressed Lieutenant Yetts, and that lovable "lower-deck" lieutenant, Jack Larmour, who was "sea-daddy" to Lord Dundonald. But, if we are to believe the latter, they were becoming rare in his day. Indeed, if we ask ourselves, as we did in the case of the captains, what manner of men were the lieutenants as a class, we must reply that they were of much the same material as their seniors, whose ranks the more fortunate or more deserving of them ultimately filled: with perhaps a rather larger proportion of "lower-deck" entry, who never struggled through the fine-meshed sieve of Influence which always tended to separate lieutenants from captains. There would naturally be, too, a rather larger proportion of disgruntled and down-at-heel officers who, starved of ambition, had "gone to seed" more than their luckier brethren, and who had, in a greater or lesser degree, substituted the stimulus of Gin for that of Ambition.

It was the Lieutenants who, as soon as there were enough

---

[1] Anyone who would view the late eighteenth-century sea-officers at first hand, should not fail to read his charming and racy *Reminiscences*, published by the Navy Records Society.

of them, formed that "mess" in the lower great cabin of the ship, which afterward came to be known as the "Ward-room Mess". The history of this well-known chamber is a complex one, and the mysteries connected with it have by no means been fully elucidated. This problem belongs rather to the study of ships than of men, and that must be our warrant for not entering into it here. In the early days of "Gentlemen Volunteers" it is probable that they shared a mess with the Lieutenants: in fact, it is so probable (in those class-conscious days) as to amount almost to a certainty that all the "gentry" on board lived together. Who the "Gentry" were differed, of course, in each ship. The Purser, for instance, might be the Lieutenant's brother or the Captain's cousin, in which cases he would certainly be allowed to set foot in the sacred circle. More cannot be said. Hard-and-fast rules, and regulations stipulating "ward-room rank", belong to the Napoleonic War period, and we shall discuss that status further when we follow the careers of the officers who were gradually aspiring to it.

### THE SUB-LIEUTENANT

Like that of Lieutenant-Commander, this title has always denoted a rank, having come into existence after "Post's" day was over. But the young gentlemen who now hold the rank have very interesting ancestors none the less. For their forebears are the "Mates"—and, almost exclusively, the "Master's Mates".

Now everybody knows what a "mate" is in ordinary life: and that is exactly what he was in the old ship. Every Head of Department among the Standing officers had his mate— his helper, second-in-command, and, if necessary, successor: sometimes, even, he had several. They were classed, in the old days, as "Inferior officers", and, when the various classes of appointment began to emerge, they were not appointed by warrant, still less by commission. They were, in fact, "ratings".

o

We cannot here enter into the early history of "mates" as a whole, but must content ourselves with following the fortunes of just one of them. As the Master was by far the most important of the Warrant Officers, so his own particular subordinates, the "Master's Mates", were more important than the other mates: so much so, in fact, that the post of Master's Mate gradually began to assume an attribute similar to that of Midshipman—it began to become a rung on the promotion ladder which led up from Lower deck to Quarterdeck: a stage in the acquisition of a "Commission". The process began at the end of the seventeenth century, and by the end of the eighteenth quite an appreciable percentage of officers who ultimately achieved a commission had served some of their apprenticeship as Master's Mates. It had already become, in fact, the post— and was rapidly becoming the rank—intermediate between Lieutenant and Midshipman.

The metamorphosis of the Master's Mate, from his old position of helper to the Master to his new one corresponding to Sub-Lieutenant, is, like all these changes, slow and often obscure. We shall catch a further glimpse of the early Master's Mate when we discuss the early Midshipman, but it was in the busy naval days of the eighteenth century that the thing was mainly done. It is clear that during all this century there were Master's Mates of both the old and the new kind. There was, even before the introduction of Second Masters into non-post ships in 1746 "an officer called Second Master who serves in lieu of a Mate"; who often, no doubt, carried out the navigational duties which properly belonged to the latter. Also, from 1731 onwards, Master's Mates were expected to keep journals in the same way as those embryo "Commission" officers, the Midshipmen. Again, Falconer, in 1769, tells us that two years' service as mate counts for promotion to lieutenant as an alternative to Midshipman's service. All these things show that Mates (or some of them) were already regarded in their new light. At the same time they were sometimes—perhaps more often than not—still the "makee-learn" masters of the old days.

In the last years of the eighteenth century, and especially during the long Revolutionary Wars, the confusion between the two sorts reached its zenith. The number of midshipmen who had passed the ordinary examination for lieutenant had become very great—much greater than the number of lieutenants' vacancies in the ships. The result was that many a "passed midshipman", especially if he commanded no influence—had to wait a weary time for a vacancy; indeed, often, never found one. Hence arose the practice of taking the examination for Master's Mate, which at least offered the consolation of a considerable rise in pay—from £2 15s. to £3 16s. But it was a gamble, because he ran a grave risk that the Authorities would interpret his move literally and side-track him permanently into the Master's branch, when he would never obtain the coveted commission. Yet things might fall out well, and then he would be promoted Lieutenant.

By the first years of the nineteenth century we find that the prefix "Master's" is usually dropped from the title of these ex-Midshipmen-Master's Mates, though retained in that of the true navigational ones. A little later—in 1824— a superior class of Petty Officer under the name of "Master's Assistant" was established, who was, in fact, in the Master's branch exactly what the Midshipman was in the Executive branch. From this time on the confusion caused by the mingling of midshipmen with the navigator's branch was remedied. In the same Order which established the Master's Assistant, the Volunteer of the Second Class was also introduced, corresponding, in the navigator's branch, to the executive First Class Volunteer. A portrait of one may be seen opposite page 96, above. In 1840, in the other camp, the position of the rather nebulous executive mate was regularized when the official title of "Mate" (unqualified) was given to the new executive rank established between Lieutenant and Midshipman. The result was the creation of two completely separate "ladders"—for the Executives, First Class Volunteer, Midshipmen, Mate, Lieutenant: for the Navigators, Second Class Volunteer, Master's Assistant, Second Master, Master.

We have thus reached, in the Executive branch, the substance—though not the nomenclature—which obtains today, for, in all but name, the First Class Volunteer is now the Naval Cadet, and the Mate (of 1840 creation) is the Sub-Lieutenant. As to the actual title of Sub-Lieutenant, it was originally invented by Earl St. Vincent in 1802, as a measure of relief to the overcrowded ranks of midshipmen. But it was only temporary then, and soon died out again, the term "mate" being retained in the sense explained above. It was only in 1861 that the "Mate" became officially "Sub-Lieutenant". He was then given his familiar "distinction lace" of one half-inch ring, thus causing Lieutenants, Commanders, and Captains—up till then distinguished by one, two and three rings respectively—all to move up one, and so to acquire the numbers they wear today. Opposite page 188 we see a Captain and a Commander wearing their earlier —and smaller—allowance of rings.

By an odd turn of Fortune's wheel, that was not the last of Mates in the Navy. In 1912, as a part of that wider twentieth-century policy of throwing all professions open to all-comers, and of giving all, as nearly as possible, an equality of opportunity, the Admiralty found it "desirable that further provision should be made so as to enable Warrant Officers and Petty Officers to attain the rank of Lieutenant at an earlier age than is possible under present regulations". A selection was therefore to be made of promising youngsters, who were, after careful preparation, to be made "Acting Mates", and, after suitable courses, confirmed in the substantive rank of "Mate"; then to be promoted Lieutenant along with the Sub-Lieutenants of the Osborne-Dartmouth-Midshipman variety; and so to merge into the ordinary flow of executive officers.

The name, but not the breed, disappeared again in 1931. Since then, instead of becoming Acting-Mate and Mate, the candidate became at once Acting-Sub-Lieutenant and Sub-Lieutenant. There was, indeed, no point in creating the distinction between Mate and Sub-Lieutenant which was so soon to be obliterated in the stage of Lieutenant, and there were obvious social advantages in mixing the young officers from the lower deck at the earliest possible moment with their new quarterdeck associates. The only possible regret to the historically-disposed mind is that Authority did not decide to call them *all* mates, and so to restore to the Sub-Lieutenant his old—and undeniably more picturesque—name. It is something of a tragedy—albeit a minor one—that neither the grand old Master nor his Mate figures any longer in His Majesty's Ships of War.

In the old days the "Mates" messed and lived in the after-cockpit on the Orlop, that deck on or below the water level which never saw the wholesome light of day. There, too, dwelt the Midshipmen, and had the pleasure of seeing their chests and other furniture used as operating tables in times of action, when the After Cockpit became the Surgery, or, alternatively, of feeding off the operating table in times of peace. And though the "Gun-room", which is now their home, was then allotted to the gunner and the Volunteers, it is significant, as a further illustration of Service conservatism, that, even then, *mutatis mutandis*, the Mate was "Sub of the Gunroom".

THE MIDSHIPMAN

Strictly speaking, the Midshipman should not appear in this chapter, since he is not—and never was—either a Commission or a Warrant Officer. Once an ordinary "rating", he is now an "Officer under Instruction". But as we do not propose to deal with ratings, as such, there is nowhere else to place him: while his inclusion here is still further justified by the fact that he took his place, long ago, in the ordinary line of promotion to the quarter-deck.

We have told, in the chapter on "Supply", something of the Midshipman's career, in so far as he played his part in the story of Entry and Training. Here we shall confine ourselves mainly to his post on board: what he once was, and how he came to be what he now is.

We mentioned the constructive proposal of Nathaniel Boteler, who, in his *Dialogues* stresses the importance of having a post on board from which future Captains and Lieutenants may be selected. His candidate for that post was not, however, the Midshipman, but the Corporal, then a comparatively new "inferior officer" charged with Ships' Police duties. Speaking of the Corporal's office, Boteler's Admiral remarks, "and withal it may lead, in a fit way, towards the making of a Lieutenant, and therefore I shall advise at sea that these corporals might be gentlemen."

It was a most perspicacious suggestion, which, being made about 1634, was well ahead of its time, and so came to nought. Yet, in essence, it was exactly what ultimately came to pass: only the Corporal was not the lucky man to receive this rise in status. That fortune fell to the Midshipman.

This elusive officer's early history is still somewhat obscure. Though he had unquestionably been known on ship-board for a very long time, the first actual mention of him there would seem to occur in Captain John Smith's *Accidence for Young Seamen*, published in October, 1626. This reference to him, together with another in the following year in a letter from Pennington to Buckingham, shows that he was already high in the hierarchy of old ship "officers". "All our pilots," says Pennington, "master's mates, middshippe men, quarter-masters and other principal officers." This does not mean, let us remember, that he was necessarily regarded then as an officer in the modern sense: but that he was already a man who held an important "office" on board ship.

We can even trace him, by inference, back into Elizabeth's reign, for, copied into Pepys's *Naval Precedents*, is a paper entitled "Ancient Customs of Queen Elizabeth's time", which contains his name in a list of "pillage-shares". He receives five—more than anybody on board save only the Captain, the Master and the Master's Mate: more even than the principal "Standing Officers"—Gunner, Boatswain and Carpenter. Boteler, too, has an identical list, which evidently comes from the same source—ancient custom. Thus, though neither document containing the information is itself Elizabethan, it is really quite safe to regard them as proof of the midshipman's existence on board in Queen Elizabeth's day.

There is, indeed, a moral certainty that we should go much further back still for his origin. In a Yorkshire Assize Roll of 36 Edward III there was presented for felonious homicide "Johannes Midschipman de Whitby". This may be a proper name, or it may be a descriptive one. If the latter, we know that the post existed as early as 1362: if the former, it is tolerably certain that it existed even earlier: for surnames cannot grow out of nothing, and the chances are evidently strong that it was the man's ancestor who was the midshipman, and that he had handed the patronymic down to homicidal John.

But it is Captain John Smith who first throws any real light on the subject. In the *Accidence* we learn that there were normally two "midshipps men" in a ship, and that they were, or had been, the Master's immediate subordinates. The rather difficult passage in which their names occur would seem to show that they were even then in the process of having Master's Mates put over their heads, in much the same way as, we have seen, the Captain and his Lieutenant were put over the Master's. But they must have been steady men, upon whom considerable responsibility was placed, or they would not have received so large a share of "pillage".

The only definite duty allotted to them by Smith is to "see the tops and yeards well manned with stones, fire-pots and brass bals, to enter them in the shrouds". But this passage, in conjunction with the information that they "ought to take charge of the first prize" perhaps gives us a clue as to their principal duty. It almost looks as though they were responsible, in Smith's time, for the whole process of "entering" the enemy, both in regard to preparation, as actual leaders of the boarding-party and as commanders of the prize when taken. Such dangerous and important duties would go far to explain the high remuneration which they received in the successful event.

We have seen the step forward which they made under the Commonwealth, and also what Pepys did for them.[1] The former made the post of midshipman the jumping-off place for a commission in theory: the latter made it so (to a great extent) in practice also.

Yet the older "rating" called Midshipman still remained. So much confusion, as a result, has existed in people's minds over the subsequent identity of the various groups collected under this title that it is worth while to attempt some disentanglement.

By the time that Pepys retired from the naval scene he had left three distinct types of midshipman, with—if we give them their full names, ultimately attained—three distinct titles:—Midshipman, Midshipman Ordinary, and Midshipman Extraordinary. Of these, the first must be further subdivided into two classes—Midshipman (old rating) and Midshipman ("Officer under instruction"). These last two were not separate posts: only some of the occupants of the post of plain "Midshipman" were of one class and some were of the other. Let us take them separately.

[1] See above, pp. 82 and 86.

(1) *Midshipman* (*old rating*).—These were, of course, the direct descendants of Captain John Smith's "midshipps men"—ratings belonging to the Master's little family—and they had certain well-defined jobs to do on board. They survived for a long time—certainly to the end of the eighteenth century. There was obviously no age-limit in their case, and some of them were very far from being of those tender years usually associated in the lay mind with the "Middy". An example of this type is—probably—Billy Culmer, who is described at some length in J. A. Gardner's *Reminiscences*. In 1791, we are told, he was fond of boasting that he was the oldest Midshipman in the Navy, having been made one by Samuel Hood in 1757. But we say "probably" because it remains conceivable that even poor Billy had once been a real "young gentleman", who hoped to become a lieutenant, and was merely an extreme instance of what happened to those who commanded no influence. Another well-known example of this type is that other "homicidal John"—Midshipman Kirke—who, in 1779, was tried and executed for the murder of his mother, a bum-boat woman, on the deck of his own ship. Yet another, perhaps—a relic surviving into a new era—was the unfortunate Midshipman Vallack. A writer, who signs himself "Lambda" in the *United Service Journal* in 1831, tells us that, when he was shipmate with Vallack in 1822, the latter's head was almost white, and his age about 65. He has scathing comments to make on a system which permitted such a thing. It is all wrong, he urges—and modern opinion will support him—that, upon the cry "Young Gentlemen", such an apparition should totter forth. And lastly, Hunt's pathetic figure, whose sad eyes and sunken cheeks faced us on page 140, is certainly no longer in his first youth, nor likely, so far as we can see, to earn promotion in the near future. Yet both these last two cases, also, may once have belonged to another class of Midshipman.

(2) *Midshipman (Officer under instruction)*. These were the "new ratings", i.e. the young men or boys on their way to the quarterdeck who occupied the post *en passant*. In theory at any rate, and sometimes perhaps in practice, such lads could only occupy the position if capable of doing the work attached to it. All the eighteenth-century *Regulations* are decisive to the verge of fierceness on the point. "Midshipmen", they declare, shall not be rated "till they have served four years and are in all respects qualified for it". A glance at the wage-tables of the period shows the reason for this edict. The "Midshipman" drew as much as £2 5s. od. a month. The "Midshipman Ordinary", who will be discussed next, drew but £1 4s. od. The point of the order was to prevent nepotist Captains from pushing their young hopefuls into skilled and responsible positions which they were quite unfit to fill.

(3) *Midshipman Ordinary*.—This, and the next, were Pepys's particular inventions. It is made perfectly plain, from 1731, when the Regulations begin, who this personage is. "None are to be rated Midshipman Ordinary but such as have served Volunteers by Order". The post is, in fact, the private perquisite of the *official* nominee: from 1676 to 1729 of the "King's Letter Boy", and thenceforward of the College-Volunteer. It follows from this that, whereas some "Midshipmen" were "makee-learn officers" and some were ordinary ratings, *all* Midshipman Ordinary were— or were supposed to be—"makee-learns". In 1816 the "rating" of Midshipman Ordinary was abolished, as being obsolete, and the "College Volunteer" was thereafter to be rated (when qualified) direct to the post of Midshipman. In theory this should have worked, but in practice, it seems, the "College" product, still none too popular with the Captains (who still did the rating) began to find himself pinched out again, being now in direct competition with the captains' own protégés. "Lambda"

tells us that, in this period, the College-trained product, when he did get his promotion, was called "Admiralty Midshipman", as opposed to "Ship Midshipman": that, once, he was universally despised, but now (1831) he was regarded as a very useful acquisition in a ship, since all the dirty work of all the "Ship Midshipmen" could be loaded off upon him! The result was that the Admiralty had to intervene once more, in 1833, in a fashion which we shall relate shortly.

(4) *Midshipmen Extraordinary.*—We have seen how Pepys drew his sharp knife clean through the original "Volunteers", the point of severance being at sixteen years old.[1] We followed the youngsters before: now we must look at the older men.

These, in 1676 when Pepys made his cut, were themselves of two distinct classes. There were, first, the real "amateurs"; the "gentlemen"; volunteers mostly for a day; "men about town", and dilettanti, for whom the practical Pepys had but little use. These were, to all intents and purposes, pinched out altogether. But there was a fairly large class of other, and far more deserving, men called by the rather un-English-sounding title of "Reformadoes". The name was borrowed from the army, and was applied to a military man who lost his place when his regiment was "re-formed" or disbanded. In the Navy the Reformado was the corresponding individual—the "quarterdeck officer" whose command had expired, as it always did, at the end of the commission; and who was therefore "out of work".

The Reformado received a ready sympathy from Pepys who created the strange post of "Midshipman Extraordinary" to accommodate him temporarily. For "Half-Pay", we must remember, was still in the cradle. No one holding less than a senior captain's post was entitled to it; and there was nothing else for the junior officer. Yet the

[1] See p. 83.

innovation arose not only from motives of charity. To
Pepys's tidy mind it was bad that anybody, even so worthy
a character as the Reformado, should be on board without
a definite "post". Irregularities had occurred: reformadoes,
serving in a ship merely as volunteers, had been promoted
captain on occasions over the heads of serving lieutenants.
Such a thing must not be allowed, and so important did
Pepys think it that he created a post with (apparently) no
defined duties attached to it in order not to violate the sacred
"post" principle. Better a sinecure than an irregularity.

As Midshipmen Extraordinary were, by hypothesis,
commission officers, often of some standing, they too
were obviously not youths. They had usually been employed
as Lieutenant, or even Master and Commander. Nor,
normally, did they mess with the Mates and Midshipmen; but probably with the Captain or the Lieutenants
according to their status.

Of these four classes of Midshipman, the second—the
officer under instruction—and the third—the College-bred
officer under instruction—soon became the most important:
especially the former, since the numbers of the latter were
always so small. The first class, as we have seen, was
gradually edged out, while the *raison d'être* of the fourth
sort ceased when Half-Pay became an adequate reality.

The term, "Midshipman Extra", however, survived into
the 1830's, but by then its meaning had changed. In the
memorandum of 1833, the Admiralty lays it down that,
if any "Admiralty" or "College" Volunteer fails to be
found a midshipman's place by his Captain, the Admiralty
will appoint him "Midshipman Extra, and he shall take the
place of one seaman". In this rather confusing way the
Admiralty stepped in to protect the interests of the College
Volunteer, deprived, since 1816, of his "reserved" post of
Midshipman Ordinary. The new Midshipman Extra is
thus the exact counterpart of the eighteenth century Midshipman Ordinary. But it was further laid down that all

other Volunteers should have places found for them as Midshipmen Extra, after four years' service. This was a distinct departure, occasioned by the post-war congestion, and was important to the aspirant, who could now be sure of becoming at least a midshipman in reasonable time. But both these new Midshipmen Extra are very far removed from the old one, who now, as a Half-Pay Commander or Lieutenant, did not go to sea at all but was supposed to be provided for by his Half-Pay.

Regulations soon began to bind the important classes. In 1677 Charles II issued orders "for the qualification of persons to enable them to become lieutenants". Three years at sea, of which one was to be served as Midshipman, was then laid down, as well as the oft-broken age-limit of 20, a certificate of good conduct and ability, and an examination conducted by three officers. These rules form the basis of all subsequent developments in the Midshipman's history. In 1703 the qualifying period was raised to six years, and in 1728 the Examination for Lieutenants was taken over by the Navy Board. But these are mere details, and they did not prevent the perpetration of many scandalous practices and subterfuges. It was, perhaps, the age-limit which proved to be the greatest source of temptation to the unscrupulous. Sir George Eliot tells us, that, in the year 1800, the porter at the door of the Navy Office kept a stock of uncompleted birth certificates, and filled them up "while you waited" at the fixed charge of five shillings.

That a very large majority of Midshipmen were the counterparts of the modern "Snotty" by 1748 is clear from the wording of the official order which put them into uniform among the very first batch of officers to receive it. "Persons", says the order, "acting as Midshipmen should likewise have a uniform cloathing in order to distinguish their Class to be in the Rank of Gentlemen." They already enjoyed the significant distinction of being allowed to "walk the quarterdeck", and, very soon after this, contemporary literature makes it clear that, in common parlance at least, the word "midshipman" is often used to mean "any officer under instruction". The whole of Falconer's article on him, for instance, is obviously based on this generic sense of the term. It is, he says, "the station in which a young volunteer is trained . . . . to qualify for a sea-officer". And again, "On his first entry into a ship of war, every Midshipman has several disadvantageous circumstances to encounter". Falconer knew, of course, that an aspirant did not enter a ship for the first time as a midshipman: he says so. But that does not prevent him from using the term elsewhere to cover the whole period of probation. Likewise Raigersfield, referring to his own position on his first voyage in 1783, calls himself "the least midshipman—indeed the least boy —in the ship", knowing full well that he was *officially* no such thing, but a "Captain's Servant". This "generic" use of the term, indeed, may almost be said to denote, in the late seventeen-hundreds, a fifth class of midshipman.

Under the heading of "Sub-Lieutenant" we have seen some of the Midshipman's tribulations in the matter of postponed promotion. So severe were they, in fact, that they nearly led to a distinct rank of "Passed Midshipmen", which is really what St. Vincent's first Sub-Lieutenant was. It soon died out, but even so we are almost justified in adding to our list of groups in which the name of "Midshipman" occurs, yet a sixth category, the "Passed Midshipman" of the Revolutionary and Napoleonic wars.

There is little to add to his story. He has not changed appreciably in status during the last hundred and forty years. As soon as the principle was established that he was there to learn how to become a commission officer, the only change in the nature of his work was the change—immense, it is true—in what was considered necessary for him to learn. And that is a side of the question which does not concern us here.

### THE NAVAL CADET

This, the most junior of the "Officers under Instruction", has already received, in the chapters on Entry, Training and Education, almost all the notice to which he is entitled. But a very few words should be added in regard to him as a person who holds a post on shipboard. He does not now go to sea, save in a training ship of his own, but of course he used to do so.

His name, like so many of the others, is military in origin and French in etymology. "Cadet" was an army term for a long time before it came officially into the Navy, which was, as we have seen, in 1843.

But the term "Naval Cadet" itself is met with quite frequently before that date. Even as early as 1769 we find Falconer in his *Marine Dictionary* describing his Midshipman as "a sort of Naval Cadet", though all he means by the phrase is, probably, "the person in the Navy who corresponds to the Cadet in the Army". In the 1820's and 1830's, however, the name, in popular parlance, was rapidly ousting "Volunteer".

His true ancestors, of course, were the Volunteers— Pepys's King's Letter Boys, or Volunteers per Order, the "College Volunteers" of the eighteenth and early nineteenth centuries, and the First Class Volunteers of 1794 and onwards: and, as well, all those variously-named young gentlemen of earlier days who had to be rated to *some* post, in the ships' books, to whom we have given the generic name of "Captain's Servants".

During the eighteenth century, he slung his hammock, in, or just outside, the Gunroom, aft on the Lower Deck, where the Gunner kept his eye on him. It was only when he passed for Midshipman that he descended to the after-cockpit to join the heterogeneous collection which occupied that not ill-named compartment.

His *raison d'être* on board was, of course, to learn as

much as he could about seamanship, and all that it became a Sea-Officer to know. But how much he learnt must have depended largely on the interest taken in him by the Captain and the First Lieutenant; and his personal comfort probably depended almost entirely on his relationship (if any) to the senior officers.

# CHAPTER XIII

# "WARRANT" OFFICERS (EXECUTIVE)

WE come next to the old "ship-officers" who originally ruled the roost before the "Fighters" came, and sank later to a humbler position. Yet these men although not of "commission" rank, never quite lost the claim to be "executive".[1] And so, when the Regulations of the eighteenth century began to lay down the order of command on board ship, in the event of accidents, we find that the four principal "ship-officers" figured in it as of right. After 1746 the Second Master—the understudy of the most important of them— also slipped in, and the "Order of Command" became— Captain, Lieutenants (First, Second, Third, etc.), Master, Second Master, Boatswain, Gunner, Carpenter. No one else is mentioned. What happened when, or if, all the above became casualties at once we are not told. The point to notice is that the other "officers"—even old-standing personalities like the Purser and the Surgeon—were regarded as being altogether too "civilian" to be considered in relation to the command of a ship of war. And the same principle holds to this day. The "order of command" of a ship goes straight through the "executives" from top to bottom, right down through commissioned, warrant and petty officers to ordinary ratings. Non-executives, even though of flag-rank, do not figure at all in the order.

This chapter deals, then, with the old warrant executives

[1] Save one—the Carpenter—in quite modern times. See below, p. 238.

—the Master, the Boatswain, the Gunner and the Carpenter. But there is a clear division between the first-named, and the rest. The Master, as we have seen,[1] though of much higher status on board than the other three, was by no means so permanent a feature of the ship. He was an officer in "inconstant employ", and he was appointed to a ship—as Commission officers were—for a commission and not for all time. The other three, however, were the officers in "constant employ"—the old "standing" officers—and normally had nothing to do with ship-commissions. The Master was a man of such intrinsic importance that he deserves a sub-heading to himself. The "Standing Officers" may be considered, for the most part, together.

## THE MASTER

Throughout his long career, from the Middle Ages when he was ruler of the merchant-ship not yet specialized for war, until his disappearance in the latter half of last century, the Master always contrived to retain one thing—the control of the ship's navigation. In the early days, when that duty was obviously the most important one, it was natural that the man who performed it should be the man who commanded the ship. But when the "gentlemen fighters" arrived, it was equally natural—in a ship of war—that he should be superseded, protesting, first by the Captain and then by an ever-increasing number of lieutenants. But he never fell further than this; and, what is more, in his own department he held his own to the last.

His social status too improved with the years. From the bluff merchant-skipper of Tudor times, he developed under the Stuarts into something of a specialist; 1675 was a great year for him, for it was then that he received substantial recognition in the shape of half-pay—before anybody else save a few captains. But also in that year there came into existence for him the possibility of a really good education.

[1] See p. 124.

In 1673 Charles II had established by Letters Patent a foundation in the already existing Christ's Hospital for "forty poor boys . . . to be taught and instructed in the art of navigation". In 1675, under the enthusiastic eye of the ubiquitous Pepys (himself a Governor of Christ's Hospital) a regular scheme of apprenticeship in the Navy was drawn up for these "poor boys". The Navigators thus acquired facilities for a good technical education a full half-century before any other officers. Nobody ever attempted to do any such thing for the "standing officers", so that the gulf between them—especially in social respects—tended to widen thereafter. Further the Master always had behind him the very strong support furnished by the Trinity House, without whose certificate he could not qualify for his post.

Though he was still appointed by Warrant from the Navy Office, and not by Commission from the Admiralty, these advantages gave him in many respects the standing of those who enjoyed the latter mode of appointment. Thus—in addition to his resemblance to them in the matter of moving from commission to commission—he was much nearer to them than to the other "Warrants" in the matter of pay; being throughout, in fact, only less favoured than the Captain in this respect. His average eighteenth-century wages were 6s. 6d. per diem, as compared with the Captain's £1 and the Lieutenant's 5s.: and he received more than twice as much as any other warrant officer on board. To measure a man's status in his profession by the amount of his pay may be crude: yet it has a way of being realistic. But in some respects besides the humbler method of his appointment he lagged behind the commission officers. He did not, for instance, receive the recognition of a naval uniform in 1748, along with the commission officers and the midshipmen; and, though he first went into one in 1787, it was not distinctive, since it was common to himself and all the other warrant officers. Still, that he was well ahead of them in other respects is shown by the fact that he was the first of

all the newcomers who, towards the end of the eighteenth
century, found their way, one by one, into the exclusive
precincts of the "Ward Room Mess". It is not possible to peg
down to a single year the date when this took place. It was
probably a gradual business, depending upon custom and
the individual breeding and antecedents of particular
Masters. But, by the turn of the century, the thing has gone
beyond custom, and he is officially referred to as being a
"Warrant Officer of Ward Room rank"; which certainly
means that he had already been so in practice for some time.
In the early eighteen-hundreds, too, he received yet more
"social" promotion at the hands of Authority. In the year
of Trafalgar he was "made eligible to become a Lieutenant":
in 1807 he was put into a distinctive uniform of his own;
and, by an order in Council of September 28, 1808, the rank
of Lieutenant was conferred upon Masters. They were to
be "junior to all Lieutenants, but taking precedence of
Surgeons". This does not mean that they *became* Lieutenants.
The Order in question is using the term "rank" in its older
and more relative sense. All that is meant is that they now
"rank with, but after, Lieutenants". The extinction of the
old name was not yet.

But it was not far off. His long innings was nearly over.
Though he had not outlived his usefulness, the day of the
"Officer Specialist" was at hand, and the Master's position,
half-way between Commission and Warrant as it was, was
rapidly becoming anomalous. He had been, in one sense,
all too successful in retaining his monopoly in navigation.
The "Gunnery Officer" could slip almost imperceptibly
over the head of the gunner: so that the latter could fit in
without undue loss of dignity under that specialist, when
the nineteenth century brought him into being. But with
the Master it was different. When the new Navigation
Specialist came, as come he must, the old Master had to go.

He went: but not without achieving a further and considerable rise in position first. In 1831 his appointment was

at length transferred from the failing grasp of the Navy
Board to the Admiralty itself, thus making him in yet another
respect like a commission officer: in 1832, the few very
senior Masters, who were employed in flagships, and called
"Masters of the Fleet", were given Commanders' uniforms
and rank: and in 1843 the ordinary Master came to be
appointed by Commission, instead of by Warrant. He was,
in all respects, a Commission Officer at last. Also we have
seen how a regular series of ranks, exactly analogous to those
of the executive branch, grew up behind him,[1] leaving him,
as the position which he had reached in 1808 indicated,
on the level of a Lieutenant. In 1864, when his sands were
all but run out, he received one more advance. For such
as had served fifteen years as Master a new rank was created,
called Staff Commander, while the "Masters of the Fleets"
were now given the rank of Staff Captain. All the branch
had, too, in the previous year, received a distinctive stripe
of light blue to be worn between the gold rings on the arm.
But this they did not retain for long. In 1879 it was taken
from them and given to the Naval Instructors.

Yet in 1867 came the beginning of the end, when all the
other old titles were finally abolished, and a new set instituted. The Master himself now became "Navigating-
Lieutenant"; the Second Master, Navigating Sub-Lieutenant; the Master's Assistant, Navigating Midshipman, and
the Second Class Volunteer (already once changed to Second
Class Naval Cadet in 1863), "Navigating Cadet".

The "Navigating Branch", as a distinct entity, continued
up to the year 1883; but after that no additions were made
to the bottom of the list. The result was that the branch
died a lingering death, as Age and Retirement claimed its
victims. The last Navigating Officer of the old school was
Staff Captain Moulton, retired on August 30, 1913.

So vanished the officer with the longest continuous record
in the Navy. He did vanish—completely, and not only in

[1] See p. 211.

name.[1] The Specialist Navigator—the "Lieutenant (N)" or the "Lieutenant-Commander (N)" of our own day—is something very different from the old Master. The former is an executive commissioned officer with a status exactly similar to that of all other executive commissioned officers save for the fact that he happens to have spent more time in the study of Navigation. But this is a description which does not fit the old Master at all. So it is a much truer statement of the facts to say that the Lieutenant (N) took his place than to try and show that the Master became the Lieutenant (N). Such a view of the change would be true enough in the civilian branches: the transition from Purser to Paymaster, for instance, is really only a change of name. But it is not so with the Master: no one ever did, and no one ever will, quite replace him in the Service. So let us give him, for an epitaph, the verdict of Ned Ward, not too ill-natured for once: "He is a Seaman every bit of him, and can no more live any while on dry land than a Lobster; and but for that he is obliged sometimes to make a step ashore, to new-rigg, and to lay in a cargo of fresh Peck and Tipple, he cares not though he never see it."

## THE "STANDING" OFFICERS

We remember our prominent statesmen, our brilliant generals and admirals, our great pro-consuls, our mighty captains of industry. But we tend, unless we are very careful, to forget the quiet work and patient care of the lesser lights —the civil servants, the regimental and ship officers, the under-managers and the head-clerks. It is not surprising: they have stolen a far smaller proportion of the thunder, and monopolized a far smaller share of the lime-light. History knows this: and it does not so much neglect them as take them for granted: which, in a small way, is almost a compliment, for it means that, while things run smoothly, there

[1] Just one exception remains, however. The *rank* has vanished, but a *post* of "Master of the Fleet" survives in the Mediterranean Fleet.

is not a great deal to say about them: it is only when the
breakdown occurs that they are sought for in the dusk of
their well-earned obscurity, and submitted to the hard light
of criticism.

All these things are true of these, our "Standing Officers":
and so seldom do they emerge on to the pages of history
that we are forced to conclude—and conclude, we are sure,
very rightly—that their ordinary standard of efficiency was
quite remarkably high. Consider for a moment the enormous handicap which invariably faced them in the material
which they had to handle: the constantly changing personnel,
often of indifferent stuff, and always untrained when they
took it in hand; with not less than 50 per cent, and sometimes as much as 80, pressed into a job they detested: honest
in the main, yet with a fair sprinkling of good-for-nothings,
and even minor criminals among them: leading a life of
squalor in unhygienic quarters; ill-fed and ill-clothed;
refused leave, and most of those simple indulgences which
make life tolerable: hard-worked and often ill-treated. This
heterogeneous collection of all sorts, classes and conditions
of essentially "short-service men" had to be welded—every
time—into a highly organized and trained crew, capable
of accomplishing a host of crafts each difficult in itself, and
of a nature very different from its neighbour. Truly, the
miracle is, not that the welders occasionally failed, but that
they ever succeeded!

For it was they and their mates who did the donkey-work.
The quality of the commission officers made, of course, a
tremendous difference, but it was the standing officers above
all who did the licking into shape—"licking" is indeed the
word. As the mainstay to the mast, they were the mainstay
to the whole system of ship economy.

Each, from the earliest times, had his own particular
coterie on board, his tried and exclusive little "clique" of
mates and permanent assistants. These small "families"
formed the core of each department, with a well-marked

allegiance to their own immediate chief—a fact of which
newly-commissioned captains often found cause to complain: for it was a loyalty which tended to cut clean across
the authority of his "commission", and to confine itself
exclusively to the "Ship" as a unit. Even the new spirit
which is visible in the *Regulations and Instructions* of 1731
did little to change this. Rather it confirmed, and made
it official: though it did do something towards breaking up
the family life of the departments when the ship was "in
ordinary", by appointing most of the "standing" crew from
the dockyards.

The custom was, as soon as the crew of a new commission
was safely on board, and before ever the ship proceeded to
sea, for the Captain to call together his First Lieutenant,
Master, Boatswain, Gunner and Carpenter, and to proceed
to "rate" the Ship's Company—assign each man, that is,
into that department where it was conceived that he would
produce the best results. Thereafter it became the duty of
each Head of Department, with his assistants' aid, to make
them into good seamen as quickly and as efficiently as
possible.

Another significant fact is noticeable in all these eighteenth-
century *Regulations*. The detailed instructions to almost
all the "officers" whose names figure therein, open with a
statement as to how they came to be there and by whom
appointed: what, in fact, is their authority. But not so the
"Standing officers". In their case alone nothing is said about
their authority: it is tacitly assumed that, since the ship is
there, they are there too. So we cannot tell from the *Regulations* who did appoint them. Oddly enough, in the
eighteenth century, that power resided, not with the Navy
Board, but with the Admiralty, who appointed them, of
course, by "warrant".

Towards the end of the century, when fleets became
numerous and the exigencies of the Service far more complicated, the inconvenience of always retaining these trusty

folk in the same ship began to increase. It would clearly be very wasteful, for instance, when the demand for efficient gunners was great, and the supply none too good, to leave a really experienced one in a ship laid up temporarily, either "in ordinary" or for repairs. So, gradually, the old custom of complete immovability was relaxed, especially perhaps in the case of the Gunner, whose duties during "repairs" would not be quite so indispensable as those of carpenter and boatswain. Thus in the last decade of the century, we find William Richardson making two or three moves in the course of his career as gunner: though even so he does not move nearly as often as the commission officers. Moreover, a standing officer could always remain in his old home if he wished. As late as 1808 the *Regulations* expressly state that no Warrant Officer is to be removed from his ship without his own consent. Even a Flag-Officer had no power to shift him.

They all three went into uniform together, along with the Master, the Surgeon and the Purser when the "Warrant-Officer's" dress was instituted in 1787, and they all achieved ultimately the *possibility* of promotion to commissioned rank when, in 1864, the titles of Chief Boatswain, Gunner and Carpenter were instituted. But they were still well behind the Master in the race, for, with them, the promotion was not automatic for the whole branch, but only the reward for the outstanding ones: whereas the *whole* of the Master's branch achieved the status of the Commissioned Officer before it disappeared. All the Commissioned Warrant Officers can now, however—in theory at least—rise to Commander's rank, though in practice very few do.

Little separate treatment is now necessary, yet we can scarcely leave them without some brief account of their various vicissitudes.

The Gunner, by far the last of the three to appear, and once the least important of them, must come first, since he is placed above the others in the modern *Navy List*. Arriving,

as we have seen, with the Big Gun, he quickly and naturally
became a personage on board, keeping pace with the importance of his special duties. He suffered, it is true, a more
or less total eclipse in the function of "command" upon the
super-imposing of the various commission officers, but that,
as we have said when dealing with the Master, perhaps
enabled him to escape the nineteenth-century fate of the
navigating expert. For when the great gun-revolution of that
period set in, and gunnery specialization began in earnest
with the establishment of H.M.S. *Excellent* and Whale Island
in 1830, he found no difficulty in falling into place under
the new type of commissioned, specialist executive officers
that emerged therefrom.

In his halcyon days, not only was he responsible for the
guns themselves, but also for the small arms which were
stacked in his own sanctum, the gun-room. And—a heavier
responsibility still—he looked after the ammunition, which,
in so combustible a contraption as the old wooden ship,
was a very serious charge, requiring a particularly careful
and sober sort of man to mind it. Perhaps it was on
account of such qualities being expected of him that he was
appointed also to look after the "youngsters", who shared
with him and his mates the after part of the Lower Deck,
called the "Gunroom".[1]

·As responsibility multiplied in the eighteenth-century ship,
there began to be a tendency, in all three "standing" departments, for certain of the lower officers of each group to turn
into a sort of lower class of warrant officer, under the head
of the department. But these men never came within measure-
able distance of their chiefs; and have in some cases
disappeared, and in others, sunk again to the status of Petty
Officer. This latter process was well on the way as early as
1808, when the *Regulations* declare that all these inferior
departmental officers, as well as the Master-at-Arms and

---

[1] This was so in big ships; in small ones, the Gun-room was usually
the Lieutenants' Mess.

the Cook, "though appointed by Warrants, are to be considered as Petty Officers". The gunner's department had two such, the Armourer and the Gun-smith, appointed from 1731, by Warrant from the Board of Ordnance. They were, however, straitly charged "to observe the gunner's orders", and their special duty was to tend the small-arms, keeping them "clean within as well as without, by frequent oyling them: but not to take them too often to pieces which destroys the Locks, Screws and other Parts".

The Boatswain, once immediately after the Master in importance—once, even, in dim Saxon days, the Commanding Officer himself—has certainly lost ground, since the most important part of his former work has been taken from him. He is, says Boteler "to take into his custody . . . all the ropes in general belonging to the ship; with her cables anchors and sails; her flags, colours and pendants. . . . He is also to take care of the long-boat and the furniture thereof, and is either himself or his Mate to go in her. . . . He is likewise to call up all the several gangs and companies of men belonging to the ship to the keeping of their watches . . . and to keep them in peace, and in order one with another. Lastly, he is (in the nature of a Provost Marshal on land) to see all offenders punctually punished, either at the Capstan, or by being put in the bilboes, or with ducking at the main yard-arm".

No wonder the early seventeenth-century boatswain was an important personage; and that even in Ned Ward's time, a century later, "let him but whistle once, and you have a hundred or more *Cartesian* Puppets pop up on deck, and run about, and straight disappear again in an instant". The sound of his silver whistle (which instrument, by the way, the Master and the Coxswain also wore) and the sight of his twine-tipped bamboo, or "rattan", were for ever keeping the poor tar up to concert pitch.

But he soon began to lose some of his many duties. The appearance of the Corporal in Charles I's time, and the blossoming forth, in 1731, of the Master-at-Arms as a full-blown Warrant Officer, relieved him of his responsibility in the matter of discipline: for though this new branch was brought into being merely "to the perfecting of the practice of the fiery weapons" (i.e. the small arms), it had, by the latter date, acquired its modern rôle of Ship's Police. Yet, even after that, the Boatswain contrived to keep in his department just one unenviable duty of a disciplinary nature. His mates remained the official wielders of the "cat". This is a very typical example of that careful specialization of functions on board ship, which, as every modern officer knows, is not at all dead today. Thus, the Master-at-Arms or his Corporals apprehended the victim and brought him to the scene of expiation; but Rope fell within the province of the Boatswain, whether it took the form of cable, of sheets or of carefully prepared, nine-tailed ends.

His old duties in connection with flags have had rather a curious history of their own. When Howe and Kempenfelt, in the last quarter of the eighteenth century, set the whole subject of signals in the Navy in its true perspective, a signalling corps became an inevitable development. After the usual delays, the "Yeoman of the Signals" was established in 1816 (though he had been there in fact for some time). The men under him were gradually organized, but he himself had only achieved one upward step—to Chief Yeoman—by 1889. Then, however, it was decided to allow these indispensable people to rise to Warrant rank; and when, in that year, a limited number of them were selected, they entered, picturesquely enough, as "Boatswains". Thus the old name of "the man in charge of flags" is still associated with the kindred department of Signals: only—now—the lists are kept separate. There are Boatswains, and there are Signal Boatswains.

Among the lesser Warrant Officers, referred to above, two appear in the eighteenth century in the Boatswain's department. They are the Sail-maker and the Rope-maker, officers

of obvious importance in the sailing ship. By the end of the
century, both were appointed by the Commissioners of the
Navy, and both were under the Boatswain. But in its earlier
years, they were far apart in station, for the Sail-maker was
apparently independent of the Boatswain and virtually head
of his own department, being appointed by Warrant from
the Navy Board; while the Rope-maker is not mentioned
as a "Warrant-Officer" at all. This is rather characteristic
of the ups and downs in the careers of these lesser "officers"
—a phenomenon which makes it impossible to keep pace
with them all in a work of this description.

The Boatswain, not unnaturally, has come in for a good
deal of chaff, not to mention criticism, from the writers of
fiction, and even from those who profess to be retailers of
history. Thus J. A. Gardner has a very pretty story about
one of the breed, a certain Johny Bone, who "was a devil
of a fellow at Cap-a-bar"—the eighteenth-century vernacu-
lar for the modern "scrounging". "It is related," he tells
us, "that the late Lord Duncan, when he commanded the
*Edgar*, once said to him, 'Whatever you do, Mr. Bone, I
hope and trust you will not take the anchors from the bows'. "
The later history of Mr. Bone is summarized in one of
Gardner's little thumb-nail sketches: "Dead, from drink."
Yet, once again, we will not let the backbiter have the last
word, but will add this touching little homage from William
Richardson to another boatswain. "We (the crew) sub-
scribed 2s. a piece to buy Mr. Cooper a silver call with
chain and plate, with a suitable inscription on it for his
kindness to the Ships' Company: and a silver pint-pot for
his wife. . . ."

But when all is said, the Boatswain's biggest loss came
with the introduction of steam. In the days of sail, he was
responsible for the motive power of the ship: in fact, this
was his most important duty. In this respect, the old Boatswain is supplanted by the new Engineer, and much of his
old glory has thus departed.

The same remarks, in rather a less degree, may apply to the Carpenter. Though his duties are now legion—far more, and more highly skilled than they were of old—yet the substitution of steel for wood has done for him what the change from sail to steam did to the Boatswain. In the wooden ship, the Carpenter was "to take upon himself the Care and Preservation of the Ship's Hull, Masts, Yards, Bulkheads and Cabbins, etc." Also "in an engagement he is frequently to pass up and down the Hold with his Crew, and to be watchful against all Leaks from shot under water, having Shot-Boards and Plugs of Wood ready, and whatever else is necessary to stop them, and likewise to fish, or otherwise secure, the Masts and Yards". He had, in the later eighteenth century, an inferior warrant officer called the Caulker to help him. But neither Carpenter nor Caulker it is to be feared, with their plugs of wood and their pitchpots, could compete with the hole made by a modern fifteen-inch shell. With the Boatswain, he "made her go" in the old days, and did his best to keep her afloat. And now, much of his glory also has departed.

He too, of course, changed with the times. He even fell one step behind his old colleagues, the Gunner and the Boatswain, who both remained "executive" officers in 1878 when he ceased to be one. Thenceforward he began to form a "civilian" branch of his own, ultimately sharing with the Naval Constructor (when afloat)[1] a silver-grey "distinction stripe" on his sleeve. And, finally, he changed his name. But it was not until the old wooden ship had completely given way to steel that the Admiralty reached the conclusion "that the titles of Carpenter-Lieutenant, Chief Carpenter and Carpenter, which no longer correspond to the duties carried out by these officers, should be revised".

This was in February 1918, and they became "Shipwrights" forthwith. It is sad when an old name goes. But the blow in this case was mitigated by the fact that the new

[1] When ashore, a Naval Constructor wears plain clothes.

THE COOK, ABOUT 1799

one was itself old in the Service. Apart from the ship-*builders* in the dockyards, who had always been called by this name, as early as 1613 we hear of the sea-going carpenter himself being known as "Timberman or Shipwright".

## THE COOK

One other of the old "standing" officers remains to be discussed—the Cook. He was—and is—an important person: for, if it be true that an Army marches upon its belly, surely a Ship may be said to sail on the same part of its anatomy. So, in the old ship, the Cook was a full-blown Warrant Officer, and Head of his own department. But in the end he fared even worse than his colleagues whom we have just discussed. Indeed, as the Service progressed, perhaps he could hardly hope to keep pace with his combatant brethren: for, in the very nature of things, the Cook found himself regarded as a "non-combatant" or "civilian" as soon as that distinction came to be made. An order of 1704, too, certainly helped him on his downward career. In future, in the appointment of Cooks, the Navy Board was "to give the preference to such cripples and maimed persons as are pensioners of the chest at Chatham". And that rule which insisted upon his being drawn from among the sick, halt, and aged remained throughout the century. So it happened that, when the "Rank of the officers in a Ship" was settled, the Cook found his name omitted; and, in the same orders, was relegated to the list of "Inferior Officers". This demotion is reflected in his pay. He was to receive only £1 5s. a month, where Boatswain, Gunner and Carpenter got £4. Though no less useful than before, he has never recovered his relative status; and Rowlandson's spirited drawing reveals more eloquently than words what a fall was there by the end of the eighteenth century.

CHAPTER XIV

# "CIVILIAN" OFFICERS

## PROFESSIONS WITHIN THE PROFESSION

THE turn of the non-military officers has now come—those men who practise a "profession within the Naval Profession". The four principal branches of them are the Pursers, the Surgeons, the Chaplains and the Schoolmasters. The vexed question of the degree of "Militarism" in the Engineering branch we will leave to a subsequent chapter.

The four officers whose functions are essentially "civilian" will have to be dealt with separately, since their stories differ very widely in both origin and subsequent growth. Thus the Purser was one of the old "standing officers", only less long-established on board than the original "Big Three"—the Master, the Boatswain and the Carpenter. The Surgeon, from the very nature of his profession, was an essential element on ship-board, and an early arrival there, though his position was, for a long time, much more anomalous than the Purser's. The Chaplain's first appearance was also very early, but his presence on board was more sporadic, and his position much more anomalous and ill-defined even than the Surgeon's: while the Schoolmaster was an early eighteenth-century innovation.

Before we pass to a more detailed discussion of each civilian group, there is a word to be said on a subject which covers them all, as well as Engineers and Executives—the subject of distinguishing marks.

Since 1748, when such things were first introduced, the Executives have always been distinguishable from all other branches—first in being the sole possessors of uniform: later in being dressed in a different uniform from the rest; and —now that all naval officers' uniforms are in their main features identical—in wearing the rank-indicating rings of gold braid sewn direct on to the cloth of their sleeves, leaving a narrow gap between each ring through which the original "navy-blue" of the cloth appears. The other branches, however, wear a strip of distinguishing coloured cloth between the rings—a colour different in each branch. This—since 1918—has been the only distinctive mark in ordinary everyday uniform: but before that date there were several others, such as a different ornamentation on the peak of the cap, and the absence, among "civilian officers", of the so-called "Executive Ring"—that complete loop of lace added to the uppermost ring on the sleeve.

This latter sartorial addition is not very old, as years go in the British Navy. It dates only from 1860. But from then until 1918 its presence did denote the "executive" branch, no one else wearing it. Yet, only four years after its appearance, the coloured strips came in for "civilian officers", and these really served much the same purpose as the Curl itself: they showed, that is, who were *not* executives. In fact, they fulfilled the distinctive function even more efficiently than the Curl, which only distinguished between "Executives" and "non-Executives", while they distinguished, *in addition*, between the various branches of non-Executives. Both were not a logical necessity, and in 1918, the less efficient method had to give way. But the Curl was not abolished: on the contrary, it was extended to *all* officers. The probable reason for this is that it had become by then a characteristic feature of naval uniform: and, where the matter was of small intrinsic importance, conservatism won, as it usually does in the Service.

Q

### THE MAN OF BUSINESS

First, the business-man and shop-keeper—later to become the Paymaster:—the Purser. We hear first of this officer as a regular member of the crew of the "King's Ships" in the fourteenth century. He was then called the "Clerk", and, a little later, the "Burser", from which the name soon changed, by easy stages, to "Purser". There is reason to think that, in these early days, he was often, in a literal sense, paymaster as well: but, if this is so, we shall see that he soon lost the duty of actually handling the wages; and only recovered it again fairly recently.

There is not much that we can note in his history during the fifteenth and sixteenth centuries. It is enough to say that, at the time of the Armada, he received in pay almost as much as the Gunner and the Cook, but rather less than the Boatswain and the Carpenter.

But, this time, we cannot afford to take his rate of pay as an assessment of his importance on board, because already it did not represent the full tally of his remuneration. There was always something of the "piece-worker" about the Purser. In this, as in several other respects, he was quite unlike the other warrant officers.

To begin with, he was almost always of a higher social standing than the rest of them. Obviously he had to possess *some* education, even from the earliest times—to be able to write, for instance, to "do sums" and to understand something of the casting of accounts. He had also to be a man of substance in a small way, since he could not even secure his position unless he were possessed of a certain initial capital. The practice of purchasing his place began, probably, in Elizabeth's reign, and this of itself is convincing proof that it was even then worth having. In James I's time, when the system was at its height, more than a hundred pounds was sometimes spent on a good "pursery". Also he always had to find sureties for the money which the Authorities were compelled to entrust to him. These sums were often considerable, for he had to have a good deal of cash to meet eventualities, as well as the power to run up bills in the Board's name. The bonds he gave in sureties of this kind sometimes ran into four figures—a very large sum for those days.

From the early seventeenth century, we begin to find him the target of the pamphleteers and critics, and his morals became a by-word even in that immoral age. But we need not necessarily believe all we read. Was he, we may ask, really such a rogue and a cheat as they say? Was a Pursery a short-cut to a fortune? And, if so, how did he work it?

The answer to the first question is, probably, that, in an epoch of rogues and cheats, he was no better than he should have been, but certainly no worse than his contemporaries. The real difference between him and his critics lay in the fact that a very bad system gave him very great opportunities which it did not give them. The principal thing to discover is what his opportunities were: what, in fact, was his accepted position on board.

As we have just seen, he was not, in the seventeenth century, a *Paymaster* at all. Save for a brief period under the Commonwealth Government, pay was neither carried nor disbursed on board, but was issued by means of tickets, cashable at the end of the commission at the Navy Office. So he never could—and never did—handle such obvious sums of cash, and therefore never could cheat the men, wholesale and direct, of their wages. But he could—and, we fear, he often did—make considerable profits out of this evil system. For he was the official keeper of the muster book from which these pay-tickets were made out, and that gave him certain glorious opportunities, particularly if—as sometimes happened—he was in collusion with the Captain who had to pass the accounts. He could—and this was very wrong—himself cash tickets at the Navy Office. There is not much evidence that he made it a custom—as the Jews and other harpies of the sea-ports did—to buy up seamen's tickets wholesale and at a discount, and then cash them in full at the Navy Office, though he may have done so occasionally. Nor were restrictions ever so lax as to allow him to fill up and cash extra tickets at will: the continued insistence (so often cited above) on the "every man his post" principle prevented that in large measure. But when a man died on board, or when he "ran"—i.e. deserted—he forfeited all his pay, even what was owing to him; and, could the Purser but conceal the facts from the Navy Office he might make out such pay-tickets none the less and cash them with impunity. Occasionally, we hear, he incited men to "run", having previously made some arrangement with them: and he is even accused of contriving to leave men behind on shore to make it appear that they had run.

Such things, of course, were gross dishonesties, punishable on detection even in those days. But they were not the principal sources of the Purser's profits. These were far more "legal" and we shall understand them best if we look upon the Purser not, as he is today, as an "Accountant Officer", but what he really was, as the privileged *shop-keeper* on board. This explains why he paid for the post in the first place. In that monopolistic age, the newcomer to the closed community of any city or borough expected to have to pay handsomely for the "freedom" of it—i.e. to be allowed to set up in business in it: and in just the same way the Purser had to pay for the privilege of his monopoly shop on board ship. His opportunities in this respect were greatly enlarged—and sanctioned—in 1623. In that year, in order "to avoyde nastie beastlyness by continuall wearinge of one suite of clothes, and therebie boddilie diseases and unwholesome ill smells", there was introduced into ships the famous "Slop-store"—that naval emporium at which the mariner was bound to replenish his wardrobe when at sea. Further, all ship's stores which did not come directly under his colleagues were in his charge; and many necessary articles—not to mention all unnecessary ones—he was entitled to purvey (and, of course, take the profits on) himself. It was even an understood thing that he should make his profit on the ordinary provisions on board, which he kept in the bulk, and of which he checked the issue. The problem of "shop-commissions" is not confined to twentieth-century housewives and their cooks! But the proceeds of this particular source did not all find their way into the Purser's pocket. He almost always had to share with the contractors, and often, as we shall see, with the Captain.

All such things were regarded—within reason—as legitimate profit, and very profitable they were. But often, it need hardly be stated, the Pursers went a good way beyond reason : which, however, was regrettable rather than surprising. The real fault clearly lay with the system which made it possible.

The odd part about it all, to modern minds, is that everybody seemed to realize the flaws in the system—even the Pursers themselves. They made no bones about their "practices". In 1639, for example, they gave a very frank picture of their activities in a petition to Sir John Pennington. "We are poor men," they wrote, "bred fit for service of consequence, but so poorly paid that we cannot exist without the continuance of what has ever been tolerated." Hollond, too, remarks significantly that the State made no attempt to bear half the expense of a Purser in a voyage, and Boteler makes his Admiral say that unless he is carefully watched, "this Purser may purse up roundly for himself, and that without all possibility of discovery". Pepys himself, who probably knew all there was to know about this officer's wiles, puts the matter in a nutshell when he says in his diary, "A purser without professed cheating is a professed loser." Stephen Pyend, himself a Purser of the Restoration Navy, went even further, and, after describing many "Purser's tricks", advocated the total abolition of the office, the Captain to take over the victualling.

But here the remedy was certainly more dangerous than the disease itself, for already the Captains—or, rather *some* Captains—had felt the temptation to share the proceeds of the Purser's irregularities. As early as 1608 the Captains seem to have been getting a finger into the pie, entering into an illicit combination which, owing to the immense powers they wielded, would have been irresistible. Ned Ward, at the end of the century, sums up this particular situation with his usual splash of vitriol. "The Purser would be a rich knave, but for him (the Captain) and the Rats together: but he will by no means let that rogue play his Pranks on board, except he pay him soundly for a Licence."

Towards the end of Charles II's reign the malpractices of the Purser were certainly notorious: so much so that we find the Captains themselves rather artlessly championing the cause of the oppressed, urging the King to abolish the post, and asking to be allowed to do the Purser's work in addition to their own. It is not now easy to estimate the sincerity of their suggestions, but it is evident that the Merry (and Cynical) Monarch was not impressed with it. He laughed at their proposition, we are told, remarking with his usual shrewdness, "When the men suffer, unto whom should they complain for justice?"

But though they failed at that time to obtain their way, designing Captains were more successful soon afterwards. A new post, that of "Captain's Clerk", was ordained: all Pursers had to pass through this office, and, as promotion thus came to rest very largely with the Captains, the post of Purser itself passed to a great extent under their control. It is not a little sinister to notice, after this change, how often the Purser bears the same surname as the Captain. So powerful a family concern must have been as impregnable as it was profitable.

Towards the end of the seventeenth century the purchasing of pursers' warrants was discontinued—at least officially— so that this particular incentive to the making of doubtful profits ceased, or at any rate was much reduced. But already, in 1683, another old "practice", hardly less deleterious, had been officially sanctioned—that of paying the Purser for "savings" on the provisions. These "savings" were manipulated in sundry and ingenious ways, but what it all came to in the end was simply this: for over a century a goodly percentage of the Purser's emoluments accrued to him—officially—from cheating the seamen of a portion of their rations. The simple sailor was slow to grasp just what was happening, and even then, for a long time, he did nothing more serious than to grouse. But in the end he mutinied, and at length got the wellnigh incredible grievance removed in 1797, as a result of the "breeze at Spithead". After that the Pursers were given an official "allowance for waste", to compensate them for their loss.

But enough of "Pursers' Tricks". Such practices are, unfortunately, more easily introduced than eliminated, and there was still much to criticize all through the eighteenth century both in the system and—sometimes—in the man who profited by it. Much of the criticism flung at him was doubtless mud, though not all: and that some of it stuck, making, in the end, the very name of Purser a term of opprobrium, is clear from the fact that, at long last, the holders of the title themselves petitioned to have it changed "because of the odium attached to it". But that was not until the nineteenth century was nearly half over, and all the real gravamen had disappeared from the charges. Yet all through the eighteenth century no change in method was made, and the results remained far from satisfactory. Nor can anyone who has the least knowledge of seventeenth- and eighteenth-century morality be surprised; for where, in virtually every walk of life, corruption and venality were rather the rule than the exception, the ordinary Purser must have conducted his "practices"—even the worst of them—almost as a matter of routine. The improvement in his moral outlook, when it came, was quite as much the result of a universal public improvement in that respect as of the tightening up of personal supervision from above.

Throughout the century he remained a "purser" and not a "paymaster", for reforms in wage-paying remained insignificant. But, like the Master, he was gradually rising in ship status. He received the uniform of Warrant Officers—for such he still was—along with the rest in 1787, but, unlike the "Standing" Officers he was finding his way at about that time into the Wardroom; after—but not long after—the Master. He did not even get his distinctive uniform in 1805, when the Surgeon did, but obtained it in 1807, at the same time as the Master; and, with the latter, found himself officially recognized in 1808 as a "Warrant Officer of Wardroom rank". Possibly this social promotion gave him scope for yet another "practice", as the following incident would seem to show. At the very end of the eighteenth century, a purser was court-martialled for selling drink to officers, contrary to the Captain's orders, under the pseudonym of "oil". He was acquitted, with a reprimand only, on the amiable grounds that he merely wished to show kindness to his messmates! Rowlandson's drawing, made at that very time, might almost be a portrait of this gentleman.

After this, the nineteenth-century process of transforming him into the modern Paymaster proceeded fairly rapidly. Up to 1814 he had retained that essential "standing officer" quality of "staying put", even when his ship was in ordinary. But in that year it was ordained that his movements were to be brought into line with those of commission officers. Thenceforward he was "paid-off" at the end, and reappointed at the beginning of a commission.

This change was responsible, too, for regularizing another important side of the Purser's activities. It had long been the custom for Flag Officers to select as their secretaries "pursers of talent and approved character". But Admiralty regulations, repeated and reinforced by an Order in Council of 1804, laid it down that only Pursers whose ships were "in

[*T. Rowlandson*

THE PURSER, ABOUT 1799

ordinary" could serve as Secretaries: never Pursers whose ships were in commission. This meant (as long as the rule was obeyed) that there could be little continuity in a Secretary's service, and that this side of a Purser's activities could not develop into a whole-time occupation, since, whenever his ship went into commission, the Purser-employed-as-Secretary had to give up his secretarial duties. The edict of 1814, however, had the effect of severing him from the old close connection with his ship, and gave him a half-pay, when not in a commissioned ship, just like the executive officer's half-pay. It was thus rendered possible for him to become, if he desired, something like a whole-time Secretary, especially after 1816, when it was laid down that a Secretary was, in future, to be allowed to receive his Purser's half-pay in addition to his Secretary's salary. "Secretarial work" thus became—as it is today—an important, and in some respects distinct, subdivision of the Purser's Branch, though it never diverged sufficiently to become a branch of its own. Nowadays a Secretary can —and, at some time or other in his career, usually does —revert to Paymaster duties. But, once started as a Secretary, he tends to spend most of his Service life as one.

In 1825 he really did begin to become a Paymaster—in function though not in name. Up till then, no seaman's wages were paid on board, but after this date a small proportion—for the men a mere four shillings a month— was to be paid, at their request, by the Purser. It was the thin end of the wedge.

The early 'forties saw two big changes. The first move came in 1842, when (at his own request) his title was changed from "Purser" to "Purser and Paymaster"—no doubt an unsatisfactory compromise from his point of view. But in 1843 he received his inevitable advance in status, and became a commissioned officer at last.

But still he was not truly a paymaster, and he went on

bearing the double title until 1852, when the opprobrious "Purser" disappeared from it.

This year saw, also, two even bigger changes. It is a fact strange yet true, that, until 1852, the Pursers had never enjoyed a regular scale of pay. They were still being remunerated by means of commissions on the goods they issued, in addition to their small "personal pay". This curious anachronism may perhaps explain why, although from 1840 onwards they were petitioning to be allowed to take over the entire payment of the crews, the Admiralty consistently refused them. If that request involved a percentage commission, on the old basis, on all their disbursement, they stood to gain considerably by the enormous addition of everybody's pay, and the Admiralty was not likely to allow that. In the end, the latter did the obvious thing and, in ordering that the Paymasters should handle and issue the wages, put them, at the same time, on to a regular scale, and abolished all commissions. They discovered at length, in fact (to quote their own words), that the old payment by percentage was "objectionable in principle, and in practice injurious to the interests of the Crown". Incidentally, this "inner profession" was also rounded off at the same time, by the introduction of Retirement at the age of 65, or 60 for those "who have not had Pursery Charge during the last ten years". The new officers thus became, in name and in fact, salaried Paymasters; and so ceased to be commission-earning middlemen.

Three years later, their status was further clarified by Orders in Council. They were henceforward to be "Accountant Officers for cash to the Accountant General of the Navy, and no longer considered exclusively under the direction of the Comptroller of Victualling". Thus, although the history of the Purser and the Paymaster is a continuous one, that officer has really undergone a radical change of function—a change reflected in the new title of his branch—the "Accountant Branch". Before, "Pursery" simply meant "Purveying".

The same Order of 1855 which made this change also co-ordinated the somewhat confused medley of offices which existed in the Paymaster's Department. There were then three embryonic grades, called "Passed Clerks" (those who had passed their examination in "Pursery", first started in 1814), "Unpassed Clerk" (those who had not), and Clerk's Assistants. They were all subdivisions of the old post of "Captain's Clerk", whose services, throughout the eighteenth century, had been utilized partly by the Purser and partly by the Captain. These were now formed into three ranks, called respectively, Assistant-Paymasters, Clerks and Assistant Clerks.

This cleared up the situation at the lower end of the scale. But a rise was in store for those at the upper end too. In 1867 it was laid down that a Paymaster of 15 years' seniority should rank with a Commander, and in 1886 a further differentiation was made when Fleet Paymasters, ranking with Commanders, were distinguished from Staff Paymasters, ranking with Lieutenants of 8 years' standing, or (as we should now say) with Lieutenant-Commanders. The Fleet Paymaster was, in effect, the old ship's Purser, and had thus attained the rank (though not yet the name) which, in common with the corresponding officers in the medical, engineering and instructor branches, it is considered that Heads of Departments in big ships should hold. So the rise went on. In the same Order Paymasters-in-Chief appear, ranking with Captains: there was a pause after this, but in March 1918 from among the Paymasters-in-Chief was selected a Paymaster-Director-General; and, three days before the Armistice, the first of these ex-warrant officers emerged to Admiral's rank, the Paymaster Director-General becoming Paymaster Rear-Admiral. At the same time all the succeeding ranks were standardized into the form which exists today. Paymasters-in-Chief became Paymaster Captains: Fleet Paymasters, Paymaster-Commanders: Staff Paymasters, Paymaster Lieutenant-Commanders: Paymasters, Paymaster-Lieutenants: Assistant Paymasters, Paymaster Sub-Lieutenants: Clerks, Paymaster Midshipmen; and Assistant Clerks, Paymaster Naval Cadets.

It was in 1864, when the Authorities were busy with the whole question of Naval Colours of all kinds that the Paymasters received their familiar white strip between the gold rings on their arms, as the distinctive badge of their branch. This is still retained, though, in 1944, the whole branch-name was changed from "Paymaster" to "Supply and Secretariat", the word Paymaster dropped from its place in front of the rank, and the letter S, in brackets, substituted after the rank. This had the effect of bringing them into line with the Engineer Officers (see below, p. 289).

THE DOCTOR

Next we have the professional medical man—the Surgeon; and the Parson will follow. As there are certain features in common between this essentially "Civilian" pair, the clergyman may be associated for the moment with the doctor in a few general remarks.

It should not come as a surprise, to anyone who has followed the story thus far, to learn that both slipped into the Service in a very haphazard manner, without much attempt being made for a long time to define their positions. But they are both necessary adjuncts to any community; especially, perhaps, to one in which wounds and death must be regarded almost as commonplace. And so, very early in the Navy's history, they appeared; and, in due course—but comparatively late in the day—they were woven into the composite fabric of naval life, the Surgeon leading the way.

The early naval representative of Medicine was probably no great ornament to his profession. Circumstances were in every way against him. Conditions of life afloat were terrible: current ideas on such subjects as ventilation, hygiene and dieting were elementary in the extreme. Apart altogether from hurts taken in action, the very risks of eating, of drinking, even of existing on board were quite amazingly great. "There are," says Pennington, in Charles I's reign, "no stores, no surgeons, no drugs, and the hammocks are infected and loathsome, and the men stink as they go, and the poor rags they have are rotten and ready to fall off"; and, forty years later, Teonge has this dreadful entry in his diary:— "March 22nd, 1679. I buried Francis Forrest, as 'tis said eaten to death with lice."

To combat all this was the Surgeon. He was nominated by the Company of Barber-Surgeons, and then pressed, often against his will, so that he frequently deserted like a common seaman. He was inadequately paid—in 1588 he received one pound per month; not enough, even in those days, to tempt a good man. And he was very inadequately provided with stores: in Charles I's reign, for instance, he could—nominally —draw drugs worth from £10 to £3, according to the size of the ship, but often complained that he did not get even these, and that what were provided were bad of their kind. Certainly there are endless complaints of his ignorance and incapacity. He "haunts the taverns every day", we are told by Coke; and Nathaniel Knott, writing in 1634, says he is usually "a denkard, a careless and deboyst fellow", and that his chest of drugs should be regularly inspected, "for if trust be reposed in him perhaps the money shall be bestowed on drunkenness".

Yet some, even then, must have been conscientious, if not skilful, men. At any rate the seamen believed in them, and, we hear, in 1627, "will do nothing without a chirurgeon, for that it puts them out of heart." In the following year the crew of the *Rainbow* actually deserted because the medicine chest was empty, although they spoke of the Surgeon himself in the highest terms. This faith is, indeed, as it should be. It reveals a very touching and deep-seated tendency in man. It is almost elemental in the simple mind to believe in the "expert", and to go on believing until experience proves (as it sometimes does) that the trust was ill-placed. The presence on board of a Surgeon and a medicine-chest—even an empty one, so long as the crew did not know it was empty—furnished at least a reed for the poor seaman to lean upon in anticipation: and if it broke in his hand when the test came, at least it *had* comforted him.

In 1626 the important practice began of allowing the Surgeon, over and above his pay, twopence a month taken from the wages of every man on board: and this rule, though confined at first to ships "in ordinary", was soon extended to ships at sea. It rendered the Surgeon's office a good deal more attractive. Nor must we forget another source of income. The seaman paid another sixpence per month from his wages to the famous "Chatham Chest", first established in 1581 at the instance of John Hawkins, and the Surgeons appear to have drawn from this fund on the basis of results—"no cure, no pay". Most of the consequent "practice" fell, probably, into the hands of Surgeons (and even local practitioners) in the dockyards and in ships in ordinary: but as the ships were normally in one or the other, this source of income must not be forgotten. What *is* forgotten sometimes in this connection is that compulsory health insurance wàs not unknown three centuries ago.

By 1675 our medical man was receiving £1 10s. a month, in addition to his twopences, and "Chatham Chest" perquisities, and the place was becoming, at last, worth while. He had by then, too, established himself among the Warrant Officers, and had a "department" of his own, which included at least one "mate", a very "inferior officer", who messed and slept in the darkest corner of the cockpit, itself the darkest and stuffiest part of the ship. The number of these mates increased rapidly in the early half of the eighteenth century, and by the middle of it five were allowed in big ships, and never less than one, even in the smallest.

And the Surgeon's position was improving still further. His pay rose during this period to £5 per month—a figure at which it remained for a long time. In 1729, the more senior ones began to receive an allowance of half-pay when not employed: and all, as we have seen, were already ranking with the Master in the matter of pensions, being, like him, men whose employment was not constant, and so receiving (in theory) their "superannuation allowance" after eight years' service. That by this time the Surgeon's branch was worth entering may be deduced from the fact that, in 1740, Smollett had found it quite expensive to buy himself the place of even a Surgeon's Mate of a Third Rate. At the same time, if we are to believe that acid writer, the contemporary naval surgeon still left much to be desired, as Roderick Random's account of Dr. Mackshane abundantly shows. But, while realizing that there is no smoke without fire, we should do well not to take his words too literally; not only because his naval pen-portraits are invariably overdrawn to the limits of caricature, but also because, for all its author's first-hand experience, *Roderick Random* is still a novel, and a novelist is quite entitled—indeed his main object often is—to create striking and amusing characters.

Before the end of the century, the Surgeon had reached the Ward-room; after the Master, probably, but before the Purser: though here again no one date can be given, since his admittance or exclusion had long depended, no doubt, on his own personality, breeding and popularity with the legitimate occupants.

Thenceforward the story of his rise kept pace with the Purser's. He received his distinctive uniform in 1805—the first of all Warrant Officers to do so—and, as a result of complaints on his part, was given relative rank with medical officers in the Army, and allowed to rank with, but subordinate to, Lieutenants in the Navy.

The first half of the nineteenth century saw the Surgeon, in common with the other "civilian" officers, emerging gradually from warrant to commissioned status, and then acquiring, also gradually, the various ranks with which we associate him today. Already for some time there had been a superior, and more responsible, medical man in ships told off as Hospitals. The "Physician" appears in the first *Regulations* (1731), to take charge of the professional arrangements in these ships, and—at least in theory—he was furnished with an adequate staff, consisting of "an able and experienced Surgeon, with four Mates, and six Men Assistants, a Servant to the Surgeon, and a Baker and four Washermen, all supernumerary to the complement". He was also supposed to visit the other ships in the fleet and inspect their medical arrangements. He was, in fact, already the "Inspector General" of the next century, or at least the "Deputy Inspector General". A man like Sir Gilbert Blane, indeed, as Physician of the Fleet to Rodney in 1782, was already a person of very considerable standing in the medical world. And though he was something of an exception, we may still affirm with confidence that the general efficiency of medical officers had risen enormously since Stuart times: as witness the career of a man like James Lind (1712–1794), the first scientific fighter against scurvy, and the first distillator of sea-water, who began life as an ordinary ship's Surgeon.

In the eighteenth century the medical man's allegiances were curiously divided between the "Commissioners of Sick and Wounded"—an old-established branch of the Navy Board—and the purely civilian Surgeon's Company. The former body appears to have been rather a broken reed at times, since it often had no medical man attached to it. When this was the case, the Surgeon's allegiance was directed towards the Physicians of Greenwich Hospital. In 1806, the business of the Sick and Wounded Office, including the appointment of Surgeons, was handed over to the new Transport Board. This arrangement did not work very well—there is no obvious reason, on the face of it, why it should. So the appointments were transferred in 1817 to the Commissioners of Victualling! This procedure also failing to satisfy, the business was at length handed over, when the old Navy Board was on its deathbed in 1831, to the Lords Commissioners of the Admiralty.

Twelve years later, the Surgeon reached Commissioned rank along with the other "civilian" officers in the big reform of 1843, and, also like them, found himself rated on the lieutenant's mark. But here their courses diverged in one particular. Unlike the Master's and the Paymaster's branches, which, as we have seen, developed a number of subordinate ranks, the Medical "Inner Profession" did not

R

do so, since, for reasons already discussed,[1] the Government has never seen its way to undertaking the initial training of doctors. But none the less the old "Surgeon"—head of department in his own ship—did achieve a rise corresponding to that of the Paymaster, and reached a rank equivalent to Commander: as did his mate, who soon reached the two-stripe mark. In 1866 the process began.

Their ranks up till then were, a Chief Medical Officer, called up to 1843, the "Physician of the Navy", and then changed to "Director General of the Medical Department of the Navy": Inspector General (changed from "Physician General" in 1840): Deputy-Inspector General (ex "Physician"): Surgeon; and Assistant Surgeon (ex-Surgeon's Mate). Now a new rank of Staff Surgeon was introduced, between Deputy-Inspector General and Surgeon. In 1873 the three lowest ranks had their titles further changed from Staff Surgeon, Surgeon, and Assistant Surgeon to Staff Surgeon, First Class, Staff Surgeon, Second Class, and Surgeon. Two years later the senior sort of Staff Surgeon acquired the title of Fleet Surgeon. The latter (who was really the old "Surgeon") had now the three stripes and the status of a Commander, like other Ship Heads of Department: the Staff Surgeon (who was in effect the First Surgeon's Mate of olden days) was a two-and-a-half striper, and the Surgeon (by now the title of the old junior mates) was a lieutenant.

The higher officers fell into line, and were given corresponding rank in 1886. The head man of all, the Medical Director General was ranked with a Vice-Admiral: the "Inspector General of Hospitals and Fleets" ranked with a Rear-Admiral, changing his name yet once more, in 1911, to Surgeon General; while the Deputy Inspector General, ranking with a Captain, changed in that year to Deputy Surgeon General. And so they all remained until 1918, when the unifying nomenclature was introduced which

[1] See above, p. 113.

turned all officers into Admirals, Captains, Commanders, Lieutenant-Commanders and Lieutenants, with only the distinguishing prefix of their branch (and, of course, the distinguishing colour between the rings on their sleeves) to differentiate them. The Surgeon's red dates, like the Purser's white, from 1864.

So far, he has not conformed with the Paymasters and the Engineers in the matter of rank-names. Though the modern equivalent of the old ship's Purser is now a Commander (S), and the chief Engineer on board a Commander (E), the Principal Medical Officer is still—1947—a Surgeon Commander.

## THE PARSON

The paternal Government of Medieval England reckoned to take care of men's souls no less than of their bodies. So it came about that the Parson stepped on board the ships of the King (when he had any) at a very early date: how early, we cannot say, but we shall be safe in presuming that, whenever any considerable number of ships were collected for the King's purposes, at least a sprinkling of clergymen were sent with them. As early as Edward I's time they were there, at the rate, probably, of one or two to a whole fleet. But then, of course, there was no naval service in the modern sense, so that the Chaplain's position on board was quite ill-defined. And the main difference between his history and that of the other officers which we have followed was that he remained in this nebulous position for much longer than they did.

When the day of "fixed jobs" came, and everybody on board had to be something, no particular consideration appears to have been paid to the Parson's cloth: none of the old writers seem to trouble about him in their "list of officers"—even of officers in the old sense. Often, of course, he simply was not there: but when he was, he was just "rated", officially and for purposes of pay, along with the ordinary men: and with the least considerable even of these, viz. the "ordinary seamen".

This is not to say that he was actually regarded as such on board. His education and the nature of his duties must have differentiated him. Still, his position was a remarkably humble one, and probably depended, in the event, on the attitude of the government of the day, or of his particular captain, to religion. Thus, at the time of the Armada, when Protestantism was a major war-issue, Authority thought fit to encourage him, and—this being in the days before the coming of regular posts—ordained for him a pay which was greater than that of anyone else on board, save only the Captain and his lieutenant.

But still his appearances on board were quite irregular. Even by Charles I's reign he had not established himself as a permanent institution, let alone as an officer of any sort. Yet, paradoxically enough, the regulations of that period insisted vigorously on the conduct of services afloat. If there was no parson on board, his duties devolved upon the Captain, and dire penalties were threatened to all who failed to attend. The Earl of Rutland, in 1623, solemnly ordained that such persons should be knocked on the head with a bucket of water and fined sixpence.

Perhaps, with a stipend of 14s. a month, parsons were hard to come by. Although Buckingham announced in 1626 that His Majesty has "given order for preachers to goe in every of his ships at sea", neither Monson nor Boteler, the naval authorities for that age, so much as mentions a specimen: and from the Chaplain's own memorandum to the Admiralty in 1628 we learn that "where there is one ship that hath a minister in it, there are ten that have none: all which", they add, "pay their monthly groat".

The sting of their protest lies in the tail. Two years previously, the Government, realizing they must give even the poor parson a living wage if they hoped to catch him, had inaugurated a new scheme. If the Surgeon was to have twopence per head per month for the cure of the seamen's bodies, no doubt they argued, it was only right that the Parson should have something for the cure of their souls: and, like good Christians, they assessed that something at fourpence. Whatever our eschatological views may be as to relative values, we may admit, perhaps, that this was not ungenerous when the award was to take the form of hard cash. But precept is a very different thing from practice, and there is plenty of evidence that, for a very long time, there was many a slip 'twixt the parson and his groats.

Indeed, the officers—both of the old and the new variety—seem to have conspired to have a down on the poor preacher, and to do everything in their power to keep his fair wages from him. Thus we find the Treasurer of the Navy himself trying to get out of paying him even his fourteen shillings, while, in the year of the above-quoted petition, the "preacher's groat" seems to have been withheld consistently from them. Someone was certainly making an exceedingly good thing out of those fourpences, cheating chaplain and seaman alike.

Into whose pockets did the money go? That is never an easy question to answer, in any age: for the first concern of peculators is always to cover their tracks. Yet we can still take a peep at a sorry picture of petty fraud, and a sordid absence of morality, even in high places. Thus we hear of one Captain Harper not only retaining the groats, but also having the effrontery to take 10 per cent commission on his chaplain's wretched wages. This, it would seem, was the normal procedure. The poor parson had no powerful friends, so that anyone could pluck him with impunity. Nor was Charles I himself ashamed to give the lead. Incredible as it may seem, he granted all the groats collected from parsonless ships to one Wells, the Keeper of Stores at Deptford. It was a disgraceful thing to do, for two reasons at least: first, because, by his own laws, all ships were supposed to carry parsons, and second, because the fourpenny deduction was made simply and solely to give the seamen the benefits of religion, and should have ceased as soon as those benefits were withheld. But Mr. Wells, who was as clever as he was close, made things even worse by claiming the groats, not only of parsonless ships, but also of parson-carrying ships at all moments when the preacher was not actually on board. Now as that rare, and therefore over-worked, specimen was expected to—and usually did—minister to all the parsonless ships in the neighbourhood, he was often out of his own ship and thereby lost his own groats: so that Mr. Wells of Deptford contrived to collect practically all of them!

This is not the only time in the Navy's history when the Chaplain was grossly defrauded, but it is perhaps the worst case. Indeed, so bad it is that one is inclined to suspect some form of concerted conspiracy against him. Can it be, perhaps, that, at a time when religious animosities within the Church of England itself were running high, the Treasurer and Captains, and perhaps the King himself, did not see eye to eye with their poor preachers on such burning questions as Bishops and the Prayer Book? It may well be so, though the uncertain status of the Chaplain on board, and the absence of any strong champion for him certainly contributed, in that greedy age, to his discomfiture.

As the century progressed, however, the lot of the chaplain improved somewhat and the first steps were taken in regularizing his position. These, like most Restoration improvements, were the work of Pepys, who deplored "how few commanders take any (chaplains), and the ill-choice generally made of those that are entertained, both for ignorance and debauching, to the great dishonour of God and the Government". So now the Chaplain, though still to be appointed, as he always had been, by the Captain, was also to be approved by the Archbishop of Canterbury and the Bishop of London. The former does not seem to have officiated in the matter, and soon dropped out. But the latter's functions became a reality. This was probably a distinct gain for the decent chaplain, since he secured thereby a patron who might—and sometimes did—champion him against the worst of his many oppressors. Pepys also got it laid down that the parson should be appointed by warrant from the Commissioners of the Admiralty, so that he became officially a "Warrant Officer", though he does not seem to have been regarded as one in practice, nor did he receive any more pay than that of seamen, which he already had; being borne still "on the establishment", and not, like the Surgeon as "supernumerary". And lastly, Pepys secured—or tried to secure—the groats from parsonless ships for the Chatham Chest—a much more equitable destination for them than the pockets of men like Wells. On the other hand this last effort on the Secretary's part seems to be a confession of failure to enforce that already ancient decree, re-emphasized by himself, that every ship should carry a preacher.

There is, in fact, evidence that the supply of real chaplains fell considerably short of a one-per-ship basis. Several instances are recorded in Pepys's papers of men officiating for complete cruises who were not in holy orders at all. One was Henry Teonge's predecessor in the *Assistance*: he did not get his groats when he applied for them, but then nor did Teonge when in the *Royal Oak*, although he certainly was a priest. Another curious case is that of a Ship's Surgeon in 1679 who had done duty for a deceased Chaplain for a whole cruise. It is interesting to notice that, in this case, the Bishop of London supported his claim, but whether he received the money we do not know, the case being referred from the Admiralty to the Navy Board. But of one thing we may be sure: had it not had the Bishop's powerful backing it would have been turned down at once, as was the fate of far more justifiable claims.

Much valuable light is thrown on the life of a chaplain on board ship in the 1670's by the valuable and amusing diary of the above-mentioned Teonge. Extreme poverty drove him to sea—a reason, one suspects, common to many seventeenth- and eighteenth-century chaplains. In order to purchase himself a bed he had to perform prodigies of financial jugglery, which included the borrowing of five shillings from his landlady to redeem his cloak from pawn, and the subsequent re-pawning of that article for forty shillings. Nor, for all his resource, could his sea-equipment be regarded as anything but sketchy, when he came on board carrying all his belongings in an old sack. But he soon exercised his ingenuity in remedying that. "And here I might tell you what Providence putt into my hands, which though littell worth of themselves yet were they of greate use to him that wanted almost everything. Early in the morning I mett with a rugged towell on the quarter deck: which I soon secured. And soon after Providence brought me a piece of an old sayle and an earthen chamber-pot."

Yet in one respect Teonge was lucky: he was probably a friend, and certainly became a favourite, of the Captain who appointed him. At any rate, he seems to have enjoyed himself on board; to have had his meals, quite often, at the Captain's table; to have had his own cabin, and in general, to have enjoyed the social, though not the official, position of a quarter-deck officer.

Ned Ward, writing thirty years later, of course belabours his Sea-Chaplain unmercifully: indeed, so wantonly that perhaps the only fact worth gleaning from him is that the Parson regularly played cards, supped and drank with the Captain. Thus he unconsciously corroborates the—comparatively—saintly Teonge, and shows that, sometimes at least, the Chaplain had left the status of ordinary seaman far behind him.

But already, when Ward wrote, the Chaplain had been once more ignored officially, and, in modern eyes, grievously wronged. We have seen how, in 1700, the other "warrant" officers, including even the Surgeon, were made eligible for "superannuation" allowance. But as regards the Chaplain the Authorities maintain a strict silence. Indeed, he was destined to wait for over a century longer before he received any "after-care" at all.

Why was this? Partly, no doubt, because he was still officially "on the establishment", and not there regarded as an officer of any sort. But this is only begging the question. That was Authority's excuse. The real question is, why was his position not higher? And the answer, we are afraid, is not to the Government's credit. It is, indeed, very hard to avoid the uncharitable conclusion that the parson was still being shamelessly exploited. There was, of course, the inevitable vicious circle. "The labourer is worthy of his hire"—so runs the unspoken argument: "but he is poor quality, and so his wages must be poor too." But that is only the first half of the circle: the second follows. His quality is so poor because his remuneration is so bad: even parsons must earn the wherewithal to live: and if we offer a wage inadequate to relieve the necessities of educated and cultured men, we shall never attract a sufficiency of them.

This treatment was no new experience for the secular clergy in all walks of English life, and over many centuries. As it was in the days of Chaucer so it remained when Wesley came on the scene. The plums all went to the privileged—those who commanded the influence: the work was done—when it was done at all—by the "povre persoune". There have always been in our Church (and, for that matter, in all Churches) a creditably large number of the latter, men prepared to work where their sympathies and their consciences bade them in spite of a hopelessly inadequate earthly reward. And the Government, we are driven to conclude, realized the existence of such Christian virtue: saw that, because of it, the supply of Sea-Chaplains would never fail them altogether: discovered that, as a class, they were less likely than others to make a fuss—and left it at that.

But, under such conditions, it must be admitted, there were not, in the Church's lean eighteenth-century days, enough good men to go round the fleet: and not only the fleet—there were certainly, in the Church on shore as well, a number of men entirely unworthy of any spiritual cure whatsoever. Some of these took the best livings which their friends could offer without any real intention to do their duty as clergymen: others were unfitted by nature for the office—ignorant men, wasters and adventurers who used their cloth as a screen to cover their nefarious schemes.

The former, of course, never found their way into the fleet: they were too snug in their family livings: but the latter did, perhaps because they could not find employment elsewhere —the reason, too, why many a better man who had no "patron" also found his way on board. Yet a tactful and well-patronized chaplain might still contrive to take a comfortable place in the entourage of his high-born Captain: as, evidently, does the reverend gentleman in Hogarth's charming picture, reproduced on p. 196.

It was probably because of the "mixed bag" thus collected as Sea-Chaplains, and their inability—or refusal—to make a fuss, that they seem to make such little progress during the eighteenth century. Throughout it, they received the pay, and retained the official status of, ordinary seamen. They do not receive recognition among the wide range of officers included in any *Regulations and Instructions*—they are scarcely mentioned in any of the eighteenth-century editions. After the mutinies of 1797, they went—relatively speaking—yet further downhill, for then the ordinary seaman's wages were raised from 19s. to 25s. 6d.; but the Chaplain's remained at 19s. (We can almost hear Authority saying, "the Chaplains will never mutiny, poor fish!")

This total lack of recognition makes it hard to say whether they received anything like their full tally of groats, as they were still supposed to do. Evidence is lacking, but it is very doubtful whether they did, for there is every reason for thinking that they were regarded, both by themselves and others, as being underpaid—which would not have been the case by any means, in a big ship at any rate, had they really received their full monthly quota of fourpences. But, be this as it may, their official position certainly remained disgraceful. As late as 1808 the Parson was still placed in the humiliating position of being at the mercy of the Commission Officers, and even of one Warrant Officer. For, before he could draw his pay, or be reappointed to another ship, he had to receive a certificate from the

Captain, the Senior Lieutenant *and* the Master, "that he had diligently attended to all the duties of his station: that he had performed divine service whenever he was directed; and that his conduct had been sober, regular and decent, and in every respect becoming the character of a clergy-man". If only there had been any guarantee that his judges themselves were "sober, regular and decent" it would not have been so bad. But unfortunately there was none, and among the responsible trio, there might well be at least one who put good-fellowship before Godliness, and who would refuse to sign *because* the clergyman had done his duty. Nothing, perhaps, shows more clearly than this nineteenth-century order, the low regard in which the Chaplains were held by the authorities.

Yet, though the Government did nothing for him, there can be little doubt that he retained, and even improved, his social position. So long as he was regarded at headquarters with such abiding suspicion his treatment on board depended inevitably upon his own character and breeding. If he behaved like a gentleman and made himself agreeable to the Captain and other officers, he was, no doubt, accepted, socially speaking, as one of themselves. Thus, as early as 1741 (unless Smollett's memory is playing him false), the singularly unpleasant specimen in *Roderick Random* lived with the officers. "He", (the chaplain in the *Thunder*), we are told, ". . . returned to his mess-mates, who were making merry in the Wardroom". But, on the other side, is the evidence of the *Sea Chaplain's Petition to the Lieutenants in the Wardroom* of 1758, where the writer, who has been forbidden to use it, relinquishes the quest with the pathetic words,

> E'er, taught the deference to Commissions due,
> Presumptuous I aspir'd to mess with you.

But this was perhaps an exceptionally "stand-offish" mess, even for 1758. The Chaplain was certainly "on the rise".

Indeed, for all his official classification, even the Lords of the Admiralty must have realized that he was really by no means a common seaman or they would never have allowed it to be stated in their regulations that he might have a servant of his own. Yet such he had—in the regulations, anyway—from 1731 onwards.

It cannot be doubted, also, that the general all-round moral level of Chaplains was fast improving towards the end of the century. But this, as in the case of the Purser, was far more due to the moral uplift of the whole community in general and of the Church in particular, than to any action on the part of the Government. He did not catch up with the Masters, Pursers and Surgeons in the 1808 order about "wardroom rank", though most of his kind had probably been inhabitants there longer even than the Masters.

But his deliverance was at hand. The Orders in Council of 1812 are the Chaplain's Charter, for it was then that his old remuneration was abolished, and a proper salary instituted. Away at last went the nineteen shillings a month, the seamen's groats, and certain insignificant bounties which he had recently acquired; and in their stead he received a salary of £150 per annum, and a pension after eight years' service—he was now apparently an officer of "inconstant employ": also an allowance for a Servant, valued at £11 8s. Nor was this all. A cabin was allotted to him "in wardroom or gunroom", where he was to "mess with the Lieutenants and be rated for victuals". And, lastly, if he was willing to act as Schoolmaster, he was to be entitled to the £20 bounty which came to them, and to the £5 "capitation fee" for each pupil taught. Every ship down to a Fifth Rate was to carry a Chaplain, and at last this old-established order seems to have been obeyed.

Though still appointed by warrant he had now achieved a position which accorded with his merits. Even in the matter of pay, when his allowances were added, he was not far behind the other civilian officers with whom he could most properly be compared. It is therefore rather surprising to find that in 1820, the Admiralty were faced with a shortage of chaplains: especially as the post-war shrinkage of the Navy was still going on. Why, so soon after receiving their just dues they should have been unwilling to come forward it is not easy to say. Perhaps the rapid rise in the cost of living had already made the salary too low: perhaps the actual posting of one to each ship, probably for the first time, had revealed the true and permanent shortage of numbers: perhaps it was only a case of one of those temporary fluctuations which have occurred from time to time in all branches. But, whatever the reason, the Admiralty had to forgo, for the time being, their age-old regulation that only Priests should be appointed. Deacons would now be accepted, though they were informed that they must take Priest's orders as soon as possible.

In 1843, in the great accession to Commissioned rank of that year, the Padre at last caught up with his fellows. And there, abruptly enough his history may cease. For, unlike all other branches, the Naval Chaplain has never split up into ranks. Nor, beyond certain minor modifications of his familiar civil dress, has he blossomed forth into uniform. His "distinctive badge" is the collar and black cloth common to all clergy: that, he conceives, is uniform enough. In these latter days, when he is not so closely confined to a ship as he used to be, this has sometimes caused him considerable inconvenience: indeed, in the Great War, his enforced presence in "military areas" sometimes compelled him, temporarily, to don a uniform whether he would or no. His objection, too, to "taking rank" is one which can only do him honour. He has felt that he will be the nearer to any individual member of his oddly assorted "parishioners" if he is not tied down to any particular label. And, seeing that his flock may range from Admiral of the Fleet to Boy, Second Class, who will dare deny the wisdom and magnanimity of his choice?

The relation between the Navy and its Chaplains having been satisfactorily settled, it remained to solve the problem of the relation between them and the Church. This was not altogether easy, the Church having always existed on a territorial basis, and its clergy being ruled by the Bishop of the diocese. But the wide seas have no Bishop. Thus, in our own century, there arose again the problem—though in a different form, and for another reason—which had reacted so unfairly on the Chaplains of the seventeenth century. They still had no direct link with the Church. That was provided for them by an Order in Council of 1902, under which the Chaplain of the Fleet was instituted by the Archbishop of Canterbury an "Archdeacon for the Royal Navy". This does not mean that naval chaplains are "in the See of Canterbury", but that they are linked direct to the Primate of the Church of England: and each one, on appointment, receives from the Archbishop a special ecclesiastical licence.

In the Second World War—for the same reasons as in the First—the Chaplain went into uniform again: a distinctive and very simple one, innocent of marks of rank which he still eschews.

### THE SCHOOLMASTER

The naval beginnings of the Purser, the Surgeon and the Chaplain are lost in antiquity, but not so the Naval Instructor. He is a contemporary of Mr. Lewis Maidwell, and his arrival on board coincides with the first faint realization of the fact that naval officers, like everybody else, may require a little schooling. And as he arrives after the others, so he remains behind them in recognition and status, and does not emerge as the modern Instructor Officer of Commissioned rank until after all the rest have reached a similar goal.

Having seen what a rough passage the Chaplain had, no one will be surprised to learn that the path of the School-master was not exactly strewn with roses. He is first mentioned in an Order in Council of 1702, when he is to receive a bounty of £20 a year for instructing the "young gentle-men". The nature of the employment designed for him may be gleaned from the fact that, before appointment, he was to pass an examination at the hands of the Master and Brethren of Trinity House: and this he continued to do for over a century. Evidently therefore his duty from the first was mainly to instruct in Navigation, though he was very soon—if not from the first—teaching Mathematics and Writing as well.

He was not a Warrant Officer; still less, of course, a Commission Officer. He was a "rating", and yet not quite so lowly a one as was the Chaplain, who, as we have seen, was a seaman. We seem to be able to detect some hesitation on the part of the Authorities as to how they are to regard their new creation, and, being in doubt, they appear to have fallen back on that office which had already proved such a standby under similar circumstances. They decided that he should be a Midshipman. The modern young gentlemen who attend their "schoolie's" classes in 1939 will be amused to learn, perhaps, that the Instructor Officer himself was once, officially, just what they are now. For such he was. When first we obtain an official view of him, in 1731, it is ordered that he "shall receive the pay of Mid-shipman, and the Captain is to keep open the vacancy of a Midshipman for that purpose: but if there be no vacancy, when the Schoolmaster appears on board, he shall never-theless be paid as Midshipman, and entered into the first vacancy". Further, although the order does not actually say so, we know from a later one that his wages were those of the worst-paid class, the Midshipman Ordinary: and this is only logical, since he would almost certainly lack the technical skill and experience to perform the duties of the full-blown variety.

His functions, as laid down in all eighteenth-century *Regulations* do not vary. "He is to employ his Time on board in instructing the Volunteers"—not, notice, the Midshipmen—"in Writing, Arithmetic and the Study of Navigation, and in whatsoever may contribute to render them Artists in that Science." He is, further—and in this he is the true ancestor of his modern namesake, the Naval Schoolmaster—"to teach the other youths of the ship". And, lastly, "he is to be early every morning at the Place of Teaching, and to represent the Names of such as are idle, or averse to learning, to the Commander, in order to his taking course for their correction".

Now, if we went by the *Regulations* alone, we might imagine that quite an admirable system of training, and, even of education, existed for the young gentlemen on board ship throughout the century. But in practice this was very far from the case, and that for two reasons. First the wretched wages granted—they work out at £34 8s. a year—combined with the utter absence of ship-status which he enjoyed, made it quite certain that the person with the right qualities would seldom if ever appear. And in fact he did not. When Hood recommended Raigersfeld

s

Senior to send his boy to a shore-school,[1] where, we must ask, was the Schoolmaster, in theory dwelling on board for the sole purpose of purveying the very goods which young Raigersfeld required? He may have been there, but, if he was, Hood ignored him, completely, and probably rightly.

On the other hand he may *not* have been there. And this brings us to the second reason why the "Schoolmaster" scheme was a total failure from a "training and education" point of view. We believe—though it is hardly possible to prove it—that very often he was *not* there: much more often than not, in fact, for all the reiterated regulations on the point. It is strange that we glean so little of him from the various writers of the century who describe life afloat. Ned Ward is silent about him: so is Smollett, and Raigersfeld: yet it would be hard to find any other ship-character who is not mentioned by one or other of these authors. It is not maintained, of course, that he was *never* there. We know he was. Mr. Carr Laughton has shown that his earliest known appearance—in one or two small ships—was 1712, where a few specimens of his class are crowded into a list of Midshipmen wherever there is space for them. And after that there are quite a number of isolated evidences of his presence, especially towards the end of the century. Gardner has one, for instance—poor Andrew Macbride, a very good mathematician and thoroughly cultured man, but a hopeless dipsomaniac. Nor must we overlook the unfortunate Mr. Mears, the mad schoolmaster of the *Pegasus*, mentioned by Byam Martin, who all but succeeded in altering the succession to the throne of England, by just failing to murder King William IV when he was a young naval officer in 1786. Indeed one almost begins to be thankful that the Schoolmaster *was* so rare, for almost all of the few specimens we know were either good scholars of this type, yet fallen on evil days, and in

[1] See above, p. 95.

the last stages of disintegration, or else more worthy young men of no particular intellectual attainments, who were "on the rise", and regarded the post of schoolmaster as a stepping stone to a "pursery" or even a lieutenancy.

Sometimes, however, the schoolmaster's duties were performed by other and more substantial officers. Indeed, it is fairly certain that thoughtful and conscientious Captains, even prior to 1702, caused their young charges to be trained, say, in navigation by the Master, or his assistants; in Scripture and perhaps the more elementary "humanities" by the Chaplain, and possibly in Arithmetic by the Purser; there may even have been occasional poor scholars, of an entirely civilian status, brought on board for the purpose. Such a one is the slightly nebulous Mr. William Jones, who is said to have taught Lord Anson mathematics. As this worthy was certainly in the Cadiz Expedition of 1702, and retired almost immediately afterwards, he can hardly have come in under the "Bounty" scheme of April of that year. And as to teaching Lord Anson, if he did so it must have been after he had left the Navy for good. Still Mr. Jones may well be the first Schoolmaster known to us by name.

We shall not be far wrong, probably, if we regard the 1702 order as a rather feeble regulating effort on the part of the Government to see that *all* Captains did their duty in future by introducing a special person to undertake the whole training side of the business. And though this scheme failed owing to the niggardliness of the provision which they made, there is still evidence—chiefly culled from the later years of the century and the early 1800's —that such instruction was sometimes given. At that period, for instance, we hear quite often of Pursers claiming, and obtaining, the Schoolmaster's bounty for having conducted classes in Arithmetic, while the wording of the "Chaplain's Charter" of 1812 makes it appear likely that, long before that date, some at least of the Parsons had been

doing their bit, and—characteristically enough—doing it
gratis. But all this really only goes to prove how weak,
both qualitatively and quantitatively, the Schoolmaster
branch was.

But when all is said, perhaps the most potent reason why
the young gentlemen went untaught at sea lay in the
obstructive attitude of the other officers themselves to what
they regarded as high-faluting and over-theoretical instruction. Even as late as the present century, and well
within the memory of officers still serving, one of the most
frequently heard plaints of the Naval Instructor was that
his pupils at sea, whenever they were supposed to be
"chasing X" with him, were always being sent for by the
Commander or "Number One" to discharge some other
duty of a more practical nature. If this was still a
factor in the education-conscious twentieth century, how
much more powerful was it a hundred and fifty years
ago?

So we pass out of the darkness of the eighteenth century
to the reforming nineteenth. In 1812, as we have seen,
the Chaplain was officially linked, if he so desired it, to the
Schoolmaster Branch. And at the same time, both he and
the Schoolmaster were to receive a bonus of £5 for each
pupil taught—or caught. These were great gains for the
schoolmaster, both in prestige and in pay. But better was
in store. In 1816 an Order in Council points out that he is
still receiving "the pay of the youngest midshipman" and
that men of adequate attainments are patently impossible
to obtain at that figure. The pay was therefore considerably
raised. Three years later, too, the old "Queen Anne's
Bounty" was raised to £30, and the entrance examination
was transferred wholly from the Trinity House to the
R.N. College, Portsmouth, where the great Dr. Inman
could be trusted to select the right material. Three years
later, again, in 1822 a compulsory knowledge of the classics
was added to the Schoolmaster's requirements. Was this

the first-fruits of Dr. Inman's influence? If so, it did not outlast him.

But meanwhile the "Schoolie" had fallen far behind the other "civilians" in official status. They were all "Warrant Officers of Ward-room Rank", but he was still a "Rating". Yet that rise soon came too. In 1836 he was given Warrant Rank—"in all respects a Wardroom Warrant Officer"— and, unless he were also a Chaplain, a uniform. Next year his title was changed to "Naval Instructor and School-master". In 1840 proper rates of pay were established for him for the first time, and the old £30 bounty abolished; and two years later his title reached the form of "Naval Instructor".

But it was in 1837 that the foundations of his future status and utility were really laid: for, upon the closing of the R.N. College at Portsmouth as a training estab-lishment for "young gentlemen", the Admiralty at length decided to give some training afloat, not only to the ex-Collegians, but to *all* volunteers.[1] And the "Naval Instructor and Schoolmaster" was the man who was to give it. From that time onwards the branch advanced rapidly both in size and status, as the improved conditions began to attract in growing numbers the class which the Admiralty sought—the University Graduate.

He fell behind his "civilian" colleagues again in 1843 when they all came to be appointed "by Commission", but he caught up once more in 1861, when he too was appointed by commission instead of "by Order". At that point in his progress, oddly enough, he went *out* of uniform again, if he desired to do so. But, if he liked to wear one, it was to be that of the "Secretary": that is, a Pay-master's uniform.

The next step, if he would keep pace with the times, was to acquire ranks within the branch. These came rapidly for the purposes of status and salary, though much more

[1] See above, p. 93.

slowly in actual titles. In 1864 there were established grades
of seniority—those of under eight years' service: those of
from eight to fifteen years', and those of over fifteen years',
with suitable rises of salary attached. In 1879, uniform
became obligatory, and the Instructor's Branch shipped
the light blue cloth stripe which had fallen from the
moribund arm of the Navigator. When that occurred the
grades fell into their natural places. The junior Naval
Instructor became the "Two Striper": the man with
eight years' seniority and over, the "Two-and-a-half
striper", and the Senior man the "Three Striper", corresponding with, though not yet called, a Commander.

Then came 1903, and the Selborne Scheme. Its sponsors
thought that the generous educational facilities now being
afforded on land would render the services of Naval
Instructors afloat completely superfluous. They therefore
closed the entries, and the days of the branch seemed
to be numbered.

But they reckoned without the ever-growing complexity
of the modern Service: and in this, as in other respects,[1]
things did not pan out exactly as they had anticipated.
In 1915, therefore—soon after the vast expansion entailed
by war had started, and with Naval Cadets hurried off to
sea after comparatively short periods of instruction at
the Colleges—new Naval Instructors began to appear, in
undiminished numbers. The only permanent results of the
break, in fact, were, first, that the old "Chaplain and
Naval Instructor", after a life of more than a century,
disappeared: and second, the old "head-money" levy
on the Naval Instructors' pupils fell into desuetude, to be
formally abolished after the War. Between 1903 and 1915,
of course, the Chaplain entry went on as usual, but since
1915 the two have been kept entirely separate.

In 1917, the most senior of the fifteen-year Naval
Instructors, hitherto known as Chief Naval Instructor,

[1] See Chap. vii, *passim.*

added a fourth gold band to his arm and ranked with a Captain. That was the highest point reached until, in 1941, the Branch acquired one Instructor Rear Admiral.

In the following year, at length abreast with all the others, the Instructor Branch took over the equivalent titles of Instructor-Captain, Commander, Lieutenant-Commander and Lieutenant: and, in 1919, all Naval Instructors became "Instructor Officers", as they are today.

There was not—and almost certainly never will be—such a person as Instructor Sub-Lieutenant or Instructor-Midshipman; for here is another obvious case in which the Navy will leave preliminary education to outside educational bodies. Yet there are "one-striper" members of the Instructor Branch, and they bear, moreover, the old and honoured title of "Schoolmasters". Their story must be briefly told.

In 1862—only one year, that is, after the new Naval Instructor became a Commissioned Officer, and only twenty years after the name "Schoolmaster" had disappeared—the new rating of "Naval Schoolmaster" came to take its place. There was need for him. We must not forget that the original schoolmaster had from the first been assigned *two* posts—the teaching both of the "young gentlemen" and of "the other youths of the ship". In the middle of last century, the efforts of Sir James Graham and Captain Harris, as we have seen, had put "training for all" very much on the map. That clumsy title "Naval Instructor and Schoolmaster" was not, therefore, quite so meaningless as it sounds at first sight; and after the differentiation was effected in 1862, the very logical result was complete. The Naval Instructors had become the Schoolies of the Quarterdeck; the Naval Schoolmasters, the Schoolies of the Lower Deck.

The last-named advanced in their turn. In 1889 the grade of Head Schoolmaster was given warrant-rank, while in 1904 the commissioned rank of Chief Schoolmaster was established. They now had ranks ranging from Warrant Officer to the equivalent of a Commander, and were called respectively Schoolmaster (Warrant Rank); Schoolmaster (Commissioned) and Senior Master (one-stripers); Headmaster Lieutenant; Headmaster Lieutenant-Commander, and Headmaster Commander. But in 1946 the whole of these outward distinctions between the old Schoolmaster and the old Instructor Officer was swept away when all became Instructor Officers, the latter class distinguished in the Navy List by the addition of a dagger before the name.

# CHAPTER XV

# THE ENGINEER

LAST, but least only in the matter of age, comes that "Cuckoo in the Nest", the Engineer.

The whole service had grown up without him. It had developed in its confused English way, yet ultimately it had crystallized along very different lines. The original amalgamation of Seamen and Fighters was, apparently, accomplished for good and all. The nest was safely built: the men who fought and the men who made the ship go had engaged their respective niches in it: members of many other leading professions had hopped in too and snuggled comfortably down therein, each in his appointed place. As far as general functions were concerned, everybody knew where he stood: all was serenity and peace, and all were busily engaged in a healthy and common growth. But then there dropped suddenly out of the blue, right into the heart of the nest, an egg—an uncompromisingly large egg —which, before anyone had time to realize it, incontinently hatched out into a vigorous and highly intelligent fowl: one, moreover, whose growth was phenomenally rapid, for a very large percentage of the food poured into the nest (in the shape of work to be done) was absorbed by him. He quickly became quite indispensable, so that no one could dream of turning him out, even had they wished to do so. And, like every other cuckoo, he immediately set the parent birds a problem of the first magnitude. In fact it would not be altogether untrue to say that they have been scratching their heads over him ever since.

Like all late-comers into the Service, the new arrival began humbly enough. When steam was first used in the Navy it was frowned upon—if not despised—and was strictly relegated to tug-boats and the small craft of the packet service. There was no hope that any of its regular attendants, even the more senior of them, would be admitted to the heights of commissioned rank.

Yet, even before the appearance of the first Royal Navy steamboat, there was, oddly enough, a functionary in the Service whose title contained the word "engineer". This was the Civil Architect and Engineer of the Navy—Sir Samuel Bentham, an "officer" of the old sort, and a very distinguished man, but not the possessor of a naval rank. He was displaced in 1814 by the "Engineer and Mechanist", an important dockyard official, as his salary of £600 indicates. He had under him a Draughtsman and a Clerk, and his duties were to superintend the Wood Mills, the Metal Mills and the Millwrights, as well as all machinery that was in, or might come into, the yards.

The original office-holder lasted until 1831: but then, the Admiralty proposing to halve the salary of his successor, the latter refused to take it, and the office was abolished.

But this first effort for the Engineer's rights seems to have been successful, for in 1835 a "Chief Engineer and Inspector of Machinery" was appointed to superintend all engineering activities, which were already important enough to require the attention of a good and well-paid man. They gave him £650 a year, a sum which made him the financial equal of the dockyard's third-in-command. But, although his titles were identical with two of those soon to be given to the higher engineer officers of the *new* sort, he was not actually one himself: his was still essentially a *post*, and he was a civilian.

A new appointment was made, however, in 1837, in the person of a "Comptroller of the Steam Machinery and Packet Department of the Navy". This was still a post, but its incumbent was to be a Naval Officer, and his place (including house) was worth nearly a thousand a year. This man was the true prototype of the modern Engineer-in-Chief.

But by 1837 engineers as a body had begun to come into their own, for from that year dates their first permanent establishment of officers, with regulated rank and pay. They were to be divided for these purposes into three classes—first, second and third—and were all appointed by Warrant of the Admiralty. This was not of itself an ungenerous provision of status, and was inevitable in 1837, when none of the "civilian" branches had reached commissioned rank. But it was further ordered that they should rank next below Carpenter: that is, last of the old "standing" officers—and indeed of all warrant officers, for the name next below theirs in the pay-list was the Cook's, by then a Petty Officer. Yet, though the highest point to which they could attain was low, we must remember that their lowest point was high: the whole corps consisted of warrant officers. Another thirty-one years were to elapse before there were any purely "engineering" petty officers or ratings. In 1837, too, they received their first uniform—that of the ordinary warrant-officer of the period: but, four years later, they were given distinctive "Engineer" buttons.

It was not perhaps a great start, but things soon improved. In 1838 their pay was raised substantially, and though they missed their commissions in 1843, it was soon felt that the right "officer" class would not be obtainable if they were withheld. So in 1847 they were reorganized in such a way that some of them at least obtained a rather grudging commission. The First-Class Engineer now assumed the remarkably un-naval sounding title of "Inspector of Machinery Afloat", and was to rank with, but after, Master of the Fleet—that is, in the hierarchy of 1847, above Master but below Commander. The Second Class acquired

the title of Chief Engineer—a rank in itself subdivided
into three classes—and was to have commissioned rank
with, but after, the Master. The Third Class was to be
called "Assistant Engineer"—also arranged in three sub-
classes—and to be appointed "by Order" (i.e. *not* Commission), ranking with but after Second Master, and above
Midshipman only.

It was not until 1852 that any of them appeared by name
in the Seniority List of the Navy; but then, the first two—
the Commissioned—classes did. It is interesting to see their
total numbers, on the eve of the Crimean War. There were
two Inspectors, fourteen First Class Chiefs, fifteen Second
Class and forty-eight Third Class, or 79 in all. This will
serve to explain the slowness of their rise, for the numbers
in the various branches have always had a good deal of
influence in dictating both the speed and the degree of their
elevation. It was the Russian War more than any other
single event which hurried forward the introduction of
steam, especially into the bigger ships; and thenceforward
the Engineer's numerical rise—and therefore his elevation
in status—proceeded apace.

In 1856 he lost his special button, but acquired in 1863
the modern mark of distinction, the purple band. But
meanwhile the heights to which he could attain were also
rising. In 1860 the Inspector of Machinery reached Commander's rank when the Master of the Fleet (with, but
after, whom he stood) was also promoted, and in the very
next year it was laid down that an Inspector of Machinery
of eight years' seniority should rank with a junior Captain:
while in 1866 the new grade of "Chief Inspector of
Machinery Afloat" was established for Inspectors of eight
years, and they were ranked with Captains of three years
and upwards.

But now, having extended so far their upward range, they
began at length to spread downwards too. In 1868 the whole
body was divided into a "professional" and a "mechanical"

class, and thereby completed the process of becoming a full-blown branch. In addition to the commissioned and warrant officers already there (professional), they now acquired petty officers and ratings (mechanical). The latter are, of course, the modern Artificers, and since then there have opened for them avenues of advancement from "Lower-deck" to "Quarter-deck", exactly analogous to those in the executive and other branches. But it is with the "professional" class, as ever, that we are mainly concerned.

The commissioned Engineer Officer had now caught up with the officers in the other civilian departments. Yet he *was* a "civilian" in the naval sense. So much had been succintly laid down in 1847 when he first received a commission. And here he paused for quite a long time, while the lower categories were finding their levels, in a complicated series of little changes which were each so short-lived as to make a close examination unnecessary. In 1877 for instance, after the Chief Inspector and the Inspector, of Senior and Junior Captain's rank respectively, we have the Chief Engineer who, according to his seniority, hovers between Commander and Senior Lieutenant, and the "Senior Engineer" who did not receive a rank, but enjoyed advantages of seniority corresponding with those granted to the eight-year Lieutenant in the executive branch. We only mention these two officers because their particular names seem to have stuck. To this day, in engine-room parlance, the "Chief" is the Head of Department in the ship, and the "Senior" is the Lieutenant-Commander immediately under him.

It was in 1886 that the "Chief" was split into three grades—Fleet Engineer, Staff Engineer and Chief Engineer. The first-named—the Head of Department in a big ship —thus acquired a name similar, and a position equal, to that of the Fleet Paymaster and the Fleet Surgeon, ranking, like them, with a Commander. The Staff and Chief Engineers remained in charge of smaller ships, and ranked with senior

Lieutenants, both wearing, like them, two-and-a-half stripes, until the former was abolished in 1900. The plain "Engineer", also, now began to approximate, for the first time, to Lieutenant, though the junior members of the rank had, for a while, to wear the rather unbalanced-looking number of one-and-a-half stripes on their arms. At the same time, too, the Assistant Engineer had his one stripe, and came to rank with the Sub-Lieutenant.

Though the head of the branch had enjoyed the title of Engineer-in-Chief since 1860, it was not until 1900 that he obtained the equivalent rank of Rear-Admiral. But then he too reached flag-rank at last.

In 1903, in the great Selborne changes, the old system of nomenclature gave place to the modern method of simply putting the word "Engineer" before the ordinary executive title. The Engineer-in-Chief also received one step more promotion (if particularly senior) and became an Engineer Vice-Admiral. The Chief Inspector of Machinery became Engineer Rear-Admiral; the Inspector of Machinery, Engineer Captain, and the Fleet Engineer, Engineer Commander. The Chief Engineer and the Engineer both became Engineer Lieutenants—corresponding, that is, with the two-and-a-half and the two-stripers in the executive branch (these being still pre-Lieutenant-Commander days). The Assistant Engineer became Engineer Sub-Lieutenant, and the Engineer Student emerged as the Engineer Cadet. The last-named was the inhabitant of the Engineering College at Keyham, Devonport. This establishment had come into existence in 1880, and, for the first eight years of its life, had run concurrently with H.M.S. *Marlborough* up till then the naval home for engineer students who were training in the yards and dockyard schools. In 1888, however, the College displaced the ship.

It was in the 'eighties and 'nineties that controversy began to grow really hot over the Engineer's position. By that time it was rapidly becoming evident that Sail was gone—or at least was going—for ever. Yet there were many people in the service—and high up in it at that—who were more than a little inclined to close their eyes to the inevitable. Such conservatism, not unnaturally perhaps, bred a certain antagonism to the Engineer, the man with the big future in a wholly steam-driven Navy. As late as 1893 we find a writer in the *St. James's Gazette*, anonymous, but claiming high service connections, who maintains that, when all is said and done, Engineer-Officers are only *Engine Drivers*. The charge, astonishing as it sounds to us, was yet considered worthy of rebutting in full, and a distinguished Chief Inspector of Machinery, Harry Williams,[1] undertook the task, demolishing his nameless opponent without undue difficulty. At the same time he put forward an interesting scheme whereby not only all Engineer Officers, but also all Engineering ratings should be trained to carry out directly military duties on board.

This was revolutionary, but then so was the problem. It was, roughly, this. The great growth in numbers of Engineer Officers made the total of "non-military" officers carried on board very large. Was this wise? And, further, was it in accordance with the facts to class the Engineer as non-military? Was he not in effect "military"? And, if military, why should he not be executive too?

The Engineer himself has usually inclined to the view that he is—or ought to be—"military", and even, in some respects, executive. As to his "military" claims, they are hard to combat.

An otherwise perfectly equipped ship which for some reason or other will not go, is admittedly a hopelessly poor military weapon. In these days when speed is a vital factor, the man who moves the ship along is quite as important

---

[1] This officer had the unique distinction of living through every phase of the Engineer's development described in this chapter. Born five years before the first establishment of 1837, he died in 1930, aged 98, five years after the "executive" decision next to be discussed.

a person as the one who controls her in action. Besides, he may argue, the *old* officer who "made her go"—the Boatswain—has always been accepted as "military", and even, when occasion demanded, as "executive". Nor, it must be observed, is the Engineer's case quite comparable with that of the recognized "non-military" branches. They are all, in their own way, indispensable, but not—militarily speaking—nearly so directly essential. To go into action without a surgeon would be very unpleasant: without a Chaplain very comfortless: without a Schoolmaster very unwise, and without a Purser very wasteful and confusing. But, none the less, one *could* go into action without any of these men, albeit with a serious loss of efficiency. But a modern ship might just as well go into action without men at the guns and the torpedo tubes as without men at the engines.

So we may admit that, in the ordinary sense of the word, the Engineer's functions are "military". But that is not nowadays—the same thing as saying that they are "executive": it is not to say that the Engineer can—or should —take command of the ship. For here the analogy with the Boatswain fails. The duties of the latter made him essentially a *deck*-officer, since *his* engines were all aloft, in the shape of masts and yards and sails. But the modern engineer is essentially a *below*-deck officer, and no man can be in two places at once. Further, if there is one man more than another, in that box-of-tricks which we call a twentieth century warship, who is a technical expert, par excellence, that man is the Engineer. He is the practitioner of a science which is constantly changing, growing, expanding: to learn thoroughly his highly specialist job, and, having learnt it, to keep abreast of its developments will take the very best of them all his time. And, this being so, there is a very strong case for considering him the last man on board who can be expected, *in addition*, to practise another profession altogether—the fighting direction of fleets and ships in action.

We have seen the attitude of the Selborne Committee to this question. Clearly they proposed to regard the new Engineer Officer as both military *and* executive. They desired to give him exactly the same status as the Executive Officer. But the question of the actual command of ships by the new officers (E) did not come up for a practical decision in 1903, nor for some years afterwards, since they were then only newly-joined naval cadets. But it did come up—when they were senior enough—in the 1920's. Until the end of the war, the new "E's" remained indistinguishable from ordinary executives. They were "military" and "executive", though the old Engineers were neither: they did not wear the distinctive purple stripe, though the old Engineers did. Then, for a brief period, both sorts were made "military", though the older sort were still "non-executive"—i.e., could not command ships. During this period the executive status of the new officers (E) hung in the balance. The difficulties involved were evidently being borne in upon Authority. They were even given a certain measure of choice. They could revert to upper-deck duties and executive command if they had begun specializing before 1918, or if they had begun specializing as Lieutenants. This system continued up till 1925, when the practical question of ship-command had to be decided one way or the other. It was decided; and the decision, in the light of actual events, was probably inevitable. The view was taken that the complexity of their engineering duties made it impossible for even the new-scheme engineers to find time to master purely executive duties. They were therefore brought out of the "Executive" list, and formed into a list of their own under the headings "Commander (E)", "Lieutenant-Commander (E)," etc., and once more they shipped the distinctive purple. So the Selborne attempt at a complete amalgamation of Executives and Engineers may be said to have broken down in 1925.

The question whether the latter are "military" has thus

T

become something of an academic one. The practical question—"are they executive?"—i.e. are they eligible to command ships at sea?—has been answered in the negative.

The story of the Engineer must end here. It has, admittedly, an unfinished appearance. Specialization is a force in the Navy which has certainly not ceased to operate. But how it will affect the Engineer of the future, it is not for us to say. This book has attempted throughout to purvey History, not Prophecy.

# INDEX

*

GEORGE ALLEN & UNWIN LTD
London: 40 Museum Street, W.C.1
Cape Town: 58-60 Long Street
Toronto: 91 Wellington Street West
Bombay: 15 Graham Road, Ballard Estate
Calcutta: 17 Central Avenue, P.O. Dharamtala,
Wellington, N.Z.: 8 Kings Crescent, Lower Hutt
Sydney, N.S.W.: Bradbury House, 55 York Street